NEW PLAYS THAT DRAMATIZE THE BLACK EXPERIENCE TODAY

THE DEATH OF MALCOLM X by LeRoi Jones
The white conspiracy to murder Malcolm.

THE RISE by Charles H. Fuller, Jr.
Brother Marcus' bold attempt to rouse Black
consciousness in America.

IN NEW ENG

A

EL

Th

FA

The genera   yesterday's Uncle Toms
and today's militants.

GROWIN' INTO BLACKNESS by Salimu
Life dedicated to building the Black nation.

SISTER SON/JI by Sonia Sanchez
An appeal for solidarity against the white community.

THE KING OF SOUL by Ben Caldwell
Otis Redding's plane crash plotted by a white man.

THE MAN WHO TRUSTED THE DEVIL TWICE
by Herbert Stokes
The whites will sell you out every time.

THE BLACK BIRD by Marvin X
Loyalty to whites means that you, too, will
BURN BABY BURN.

WE RIGHTEOUS BOMBERS by Kingsley B. Bass, Jr.
The Black revolution to liberate all Americans.

BIOGRAPHICAL INFORMATION

KINGSLEY B. BASS, JR. was a 24-year-old Blackman murdered by Detroit police during the uprising.

ED BULLINS is the Resident Playwright at the New Lafayette Theatre. He is also the editor of BLACK THEATRE magazine, published by the New Lafayette Theatre.

BEN CALDWELL is a Harlem essayist-playwright-artist. His plays have been presented at Newark's Spirit House and on the West Coast by the Black Arts Alliance.

N. R. DAVIDSON, JR. was born in New Orleans in 1940. He received a B.A. from Dillard University and a Master of Fine Arts from Stanford University. He is now the Resident Playwright at the Dashiki Project Theatre, a new Black Theatre in New Orleans.

CHARLES H. FULLER, JR. is a Housing Inspector in Philadelphia. His play, THE PERFECT PARTY (A PLAY ABOUT FRIENDS), is now in production for off-Broadway.

LEROI JONES (traditional name: IMAMO AMEER BARAKA) is a Black Nationalist artist and spiritual leader ("imamu") of the Cultural Nationalist Movement.

SONIA SANCHEZ, born in Birmingham 33 years ago, has three children—a beautiful daughter and twin warriors. HOMECOMING, her book of poetry, was published recently.

HERBERT STOKES is a 17-year-old actor-poet who has worked closely with LeRoi Jones at the Spirit House in Newark.

MARVIN X is a Black Muslim.

New Plays From The Black Theatre

An anthology
edited and with an
Introduction
by Ed Bullins

BANTAM BOOKS

TORONTO · NEW YORK · LONDON

A NATIONAL GENERAL COMPANY

FOR TRIXIE

NEW PLAYS FROM THE BLACK THEATRE
A Bantam World Drama Book / published November 1969
2nd printing
3rd printing

PS
634
B8

Library of Congress Catalog Card Number: 70–98971

Published simultaneously in the United States and Canada

Bantam Books are published by Bantam Books, Inc., a National General company. Its trade-mark, consisting of the words "Bantam Books" and the portrayal of a bantam, is registered in the United States Patent Office and in other countries. Marca Registrada. Bantam Books, Inc., 666 Fifth Avenue, New York, N.Y. 10019.

PRINTED IN THE UNITED STATES OF AMERICA

33788

Contents

interview with
Ed Bullins

by Marvin X

---

*How did you select the plays for this
anthology?*

These plays are typical of the plays being done in Black
theatres in the Black community for Black people by Black
writers and Black playwrights generally of the younger generation across the country. They include a wide range of
plays, from revolutionary plays like Brother LeRoi Jones'
and Sister Sonia's to historical plays like Brother Fuller's and
Brother Davidson's, to plays on the Black Experience and life
style such as my own play and Sister Salimu's. That play is
also a very revolutionary and sophisticated type of play
in a very subtle vein.

*What is the connection between your
plays* IN NEW ENGLAND WINTER
and IN THE WINE TIME?

IN NEW ENGLAND WINTER is a continuation of the life
of Cliff Dawson, one of the characters of IN THE WINE
TIME. In IN NEW ENGLAND WINTER, Cliff is older,
and the play presents a different side of his character. The

play goes into the type of person Cliff's half-brother is and how he differs from Cliff. It describes some of the problems he gets into and goes through, and how he gets out of them through the aid of Cliff. Cliff is more resigned to the reality of his identity, so now he is just "living through it." So, the second play just takes us further in time and flashes back to a previous time and introduces another character in the complete cycle that I have been working on, which is devoted to a group of Black characters and a family.

How do you feel about all the new Black theatres that are emerging?

I feel good! I feel good! I moved into the theatre for a number of reasons. But I guess it was a natural move because I was writing a number of things. I was busting my head trying to write novels and felt somehow that my people don't read novels. My family doesn't, except for my mother and some of the young kids who are now going to school. But for the great bulk of them, they don't read novels. But when they are in the theatre, then I've got them. Or like TV. You know, my ideas can get to them. So, I moved away from prose forms and into theatre. Black literature has been available for years, but it has been circulating in a closed circle—the Black Arts circle and the colleges. It hasn't been getting down to the people. But now in the theatre, we can go right into the Black community and have a literature for the people, for the "people-people," as Bob Macbeth says—for the great masses of Black people. I think this is the reason that more Black plays are being written and seen, and the reason that more Black theatres are springing up. Through the efforts of certain Black artists, people are beginning to realize the importance of Black theatre. LeRoi began this movement through his Black Arts project in Harlem and now with the Spirit House in Newark which takes his plays across the country. Other groups such as the old Black Arts/West on the Coast which we had a hand in, the Aldridge Players/West also on the Coast, the Free Southern Theatre, Concept East in Detroit, and now the New Lafayette in Harlem have tried to continue what LeRoi began. As a result of these efforts, theatre is becoming more acceptable to Black people on the whole. It is less of a novelty and becoming a necessary part of their cultural life. More young people are writing plays and more Black theatre workers think of doing for their people and for themselves. There is a great deal more activity than in '65. There was no Black theatre to do your plays in then. If you were in San Francisco, as we were, you knew there was nobody to do FLOWERS FOR THE TRASHMAN. Black people had to come together and create our own theatre. This has had great reverberations. Many things have come from it. It's like dropping a rock in a pool; the waves haven't stopped yet.

How do you see the whole Black Arts
experience?

On the West Coast?

Yes.

It came at a time when my life changed a great deal. I was a very frustrated and evil cat. I wasn't at peace with myself, as an artist, as a person. And I think many of us came into Black Arts in similar states of agitation and hostility and madness. It was a purging experience to go through, to start a theatre on nothing and make it work, to put all our energies and lives into it and to have our people—our Black people—appreciate it was a gas, to have *our* people, not the supposedly distinguished or knowledgeable, not the Jackie Robinsons of the world or the Adam Clayton Powells, or anything like that, but our people, our people on Fillmore Street in San Francisco, who would come up to us the next day in the street and say, "Man, that was boss." And you can go out there now, and the people still say, "Man, when you gonna do some more plays," still remembering and looking forward to more work to be done by Black groups now functioning like Mel Khalim and the Bantu Players. Moving my whole art back into my original reference which is my people, my community fulfills me and makes me want to work. It makes me a peaceful, creative brother who wants to build, to create for the Black people and nation, where before I was like a very, very disturbed cat—I was a misfit, a Western, Negro/

artist misfit. To paraphrase Brother Mao, those writers and artists who pursue bourgeois art become misfits because they separate themselves from the people to become dilettantes, personifying decadent culture instead of exposing and examining it. To extol decadence is to become decadent.

What about the idea of a National Black
Theatre? What would be its purpose, as
you see it?

It would be a medium for communication to raise the consciousness throughout the nation for Black artistic, political, and cultural consciousness. It would keep a hell of a lot of people working—Black theatre people—and doing what they have to do. And it would be an institution for the Black people in America who are a nation within a nation. It would be an institutional base to lay the foundations of our society and our culture and our nation. It would be an institutional form like Black schools, which are becoming more prominent. The Black theatre would be power in a sense, power in pure terms of capitalist facilities—buildings, things, places—and power, in another sense, to control people's minds, to educate them, and to persuade them. It would be power in the sense of welding together Black artists of many disciplines, because the theatre is a collective effort of many arts which come together to get the spirit going. And we would get some unity that way. When you have a Black theatre and you have a Black audience and a Black artist, then the idea of getting people back together will be *passe*. The people will be together and all you will have to do while they are together will be to tell them things which are beneficial and progressive and revolutionary. Those are some of the aspects of a National Black Theatre. I believe a National Black Theatre is possible at this very moment. It just takes people to get together and to commit themselves and to realize that, like LeRoi says, they need only the heart to do it. And they have it. All they have to do is realize it. And they can do it. Because there are enough Black theatre administrators, Black theatre technicians, enough Black managers of Black entertainers, orchestras and traveling troupes.

The know-how within the body of the Black people is there. It is just a matter of getting them and organizing them on a consistent basis to do the thing. We have information we have gathered over the past years, such as the kinds of Black educational institutions, many of whom want Black theatre groups and could benefit from them. We know most of the Black cultural organizations throughout the country that are doing anything. And many of us know each other. It's just getting together and getting us to utilize our knowledge. We are hoping to do that at conferences and other projects we will be doing this year. So it's a possibility. It's just getting it going. You know, before there was a Black Arts theatre, people thought it wasn't possible. Before there was a Spirit House, Black people thought it wasn't possible. Before the New Lafayette, Black people thought we couldn't have a theatre. But, now we know it is all possible and it only takes enough pride, application, and work to do these things. So we are going to use a little elbow grease to get a Black National Theatre together in the coming months, so we'll have a circuit across this country through which we can go to the people.

As a playwright, what have you gained from your association with the New Lafayette Theatre?

I don't get as much from watching my plays as I used to. After I finish a play now, I can't really read it for some months. I only start thinking about it after it's done. It's from the association with the New Lafayette Theatre—working with all the actors and directors, seeing how things are put together, working on BLACK THEATRE MAGAZINE (a magazine which is concerned with what we are doing in the New Lafayette and in other Black theatres across the country)—that I gain the greatest advantage right now. The association with other Black artists—being stimulated and growing as I am growing, knowing who we are working for, and perceiving in some way how we are working, what things we are bringing into our work, and what we are struggling through to make our art more consistent and correct for the needs of our people at this time—these are the most important aspects of my work. We don't want to have a higher form of white art in black-face. We are working towards something entirely different and new that encompasses the soul and spirit of Black people, and that represents the whole experience of our being here in this oppressive land. We are attempting to take all the things that are positive in us, our music, our very strong religious expression, our own life style, and incorporate them into our art on a collective basis. Our aim is not only to become better artists, individually and collectively, but to create a uniform positive art. In ten years, the things we do now will be recognizable, but we will be far beyond them. By then, I think our art will be completely different from white Anglo-Saxon Western art. It will be totally Black!

Were you satisfied with the New Lafay-
ette's production of IN THE WINE
                               TIME?

Yes, I was very satisfied with it. It could have been done in other ways, but the production came out very positive. I liked the way the audience responded. I know I could not have gotten a production of the same quality downtown, down in Madland, off-Broadway or wherever that other thing is, or anywhere else on this earth at this time. I am very pleased to have a whole theatre in my corner, encouraging me to write for them, wanting to do my plays the best they can, not each wanting to be stars and running off with the thing, and not having the director an emotional cripple, twisted and trying to find the latest fad that the faggots are trying to make a new HAIR out of . . . BLACK HAIR . . . it could be called . . . or something. It was done Black and that is the only way I could see it, and I am very happy with it.

How do you feel being called America's
                      greatest playwright?

Who called me that?

It's been in print.

Well, I don't know what that means because that makes me feel like a traitor. First, I don't feel like an American. And then, I don't understand the criteria that may be used to measure my soul with a soulless folk. It puts me very up-tight. I don't really know what that means. It is only because I'm up here working and not downtown. If I was down there, their audience wouldn't even understand me. Their critics have no conception of what Black is or the nuances of my mind which is a Black mind, or the strengths and weaknesses of my spirit. Consequently, it would be a different tale. I don't know how to answer the question, except that it's distressing.

What people have influenced you?

I guess LeRoi Jones influenced me most directly as a playwright. Bob Macbeth influenced me very profoundly and pervasively but more subtly. LeRoi was my first influence. I had heard about LeRoi's plays and read them before I actually saw them. I was reading a lot of plays and I was going to a lot of plays, as many as I could in San Francisco, which isn't a theatre town. And I wanted to write a play. For a whole year, I wanted to write a play, but I thought it would be a big complicated mess. You had to know this and that. So I started reading plays. I read the Absurd people, and I read some of the contemporary plays which aren't really contemporary. I became familiar with who was writing and who was doing what. And then I got drunk one night and I wrote HOW DO YOU DO. So since I had written one play, I had to write another one. Two weeks late, I wrote DIALECT DETERMINISM. Then it was time to get my plays produced. It's not good to let plays just sit on the desk. This was 1965. I took them around to different places, including Aldridge Players/West. People said the plays were obscene. So I took them around to different places in San Francisco, but nobody would go for my plays, Black or white. So then I said, "Well, I'll do them myself!" Buck Hartman was going to direct them. He knew Martin Ponch who had the Firehouse Repertory Theatre. Hartman and I were calling ourselves the San Francisco Drama Circle, a name we got off some defunct outfit with which Hartman had previously been associated. He was directing and fronting. I was hustling the capital and getting the company together and breathing the spirit into the thing. Then Ponch, who was a kind of third-rate producer in the scheme, wanted to put on another play, written by himself or some other white cat that was atrocious about Black-white relations. I wouldn't let him do it. So we needed another play to fill the bill. So I sat down and wrote CLARA'S OLE MAN. While we were rehearsing and trying to get it together, an angel came in and wanted us to move to a bigger theatre, with promises of money, complete backing, etc. We had an argument with Ponch who smelled money and took us through changes. So we moved and went to another theatre, The Contemporary Theatre in San Francisco. We were going to do it there, but then they told us it would be bad for business since THE TOILET and DUTCHMAN were in town. So the whole deal was squelched. The angel fled. We were left with no theatre. We were rehearsing in lofts and other places, but we kept together and kept rehearsing. Finally, we went back to the Firehouse and got exploited but did the plays. Several months later, I started Black Arts/West with you, Marvin, Hillery X Broadus, and Duncan Barber, Jr. But before that, when the former group was hassling with white shysters, opportunists, and exploiters, I went to see THE TOILET and DUTCHMAN, and a whole new world opened up to me. Until I saw THE TOILET, I didn't realize how right I was in what I had done in CLARA'S OLE MAN. I knew CLARA was a radical departure from the work of those Black playwrights I had read. It was radical in its depiction of Black people, but I didn't realize how right it was in a deep and profoundly revolutionary sense, until I saw THE TOILET. After that, I could say to myself that I had written CLARA'S OLE MAN, and it was good. I was able to settle that, come hell or high water, my way is the way it's going to be. I am the single critic of my work that I trust.

At the same time of seeing THE TOILET, however, I still didn't know what I was going to do about my work in terms of the overall thing that I wanted to create. I had nothing to connect with, no stable association. But now that's why the New Lafayette Theatre has been so great. Through it, I have some feedback, something with which to gauge my work. I hadn't really found myself until I saw what the other young Black playwrights were doing. Then I was able to give up working on my novels, essays, and short stories and go back to my plays. The Black theatre has been the great, current influence on my life. My work is my life and my life is my work.

LeRoi has greatly influenced many young Black artists. I say without reservation that LeRoi is one of the most important, most significant figures in American theatre. Hardly anybody realizes this now except Black playwrights and artists. We know that the Man (LeRoi) has changed theatre in this country. His contribution to Black theatre will have a great effect on all theatre in this country. If people say that I'm the greatest American playwright, then they must also admit and acknowledge that LeRoi Jones is one of the most significant figures in American, world, and Black theatre. He created me as a playwright and created many other young Black playwrights including many that you will find in this book, NEW PLAYS FROM THE BLACK THEATRE.

Harlem
January 1969

The
Death
of
Malcolm
X

by LeRoi Jones

Inner chambers of Uncle Sam Central.
Men in Uncle Sam suits, some with long
hats. The officers with fake beards to
signify their rank. Some walking rapidly.
Some talking animatedly. Busy office . . .
staging area for para-military operation.

Operating room. Crystal tank for body
submersion. Drugged Negroes lying almost at random around the room, strapped
to tables . . . some nodding as if to come
out of it.

Still another level downstairs. Slick bo-
hemian . . . or arty nice white girls stroll
in and out. Sign in place points out
"Staging Area."

Still another level of facade of 1st level
is mock coffee shop, beer joint, &c. Special exits, &c. Loud music . . . interracial
couples, &c.

A tall white girl bends to kiss one
drugged black figure on a stretcher, before he's wheeled away down the corridor to the operating room. Sign in
corridor and outside hall reads "I.A.B.S."
Institute for Advanced Black Studies.

Closeup of doctors operating on black
boy, taking out his mindsoul, replacing
it. They take out a black brain, substi-
tute a white one for it.

Into a classroom. Just off staging area.
Four Negroes stare glassy eyed at a black-
board upon which a white man in an
Uncle Sam suit is writing certain instructions: "White is Right" (writes on
board).

INSTRUCTOR. Now repeat after me. *(They repeat.)* White is
  Right. Right?
NEGROES. *(They answer).* Right!
INST. This is why the white man is so cool. This is why the
  white man is so great. *(He is pounding the board with
  his chalk for emphasis. The dazed* BLACKS *repeat his
  phrases deadly.)*

In a war room of the staging area. Another white man is pointing at plans for
a large hotel. He points at each black
man in the room. "Now, 'A,' what do
you do?"

A. I stage the commotion.
WHITE MAN. "B"?
B. I lead my men up the side hallway and through the front
  aisle, blasting after the first shot.
WHITE MAN. "C"?
C. I get the four bodyguards out of the way, chasing the
  commotion with an order.

Back in the classroom they are showing
movies of a black caricature, now minstrel, now laughing insanely, now walking hunchbacked and meek, and whining
over his fate. The blacks in the audience
boo and cheer, stomp their feet and
wring their hands.
"Save us master . . . save us." Some of the
blacks are screaming, stomping, pounding on the chairs. When the film is over

these blacks will sit stiff with dazed staring eyes.

War room. "O.K. A, B, C, let's hear it again." The white instructor pointing with his stick.

The inner sanctum. The USam chiefs all dressed like Sam . . . some of the higher ranked with crowns and scepters, or dressed like George Washington image with bandage wrapped around his head, some with Roman togas, some with Greek dress, a cave man, Vikings, Cortes' people, &c., sit around discussing some issue quietly to themselves. While the chief, a young blond man with a neat goatee and sunglasses, is talking very animatedly on a television phone. He is talking to a fat dragon klansman. (If black and white film, suddenly switch to color to get the crimson, green, and gold gown.) The klansman sits in a luxuriously furnished room, surrounded by human bones and skeletons. Out a window behind him, the capitol bldg., or Washington Monument . . . some indication that it is Washington, D.C.

KLANSMAN. Well, what's holding things up then?
HP (HIPPY PRESIDENT). Authorization . . . but we'll get that probably this evening.
K. You only got a little while, friend . . . you guys better not throw this chance away, don't you know. Lotta people counting on you. *(Smiles/leers.)*
HP. Don't worry . . . Don't worry . . . you just make sure your section has their end taken care of. You talk to the old man again?
K. That ol' nigger's giving us trouble . . . but don't you worry about that. It'll be taken care of in the usual way.

(Rubs fingers together signifying money.) But you know all that . . . I seen one of your men hanging around me for the last week! *(Laughs.)*

Classroom. A slide on the board of the Praxiteles . . . other Greek sculptures. Dazed blacks scream, "The beginning of thought . . . The beginning of Culture . . . God! God!"

INST. Yes . . . Yes . . . you're getting it now . . . *(Eyes wild w/joy, he and* BLACKS *foaming at the mouth.)* Yes! Yr getting it now!! *(A group of half-naked white girls dance across the screen.)*

HP's office. Goateed man w/dark glasses kisses telescreen, as he turns it off. He turns from the screen and moves through the crowd, and all the assembled touch him. There are sex-senuous cries and love moans . . . i.e., from the Greek, the Roman, the Viking, &c.

Operating room. Closeup of scalpel cutting into black flesh . . . Faces of the assembled.

Tall lump faced man in a white 100 Stetson twirls rope in rodeo fashion, sings—"I'm a cracker / A dumb cracker too / I'm a cracker / A crackeroo." Repeats, ending with a long "Whoooooo," twirling rope, and leaping in the air. A crowd applauds. They hoist signs, of weird origins . . . e.g., one says "Hip White Stuff," another, "We want a lasting piece," dollar bills surrounding the lettering. One dazed black has a sign, "Please cool me out, white daddy." But most of the signs are admiring, e.g.,

"Hail to Lumpy Jaws." But in the background black protest signs are raised higher than all. "Freedom or Death" &c.

The door of an apartment is being beaten down. The man inside is dressed like an artist. His long haired, round eyeglassed woman sits on the bed, smoking nervously.

WOMAN.   Louis ... what ... ???

LOUIS.   Get the weapons quickly! (*The door crashes in,* BLACK MEN *screaming with spears and swords crash through the door! They attack ... On the wall of the room a picture of the man with dark glasses and goatee.*)

A white cop in a black neighborhood looks up suddenly, and a garbage can is speeding for his head. He screams! Scene is repeated several times.

The klansman grinning ... looking out his window at the capitol ... talking on the phone. "Look, you ol' nigger. . . I told you you'd be taken care of. God damn it. Look, we can't talk like this ... I know this is a special phone... but it's tapped too! When? Nigger sometimes you make me mad. You carry that poppycock of yours too far. That stuff's only for niggers. You keep them spirits to yrself." (Laughs ... grows quickly sullen ...) "Now, look ... you do what I tell you or you won't have any following at all. Yeh ... that's right ... He's got to die!"

War room. White man in US suit speaking. "All right you men go upstairs check your plans and routes, then get some sleep. You'll have to be on your way by

0900 tomorrow. There's a lot to do, before that. (On the wall a movie of lightskinned Negroes dancing a cotillion. On the arch where they pass under a huge sign says "Klugteufel Beer.") The black men raise their arms and shuffle woodenly out of the room, murmuring ecstatically.

Long rows of rolling stretchers, moving down a narrow corridor. Blacks to be operated on. Coming out of the other side of the operating room another long line ... those already altered. Some stirring, smiling. Some blowing kisses. The attendants pointing.

The fat klansman with a blonde riding on his shoulders around the room. He has the top of his klansuit down, leaving his chest naked. She is licking his shoulder. She is screaming, "Giddyap, big pappa ... giddyap!" He makes whinnying sounds, like a horse, and bucks stupidly.

Man w/goatee in his private office talking silently, on phone, curled in chair. Jazz playing quietly on box, in the walls. He rocks back and forth in an upholstered rocker. Puts phone down ... buzzer sounds ... he touches box at his elbow, "Yes" ... (answer over intercom, "Col. Walters, sir.") "Send him in!"
White man in US suit who was in war room comes in with papers, writing board, &c.

HP.   Walters *(Extends hand.)* sit down for Christ's sake.
WALTERS.   Yes, sir.

HP.   Well, what's happening, Walt?

W.   Everything's together, sir. Project Sambo looks like it'll go off without a hitch.

HP   *(turns meditatively in chair, looking out window at Washington. Speaks quietly and with great satisfaction).* Yes ... good ... good ... only one more project to be completed before the main one. Hummm, just one possible hangup ...

W.   That ol' witchdoctor ...

HP.   Yes, but he's no problem at all, really. Our fat friend has the keys to his heart *(Rubs fingers together in money sign.)* ... that *(laughing.)* and the Gandhi syndrome. (W. *laughs.*)

HP *(cont.).*   But the quote followers unquote are ready? You've done yr job?

W *(sobers).*   Yes sir. They're ready now to kill.

HP.   Good ... They'll have their chance very soon.

Main intelligence gathering room at USam Central. Huge room with television sets all over the walls. Radio voices beaming in. From far flung lands ... murders ... coups ... treachery ... jokes ... murder voices cackling on and on. Men and women march around in Uncle Sam suits, tending to their business. Camera covers the room showing various information gathering activity. People reporting, rank delineation, &c.

Klansman sprawled on woman, talking, laughing. Image of capitol over his shoulder.

KLANSMAN.   Yes, tomorrow's a big day, baby, a big day ... Ha, ha, and in my humble capacity let's say, I'm a heavy contributor.

GIRL *(laughs, squeals).*   Oh, oh, oh, you're so important ... I've never known anyone quite like you ... you're Godlike ... that's what I think ... I think you're Godlike. (KLANS-

MAN *laughs, squirming and rocking his butt. His hand shoves out to turn on the television.*)

Television studio. A panel show is in progress ... two white men seated flanking a tall hard jawed black man with rimless sunglasses. The black man is speaking ... shaking his finger at the moderator and the tv cameras.

MALCOLM. No, finally it is the fact that you are evil. Evil. It is that simple fact that will animate the rest of the world against you! That simple alarming fact of your unredeemable evil. You are all disqualified as human beings (*Voice rises sharply.*), disqualified by your inhuman acts ...

Klansman's bedroom. (Malcolm's voice is droning over the television, "by your inhuman acts ... your filth and your evil.") Klansman looks up at tv, stares hard at the words and the (unseen) face, his face twisted in a leering grimace, then he begins to laugh.

KLANSMAN. Hahaha ... yr right nigger ... yr right ... hahaha ... by our evil ... hahaha ... but what good will it do you ... (*laughing hysterically ... his female companion follows with highpitched shrieks.*)

Out the window, down the street. A crowd of civil rights marchers, the Negroes impeccably clad. They are chanting mindlessly, "LET US BE AMERICANS." It is an integrated picket line, fat white ladies with sparkling necklaces ... priests and ministers ogling each other. They are led by a tall "distinguished" looking Negro with greying temples. He is walking in long gallant strides, turning his head from one side to the other to take in the applause (and abuse). The streets are lined with white people.

Shots of the windows of the official offices. Laughing fat faces, pointing and ridiculous. There is music with the marchers. Some of the marchers are singing "WE SHALL BE WHITE" in a spiritual vein . . . "WE SHALL BE WHITE" . . . they walk down the street with a militancy . . . but bereft of humanity. Beautiful automatons. "WE SHALL ALL BE WHITE." The rich ladies scream with laughter. Bohemians promenade. Cops line both sides of the street, some snarling and baring their teeth. Most of the people that line the streets are in USam suits and cop suits.

As the crowd of marchers passes down the street chanting their slogan, we begin to see a crowd of policemen and plainclothesmen gathering slowly at a point in advance of the marchers.

Some of the marchers we recognize from the classroom or the operating room. And as the procession moves down the street . . . employees of the USam bureau are going in and out.

Cops and plainclothesmen stop marchers . . . They kneel and begin to pray. "Oh, white Northamerican God, help us . . . help us to be like you and your loved ones." The marchers repeat their whines. They begin to weep en masse, the leader bawling like a baby. All praying, hands to chin, rolling their eyes. The policemen's clubs and billies beating the demonstrators in agonizing slow motion. Camera moves away from the scene, widening the shot, to include the whole ritual-like melee.

Television studio. Guards standing around in presence of a speaker ... Secret Service types. A voice announces, "Ladies and gentlemen the president of the United States." Assembled people applaud. Closeup of a handpuppet speaking into the cameras, gesturing, like a speaker, like a president making a state of the union message, or at an official press conference.

PRESIDENT *(in cowboy accent).* "Friends, violence ... *(Aside.)* to us ... hahaha, is not the answer. The only answer is the law, and law abiding citizens. Rome wasn't ... hahaha ... built in a day. *(Aside.)* Nor without slaves ... hahaha ... We will have an equitable society, a beautiful society, but it must be built through the laws of the land ... by strengthening those laws not marching in defiance of them!! America is a beautiful country ... a beautiful idea ... America will exist forever.

(Applause from people out on the street, watching tv's in an appliance store window.)

Police beating the marchers. The grey-haired man stands, untouched, at the center of the melee. He is beatified, a red white and blue halo appears illuminating around his head. Now he turns and addresses the embroiled marchers. With his arms still spread, as if to bless them, he says in the midst of the turmoil: "Go home my children ... we have proven our point, that love is stronger than hate!" People's heads are being cracked open

. . . women are wrestling with policemen.
The greyhaired man goes on: "Go home,
my children . . . we have beaten them,
I say, we are this day blessed! We will be
white . . . We will be whiter than them"
(points at the policemen; at the white
crowd). "Whiter, much whiter." He says
the last words into a wrist radio.
Instructor in classroom, white man in
war room, bearded pres., klansman, all
pick up on what's being said, through
speakers in their offices. Come to focus
closeup of bearded man and klansman,
each with their different laughter. Final
image of handpuppet, listening to wrist
radio, breaking up with weird puppet
laughter.

Night: The sky is a monstrous American flag, illuminated as if in neon, the
red, the white, the blue . . . the stars, in
the flag, glowing.
Underneath, an occasional scream or
bomb. To break up the silence with the
character of a quietly hysterical American night. The feeling must be given of
unbelievable agonies going on . . . above
them, the shrill laughter. The occasional
burst of fire.

Dawn to morning, the flag of American
sky grows dim and breaks up into white
clouds. It is Sunday morning. A calm
over the cities. Washington/New York.
We see white people going to church,
starched and stiff, the black people going
into their churches. The otherwise quiet
streets. Shops, businesses closed.
At the USam offices, however, people
are moving back and forth. There is an

anteroom, where the men take off their
outside clothes, revealing USam suits.
The women in another chamber, the top
hats collapsible ones they take out of
their pockets or pull out of the lockers.

Airplane interior. The dazed Negroes
sitting inside being talked to by the war
room officer, "Now let's go over the details one more time."

ATTENDANT.   Sir, we'll be in New York in 15 minutes.
INSTRUCTOR.   All right men, check your weapons . . . and go
over your assignments for me one more time.
NEGROES.   "I get the guards out of the way." "I stage the
commotion." "I lead my men up the side hallway and
through the front aisle, blasting after the first shot."
After the briefing . . . attendant comes
back, "5 minutes."
INST.   O.K. . . . uh . . . men. (*Loudspeaker starts playing
Star Spangled Banner.* NEGROES *fall on floor licking the*
WHITE MAN'S *shoes one at a time, in perfect order. The
plane, seen from the outside, speeds on.*)

As the plane lands, and the men get out
and are picked up in cars, which speed
off towards the city, the tall bearded
black man with the rimless glasses is just
getting out of bed. Knock on the door
of the room.

MALCOLM.   Come.
S (M's *aide comes in*).   Morning.
M.   Morning.
S.   Sir, we've got to get started . . . we're sort of running
behind schedule . . . as it is.
M.   O.K., O.K., my egg and juice ready (*Calling out into
the hall.*)??
WIFE'S VOICE (*from out in the hall*).   Sure they're ready. The
kids are up too. Only thing not functioning in here is you.

(Laughs. Voices of kids, "Daddy's up . . . daddy's awake . . . daddy's awake.")

S.   We're supposed to be at the hall in about an hour. It's 30 minutes just to get to the city.

M.   Yeh . . . yeh . . . we'll make it. *(Starts to get himself together.)* Say what's happening in the world this morning?

S *(w/newspaper).*   Same ol'. Same ol'. Charles still knocking people off. People still not together . . . makes the meatball's attitude much safer and stronger.

M.   And much more deadly. Well today is a historic date, of some kind. Got a lot of things to say this morning. *(Laughs, dressing.)*

S *(laughs).*   I know. I know.

House bell rings . . . wife calls out, "Malcolm, Price and the others are here."

M.   O.K.

S.   I'll see to them.

M   *(S exits, M humming to himself, tying tie &c., looking over a speech he is to give at the ballroom . . . just a few words are audible).* ". . . is mass murderer. I got proof." *(Laughs.)* Hmmm . . . that ought to shake up a whole lot of devils. Shake 'em very hard.

S *(calling from next room.)*   Brother Malcolm, we gonna be late . . . *(Laughs.)* again.

M *(finishing up going over his speech).* Just keeping the stereotype, brother, that's all, just keeping the stereotype. *(He enters dining room, six* MEN *sitting around the table stand when he enters.)*

ALL.   Greetings, Bro. M. Morning.

M.   Sit Sit . . . get that grease and let's split. *(All laugh and begin eating.)*

BEARDED HP *(talking on phone).* Yes . . . yes . . . that's right. About 45 minutes, unless he's late. Right. It's done. *(Turns away from phone, punches intercom.)* Ross, turn on the television to any news broadcast . . . let me know at once if anything . . . uh . . . important happens.

Ross.   Yes, sir.

Fat klansman disturbed by phone . . .
waddles out of bed . . . girl in bed moan-
ing about the disturbance . . . "Oh, God
. . . baby, why do you have to leave me?"

KLANSMAN. Bizness . . . I trust . . . bizness (*Picks up
phone.*). Yeh . . . Of course . . . it's taken care of in one
half hour, I get here . . . unless the nigger's late. I
(*Laughs.*). Right (*Laughs.*). The old man is O.K. . . . I fixed
it. It's up to yr people now. Right! (*Hangs up phone. Calls
to* GIRL.) GobbleGobble . . . GobbleGobble . . .

GIRL.   Yes, God, baby.

K.   Turn on the tv . . . get a news program. Something nice
is gonna happen in a few minutes. A historic event.

G.   Wheeee . . . oh, baby . . . that's what I like about you . . .
yr in on everything.

Elegant inner office of elegant mansion.
Stacks of bank notes lie all over the place,
though neatly stacked. Gold bullion on
the floor. A portrait of Uncle Sam
dressed in gold.
Fat bald white banker sits surrounded by
money, talking on phone.

BANKER.   Looter, here. Yes . . . everything in readiness?? Yes,
O.K. I have my suit pressed for the occasion. A little party
at my place afterwards . . . Yes . . . wear your good clothes
. . . Haha . . . the rite goes on, eh? Good . . . O.K. O.K.
(*Knock at the door.*) O.K., got to leave now; right . . . 15 or
so minutes, huh?? O.K. right . . . see you this evening . . . the
good Lord willing. (*Hangs up.*) Come in. (SERVANT *comes
in dragging huge sack of money.*) Just drop it in the corner
. . . no, better . . . just dump it on the floor. (*Dumps gold
coins on floor.*) Beautiful . . . beautiful. That'll be all.
(*Room is furnished like study, library, rumpus room, with
trophies, black man's shrunken head like Patrice Lumumba
on wall.*) Beautiful. (*Goes, looking at his watch, to turn on*

*tv, then goes back and sprawls in the gold, wallowing
drunkenly.)*

The greyhaired Negro standing before a
banquet audience. A huge white man
handing him an award; says, as he
hands it to him, "For Meritorious Service." The assembled white audience applauds and cheers.

The Audubon Ballroom. Black people
going in, white police around. We see
the four black traitors arrive separately,
one looks at one of the policemen, sig-
nificantly.
M's cars arrive. The men get out walking casually in front and in back of him.
M turns to make sure his wife and children get out and are walking beside
him.

M.   Beautiful . . . Beautiful day . . . The sun is strong medi-
    cine.

(People greet him: "Good afternoon,
Brother M.")

M.   Good to see you, on this beautiful day.

*(One old lady gives him flowers and a
sudden kiss on the cheek.)*

M *(jokingly).* Easy madam, my wife's here. *(All laugh . . .
    He goes in, greeting people.)*

The greyhaired Negro is receiving his
award. The crowd applauds. His wife
comes to embrace him. She is dressed in
a civil war ball gown. Closeup of the

crowd applauding each other. The other speakers on the stage, the Negro grinning from ear to ear. The award he has received is a life sized watermelon made of precious stones and gold.

At klansman's. Km has his klan suit on, also, the girl has taken from a newly unwrapped box, two dresses ... one is the green and maroon feminine pairing of his costume, another dress made out of an American flag, just like the USam suits. They have been practicing putting on a small tee. The fat man is putting, now watching tv. At this point the screen (which does not have to be seen): "We interrupt this program to bring you a special bulletin ..."

Banker's home. The banker spins on his heel, while counting the money ... at the same announcement.

Audubon. M is walking onto the stage ... people are being seated. His bodyguard has formed where they are supposed to. Four in front of the stage. Stationed in balcony, and at back of hall. The assembled applaud as M approaches the podium.

Bearded Hp and his staff sit now, in front of tv, sipping drinks. Instructor and his staff and war room staff sit, joking quietly, taciturn and tensed.
Office of USam: People aware more or less of something impending momentarily. The US uniforms pausing, perhaps, to whisper to each other, keeping eyes

on clock, some eyeing television screens, or listening to small radios . . . still going through the motions of their work.

Empty war room. W/black board upon which is written OPERATION SAMBO, also times; operators' code names; trans instructions; ops officer in charge, &c.

Audubon. Also from radios, USam tv's. M is speaking: "They are evil people because they benefit by being evil . . . or they think they benefit . . . finally, they will not benefit by it at all. Not at all. (Applause.) We speak of revolution and don't even know what it is. A revolution means land. (Audience responds with "Speak Brother," "Go ahead"... "Amen.") A revolution also means bloodshed. There is no revolution without bloodshed."
(The man in the middle of the hall begins a rumble . . . M's bodyguards move forward on a signal from one man who seems to be in Malcolm's guard. The killers in the audience start to move. He holds up his hands . . . in peace.)

M.   Oh, O.K., cool it brothers . . . everything's gonna be O.K.

(The shooting begins. The killers move up the aisles, blasting away . . . Closeup of Malcolm's face. He grabs his chest. People scream.)

The news on tv, in all the rooms. The white men howling with laughter or snickering, or grinning half embarrassed at their victory. As the news is announced all the ofays begin to change clothes, and put on Uncle Sam suits, top hats and chin beards. The banker begins to call people about his party.

Malcolm is falling. People screaming. The assassins disappearing in a prearranged manner. Into cars . . . to an abandoned part of town . . . since it is Sunday. Then to a waiting helicopter and off.

Malcolm's body in closeup. The bullets hitting him again, him clutching his chest.

Now a shot of black people (and Africans and Asians and Latinamericans) clutching their breasts, as if shot, at the same time.

The greyhaired Negro is finishing buttoning on his USam suit. The audience still applauding.

Malcolm dead on floor with weeping hysterical mourners. We hear the tv announcer: "Today black extremist Malcolm X was killed by his own violence."

Klansman is laughing, fingering the girl's snatch, &c.

Last image is of all the featured ofays together at a party in USam suits, celebrating and making jokes, later going through a weird historic ritual, with the Viking, Conquistador, Caveman, Roman, Greek, leading a slow weird dance as

they put on USam suits, making growl-
ing unintelligible noises, but ending each
phrase   rhythmically   with   "White!"
"White!" "White!!" "White!!" &c.

                    –Black–

We Righteous Bombers

by
Kingsley B. Bass, Jr.

ACT I

(The stage is black. Noise begins low and gradually builds. The noise is of varied things: engines, buses, jets, trains, gunfire, explosions, dogs barking, men fighting, human moans, women screaming, human hysteria—Black music counterpoints. Simultaneously, faint lights show on the several screens arranged around and in the playing areas. The lights are red, blue and orange. They change into and swirl together in abstract shapes and patterns as the sound rises and the red becomes more pronounced. An effect of rapid acceleration starts and increases, created through sound, lights and screen projections. Upon the screen are fuzzy images suggesting crowd activity—rioting, disorder, large groups being detained in wired, outside enclosures. Images of fences, walls, closed gates. Of bomb craters, gutted buildings, weed-choked railroad tracks, overturned cars. Of social and political chaos.

Lights rise and show the dim shape of MURRAY JACKSON *sitting in his cell. The cell is merely an iron grate that* JACKSON *remains behind, but is open on the sides and back so that other actors can freely move around and with him. In other areas numerous less distinguishable shapes move, and make sounds—choking, gagging, hisses, laughter, whimpers, coughs, etc.*

A VOICE *begins to speak over the loud-speaker. As the loudspeaker broadcasts, the stage should be vibrating with dark, sinister movement in the shadows; with the combined effects of light, sound, film and motion. One of the screens lights up and a* BLACKMAN *speaking in the voice of a whiteman and wearing a uniform suggestive of a military auxiliary unit appears.)*

ANNOUNCER.   And folks . . . this about ends our daily bulletin from your government information bureau. To sum up: there is evidence of increased guerrilla activity in the Western Sector of the Northeastern Command . . . near the 9th Military Pacification Area that was formerly known as Pittsburgh. In the ensuing action there were four hundred twenty-three enemy Black Revolutionary bandits killed, and our loyal government forces lost a total of forty-one whitemen killed and wounded . . . and ninety-seven of our loyal negro mercenaries killed in combat with the enemy Blacks. Of course, most of the latter casualties were caused by sniping and by bombs . . . thrown by Black Revolutionary suicide personnel and planted in various locations in the Black pacified areas that negro mercenaries police . . . For as everyone knows . . . it is your government's policy . . . Black and white do not mix . . . Even the negro mercenary combat units that are loyal to your government work and live exclusively in Black areas that are totally surrounded by electrified barbed wire and policed by combat veterans, white police and military detachments and dogs. By the Black controlling their areas and manning their own military, police and bureaucratic positions of government under our present martial law and apartheid system of government . . . they have the fullest range of freedom . . . that is allowed to any man in these times . . . Black or white.

(The moans and wails in the shadows rise as if in protest. There is automatic gun-

*fire, punctuated by flashes of light, and
the picture on the screen momentarily
goes out of focus.)*

To complete our news summary ... the Controlling Military Council announced today that all Black Revolutionaries would soon be captured and destroyed and the government would in the near future be handed back to the free peoples of America and free elections would be reinstated ... and the end of official apartheid and martial law is soon in sight for our peoples. But in these times of crisis it is vital that all citizens understand that the negroes must lose their civil and constitutional rights, so not to give aid and comfort to the Black terrorists and rebels that seek comfort in their midst. But rest assured people of America ... both negro and white ... These vicious beasts that trample American freedom, the American flag itself, will soon be brought to bay, and they will feel the full weight of American justice and vengeance.

VOICE OF GUARD *(off)*. ATTENTION ON DECK! ATTENTION! ALL RADIOS AND VIDEOS OFF! ALL RADIOS AND VIDEOS OFF!

ANNOUNCER. And the Controlling Military Council wishes to praise today the inspired leadership of the negro prefects of the Black sectors who police their districts so thoroughly ...

VOICE OF GUARD *(coming closer)*. ALL HANDS OFF YOUR SEATS AND ON YOUR FEETS! THAT'S ALL HANDS, YAWHL HARE? YOU MAHTHAFUKKERS OVER THERE IN DEATH ROW HIT YO FEETS ... YAWHL HEAR WHAT I SAID! ... WRING IT OUT ... BLACK MAHTHAFUKKERS!

*(MURRAY JACKSON stirs. The lights slowly
rise to reveal him in black pajama-like
dress. His shirt should suggest a cheap,
black dashiki; his pants are large and
loose fitting. His head is shaven. The
sounds and movements of the others on*

stage counterpoint the action of the scene.)

ANNOUNCER. And we congratulate our courageous and loyal negro Seek and Kill teams whose job it is to enter the dreaded Black no-man's-land and rout out the Black enemies of American Freedom.

GUARD *(comes on; light on him).* STAND BY FOR COUNT. STAND BY. WHEN I CALL YOUR NAME, SPEAK UP! (GUARD *freezes in tableau.)*

BONNIE BROWN *(faint light in shadows; unreal).* Speak up when you're called . . . he says. Well, you can call me Bonnie Brown . . . I'm just a sister . . . *(Soft snort.)* Huh huh . . . a sister, really . . . a stone revolutionary soul sister . . . ha ha . . . an' kinda foxy . . . yeah, that's me. *(Walks forward a few steps into light.)* Yeah . . . I'm just a down to the nitty Blackbitch . . . I can't even stand fancy clothes. Look at what I'm wearing now . . . Look! Some ole jive actress's ole thrown-away buba. Not even naturally Afro . . . really . . . nothin' like that . . . Just my nappy wig, that's natural . . . like me . . . nothin' jive. And I'm gonna be with yawhl this evening as we go through some Black Revolutionary changes . . . But yawhl remember . . . I'm just plain ole me . . . Sister Bonnie Mae Brown. *(She moves out of the light.)*

GUARD *(reality).* STAND BY FOR COUNT. STAND BY. WHEN I CALL YOUR NAME, SPEAK UP!

(GUARD *freezes; lights change.)*

ELTON "L" CLEVELAND *(unreality; steps from the shadows).* We are righteous Blackmen, brothers and sisters. Righteous bombers. We do not fear death as the whiteman does. Each moment of our lives we build until the second of death . . . That way we meet death like the Black heroes we are . . . fighting to the end.

(Images on the screen speed up as the speeches go on; sound and movement continue. Lights change.)

GUARD (*reality*).   STAND BY FOR COUNT, PRISONERS.
STAND BY. WHEN I CALL . . . SPEAK UP!

(GUARD *freezes; unreality.*)

SISSIE WILLIAMS (*reciting at attention*).   Black Revolutionary
Codes of War: . . .

(MURRAY JACKSON, BONNIE BROWN, ELTON
CLEVELAND, HARRISON BANES *and* KEN-
NETH BURK *snap to attention.*)

SISSIE WILLIAMS.   Article Eight: sub-section four (Terrorists,
Spies, Saboteurs, Special Forces, Assassins and related
Black Liberation Freedom Fighters): . . .

(MURRAY JACKSON, BONNIE BROWN, ELTON
CLEVELAND, HARRISON BANES *and* KEN-
NETH BURK *speak the lines with* SISSIE,
at attention. The GUARD *remains frozen,
in the shadows.*)

THE REVOLUTIONARIES (*together*).   . . . THE OATH: We
Righteous Bombers . . . Righteous in the Grace of the
Supreme Black Spirit, Oneness, Allah, We do His bidding
so as to liberate the BLACK PEOPLES of the Conscious
Universe, of this planet, Earth . . . *by any means necessary.*

(*Lights change;* GUARD *moves.*)

GUARD.   STAND BY. WHEN I SAY . . . SAY YOUR
NAME.
SISSIE WILLIAMS.   Sissie Williams . . . sir.
HARRISON BANES.   Harrison goddammit . . . it's Harrison
Banes . . .

(GUARD *moves among them, acknowledg-
ing their presence, but the atmosphere
is not quite real.*)

. . . And yeah . . . I know it's hard and brutal . . . murder, maimings and death . . . and all that. But I'm brutal 'cause that's the way it is. For me hatred is not a game. Brothers! . . . and sisters . . . we haven't joined together to admire each other's blackness . . . But to bring our people freedom, justice and self-determination. We have joined to-gether *to get something done*. To get something done for Black people . . . *by any means necessary*.

SISSIE.   All praises due to the Blackman!

GUARD.   YOUR NAMES!

HARRISON.   Sorry . . . but I don't have a tender heart. That kinda shit cuts no ice with *me*! . . . tender heart . . . for the whiteman and his pet negroes? . . . WE HAVE A WAR TO WIN, BROTHERS! . . . And not until the day comes when we stop sentimentalizing about a golden past that niggers never had here in America will the revolution tri-umph. This is the last half of the last century for the white-man, brothers! We have to start takin' care of business.

GUARD.   SPEAK UP . . . YOU BLACK BASTARDS!

(The group weave in and around the playing area; the movement surrounds MURRAY JACKSON's *cage. Music, screen projections, moans and whimpers accom-pany the action.)*

KENNETH BURK *(humble).*   I've always been afraid . . .

*(*BONNIE BROWN *laughs hysterically.* SIS-SIE WILLIAMS *weeps.)*

I'm just not made for this. I'm not a terrorist. I realize that now. The best thing for me to do is to make it . . . to split. I'll do my thing in propaganda, on revolutionary committees . . . and shit like that.

BONNIE *(straining it out, pleading).*   I want the next bomb, brothers.

BURK. You don't see what happens on a committee. It's far
from slicing throats. It's easy to attend meetings, work out
plans, and then pass orders for the carrying out of those
orders. You risk your life, of course, for the penalty is
death for *any* revolutionary activity, but there's a sort of
shield between you and the . . . the blood and flesh.

BONNIE. Give me the next bomb.

GUARD. I WANT NAMES! . . . SPEAK UP!

BURK. It's somethin' else again . . . goin' down into the
street when night is fallin' on Harlem, takin' your stand
among the crowds of people out on the corners or hurrying
from the subway exits and buses to their evenin' meals,
their children, the wife who's waitin' and watchin' from
her window—and havin' to stand there, evil lookin' and
silent, with the pull of the bomb on your arm—and knowin'
that in only minutes, perhaps in seconds, you'll race out
toward a car, bomb in your hand.

BONNIE. Give it to me.

BURK. That's what terrorist activity means and I know now
that I couldn't start it all over again without feeling all the
blood drained from my veins.

GUARD. GET READY FOR ROLL CALL . . . WHEN I
SAY YOUR NAME . . . ANSWER UP! . . . AN' I BET-
TER HEAR YA SAY "SIR" ON THE END . . . OR I'LL
COME INTO YOUR CELL TONIGHT AN' KICK YO'
ASS 'TIL I GET TIRED . . . YA UNDERSTAND?

(Silence.)

I SAID DID YOU UNDERSTAND?

ALL *(together).* YES, SIR!

GUARD. GOOD! . . . THEN LISTEN UP! . . . BONNIE
MAE BROWN!

BONNIE BROWN. Here, sir.

GUARD. SISSIE ANN WILLIAMS!

SISSIE. Here, sir.

GUARD. ELTON "L" CLEVELAND!

CLEVELAND. Here, sir.

GUARD. KENNETH BURK!

BURK. Here, sir.
GUARD. HARRISON BANES!
BANES. Here . . . sir.
GUARD. WHAT DID YOU SAY?

(Lights change; they dim to dark around the edges as the group moves away into the shadows, except for MURRAY JACKSON. *Sound and screen projections subside. Lights gradually come up on* JACKSON's *cell. He relaxes and sits. The others are in the shadows now, moving and speaking.)*

BANES. I said . . . here, sir.
GUARD. Repeat.
BANES. Here, sir.
GUARD. Louder!
BANES *(a bit louder)*. Here, sir!
GUARD. I can't hear you!
BANES. HERE, SIR!
GUARD. Fall out.

(Silence. Lights change. Images on screen of night skies. Stars. The moon in varied phases. Clouds scudding through night/lit space. Images out. JACKSON *rises and looks toward the cell door. The* GUARD *enters, followed by a prisoner carrying a mop and bucket.)*

GUARD *(opens cell door, to* PRISONER*)*. Okay now. Get with it.

(The GUARD *takes a seat nearby and takes out a copy of* Playboy *magazine with a Black bunny on the cover, and begins reading.* FOSTER, *the prisoner, begins to wash the floor; he takes no notice of* JACKSON. *A short silence.)*

JACKSON.   What's your name, brother?

FOSTER.   Foster.

JACKSON: Are you a convict?

FOSTER.   Am I a water buffalo? What the hell else do you think I could be?

(Short silence.)

JACKSON.   What are you in for?

FOSTER.   I killed a black mathafukker who was messin' round with my ole lady.

JACKSON.   You mean he was attacking her . . . And you protected her?

GUARD.   Ssssssh. Hey, not so loud.

JACKSON.   What?

GUARD.   What did you say?

JACKSON *(confused, then understanding).*   . . . I said, "What, sir?"

GUARD *(satisfied).*   Okay . . . Now don't speak so loud. It's against the rules for you to be talkin' at all. So I'd advise you to talk quietly, like ole man Foster.

JACKSON.   Yes, sir . . . *(Pause, to* FOSTER.*)* Is that why you killed . . . to protect your loved one?

FOSTER.   Protect hell . . . they had been foolin' round together for years.

JACKSON.   They had?

FOSTER.   Sho had. I got drunk one day and came in and she was gone somewhere . . . hadn't even left supper on the stove.

JACKSON.   Yeah? And then?

FOSTER.   So I figured where the bitch was. Some little after-hour joint usta be over on Seventh Avenue and 137th Street. I had an ole cane knife . . . a long curved thing. Usta use it when I was in Louisiana. Well, I just picked it up, and went over there . . . walked in and just started swingin' at anything that moved. Killed six of 'em, they tell me, her included. But the nigger she was with got away.

(JACKSON stares at him.)

Ohhh . . . my young friend, I see you don't call me brother no more. My little story cooled you out?

JACKSON (*hurriedly*). No, it hasn't. I've killed too.

FOSTER. How many?

JACKSON. I'll let you know, brother, if you want to know. But tell me . . . well . . . you're sorry for what you did, aren't you?

FOSTER. Sure, I'm sorry. Seventy-five years hard labor, that's quite a stretch, youngblood. I've been here thirty years already. That's enough to make anybody feel sorry.

JACKSON. Seventy-five years! I come here when I'm twenty-three—and when I go out . . . even with time off for . . .

FOSTER. Oh, cheer up . . . there's ways of getting a lot of time cut off your sentence. And there's no knowing what a judge will do; if his ole lady was nice to him the night before that means a lot. Maybe he'll be in a good mood and let you off easy. And then you look pretty smart. Well educated and all that. If you have some pull . . . you know, juice . . . you know it ain't the same when you got connections outside, not like me. You'll get off with almost no time.

JACKSON. I doubt that. And anyhow I don't want to. Feeling guilt and shame for all those years. That would be horrible.

FOSTER. Guilt! Shame! Where does all that come in? That's just one of those bullshit notions you young studs have . . . How many people did you kill?

JACKSON. One man.

FOSTER. One man? Hummmp! . . . was he Black or white?

JACKSON. Black.

FOSTER. Why, that's nothin'. You'll be out in no time. They might even give you a medal . . . if it was the right nigger.

JACKSON. He was the Grand Prefect.

FOSTER. He was?

JACKSON. Yeah.

FOSTER. The *Grand* Prefect?

JACKSON. Yeah.

(*Lights off* JACKSON, FOSTER *and* GUARD.

Up on HARRISON, CLEVELAND, SISSIE *and*
BONNIE.)

HARRISON (*looks at* CLEVELAND).   We gonna kill that mathafukker, ain't we?

CLEVELAND.   We gonna kill him.

SISSIE.   You heard what I said, Harrison, about them nasty
white girls up there in Canada.

BONNIE.   Quiet, sister. Let the brothers talk. You know better than to be runnin' your mouth all the time like that.

HARRISON.   We gonna kill that Uncle Tom nigger, right!
Dammit to hell! You're the leader, Big L, and anything
you say, man, is good enough by me. Just as long as we
kill that (*Derisive.*) negro.

CLEVELAND.   I don't need your promise, man. We're all
brothers.

SISSIE.   Don't forget us sisters.

HARRISON.   But discipline's essential. That's something I
learned for myself at the concentration camp. The Black
Revolutionary Organization cannot do without discipline.
We all must be disciplined if we're gonna kill the Prefect
and set back tyranny and terrorism of Harlem and the
Black peoples of America and the world.

BONNIE (*goes to him*).   Sit down, brother. You must be tired
after that long trip.

HARRISON.   I ain't never tired. I'd walk from Canada if I
had to be able to be in on this kill.

SISSIE.   Haven't you eaten, brother? I got some bean pie I
made yesterday.

HARRISON.   Yeah . . . that sounds boss, sister.

(*She goes for the pie.* BONNIE *sits.* HAR-
RISON *and* CLEVELAND *face each other.*)

CLEVELAND.   Now.

HARRISON.   Is everything ready, man?

CLEVELAND (*in a brisker manner*).   Yeah, everything's ready.
We've been waiting too long for us to fuck-up from lack
of planning.

BONNIE.   Yes, we have been waiting so long.

HARRISON. Yeah, I was just a kid back in the sixties when the riots . . .

BONNIE. Riots?

HARRISON. Sorry, sister, I forget sometimes. You know I meant to say the revolution. You know how they tried to brainwash us in those white schools . . . and I can't even describe the horror of the camps to you.

BONNIE. Yes, I remember . . . I remember how they tried to turn all us Black children into white things in their schools . . .

HARRISON. And they succeeded sometimes . . .

BONNIE. Yes . . . yes . . . but don't push yourself too far now, brother.

CLEVELAND. Go on, Harrison.

HARRISON. I will, brother. Like I was sayin' . . . I was only a kid . . . like all of us who are old enough to remember when the revolution began for real back in the mid-sixties.

BONNIE (*murmurs*). I was born in Watts, remember? I remember my mother holding me by the hand when I was a little girl while the city burned around us.

HARRISON. And each summer the intensity of the revolution picked up.

CLEVELAND. Yeah.

HARRISON. And the power structure became frightened for they were fighting a foreign war in Vietnam then . . . and preparing for their war with China.

BONNIE. Go on, brother, teach.

HARRISON. And first there was the silencing of the artists, the Black artists . . .

SISSIE. Brother LeRoi.

BONNIE. Remember Malcolm, brother.

CLEVELAND. Yes, remember.

HARRISON. I won't abandon him.

BONNIE. Thank you, brother.

HARRISON. And then the leaders were systematically tracked down and . . . and . . .

CLEVELAND. *Exterminated* . . . exterminated by *beasts* as if they were beasts.

SISSIE. So terrible . . . so terrible . . . what they did to our people.

BONNIE.   They were killed like Jews . . . like niggers in the Georgia night.

HARRISON.   And after that came what the whiteman called martial law and community pacification.

BONNIE.   Yes, we had to have passes to go from one neighborhood to another.

CLEVELAND.   In the following years walls of electrified barbed wire were put up around every Black community in America.

SISSIE.   Like pigs . . . like filthy . . . foul swine in pens . . . that's how those beasts tried to make us.

BONNIE.   We in Harlem couldn't even go to the Bronx . . . or to Brooklyn . . .

SISSIE.   My mother tells me that the bridges that go to the Bronx didn't have guards or gates . . .

BONNIE.   . . . We couldn't visit our families and friends without official papers from the police.

HARRISON.   Yeah . . . the military pacified the entire nation. Blacks were physically separated from whites by walls and fences.

CLEVELAND.   American apartheid became official government policy soon after the burning of Washington and the razing of the White House.

(SISSIE *begins to softly chant a Moslem prayer. From the dark surrounding areas cries and groans come.*)

BONNIE.   And the Black purges were instituted and the Black concentration camps were activated immediately after the assassination attempt upon the President.

(*Images upon the screens document the narration.*)

CLEVELAND.   All the measures were legal and constitutional under the whiteman's law . . . the McCarran Act . . .

BONNIE.   And the Presidential decrees.

HARRISON.   And after each and every Black community came

under federal military law Blackmen were placed over each
community to govern it by whiteman's law.

BONNIE. Yea, negroes were appointed to carry out the
slavemaster's will. Negroes who are called prefects . . .

(SISSIE *appears to be in a semi-trance as
she recites. Images upon the screen of
various Hollywood negro comedians: Ro-
chester, Stepin Fetchit, Man Tan Mor-
land, Kingfish, Pig Meat Markham, Hat-
tie McDaniels, etc.*)

BONNIE. . . . negroes who are more white than the whitest
whiteman, negroes who grind the blood, marrow and juices
from the Black people to feed the vampire whiteman.

CLEVELAND. Hell must be policed by Black prefects.

HARRISON. The only hell we'll ever know is this one here
on earth, brother. But our children will inherit the heaven
that we build the foundations for now in our revolution
against the whiteman.

BONNIE. Teach, brother.

SISSIE (*moans, coming back*). Prefects . . . Black killers of
their own . . . evil . . . the most evil, the most unrighteous.

BONNIE. Yes, sister, and Harlem has the most evil and unrighteous one . . . we have the *Grand* Prefect.

(*Lights down on group; up on* JACKSON,
FOSTER *and the* GUARD. *Images on screen
go off.*)

FOSTER (*chuckles*). Well, I'll be goddamned. You young
squirts don't know where to leave off, do you?

JACKSON. No, I guess we don't.

FOSTER. Yeah, it sho looks black for you, son. Ha ha ha . . .

JACKSON. Black?

FOSTER. Uumhmmm . . . very black.

JACKSON. Oh . . . I see. Yeah, very black. But really white,
wouldn't you say, brother?

FOSTER (*slowly perceiving*). . . . Aha . . . aha . . . oh, yeah

. . . Hey, you's quite a card, sonny . . . Ha ha . . . But why'd you have to go kill *him* for?

JACKSON. But I had to do it. It had to be done.

FOSTER. Oh . . . so you believe you got the right nigger after all. Why? What business does a fine young man like you have in gettin' hisself into a mess like this? Oh, yeah . . . now I know. It was over some bitch, huh? A black bitch, I bet.

JACKSON (*indignant*). A what?

FOSTER. You know . . . a woman . . . a black gal. A good-lookin' boy like you . . . I can see it all now. She was his daughter, wasn't she? . . . Or his niece . . .

JACKSON. Sir, I am a Revolutionary! Our beautiful sisters shouldn't be spoken of . . .

FOSTER. Shssss . . . not so loud, boy.

JACKSON (*deliberately raising his voice*). I am a Black Revolutionary!

GUARD. And if I have to come in there . . . you gonna be a quiet one.

JACKSON. Yes, sir.

FOSTER (*low*). What kinda bullshit is dat? What did you have to be that for . . . whatever you just said you were? All you had to do was be cool, little sucker, and you would have had it made. The world is okay for you boys who got some education . . . you could'a been an administrator . . . or sumpten' . . . in civil service . . . with a good lifetime job.

JACKSON. An administrator? Work for the whiteman all my life? You mean be in the pay of the white power structure and help keep my own Black people imprisoned and enslaved . . . No, never!

FOSTER. But you would have had it made, son.

JACKSON. No. Not me. It's made for *you*, old uncle. There are too many crimes against our people, too many submerged in poverty, starvation and ignorance caused by the whiteman. But when that day comes when there will be only a world by, for and of Blackmen, then my brother . . .

FOSTER (*ridicule*). Save it, please.

JACKSON. If Black people were free you would not be here, old man.

FOSTER. Maybe so . . . maybe not. But one thing's sure: whether free or no, you better always be able to hold your liquor. Even a slave should hold his liquor . . . And I couldn't.

JACKSON. Yeah, that's right. But a man usually gets caught up in alcohol or drugs because he is oppressed. A day will come when there's no more point in getting drunk or being on the needle, when no Blackman will feel ashamed for being Black . . . or being anything but what he is, a brother. We will all be brothers and freedom, justice and self-determination will make our souls glow. Do you know what I'm talking about, brother?

FOSTER. Yeah, I think I know what you're talking about. (*Ridicule.*) You're talkin' about dreams.

JACKSON (*hurt*). Brother . . . not dreams.

FOSTER. Yeah. The Kingdom of God, they call it.

GUARD. Shut your fucken mouths. I'm not gonna tell ya any more, ya hear?

JACKSON. No, you're wrong, brother. God can't do anything to help; unless we recognize who God is. I follow Allah . . . the spirit and soul of the Black people. Freedom, justice and self-determination is *our* concern.

(*A short silence.*)

Don't you understand? Do you know that old African tale about the most high prince and the great spirit?

FOSTER. Nawh . . . I don't know nothin' bout no Africans.

JACKSON. The most highest and greatest prince of all Africa . . . this was before the European came to Africa . . . the prince had made an appointment to meet the great spirit . . . the greatest spirit of them all. When he was on his way to keep the appointment he came upon a great elephant who was stuck in a mudhole. And the great prince stopped to help the great elephant. The mud was deep and thick and the elephant's whole body was submerged, legs, tail and all, and it took the great prince, as great as he was, the better part of the day helping to get the elephant out. When this was done the great prince hurried to the meeting place. But it was too late. Allah had gone.

FOSTER. And then what?

JACKSON. What? . . . well there are those who always get there too late. Too many elephants in their path, too many brothers to help out of the mire.

(FOSTER *fidgets uneasily.*)

What's the matter?

GUARD. That's the way I want it in there . . . quiet. And you, old man, stop bullshitting around. You've had time enough size him up.

FOSTER. Somethin' ain't right. It ain't natural, all that stuff about African princes and spirits and elephants and whatnot. Sounds crazy to me, and you got yourself put in prison for stuff like that. And then, there's somethin' else.

JACKSON (*looks at him*). Something else? What is it?

FOSTER. Now what's done to people who kill prefects, grand or no?

JACKSON. They're hanged.

FOSTER. You've said it, not me.

(*He begins to move away. The* GUARD, *who has been grinning, moves closer and gives a loud guffaw.*)

JACKSON. Stop! What have you got against me, brother?

FOSTER. Nothin'. Only, fine young men like you are, well, I don't like to make a fool of you. It's okay talkin' like we've been doin' just to pass the time—but if you're goin' to be hung, and, no, it ain't right, it ain't playin' fair, as I see it.

JACKSON. Why not?

GUARD (*laughs*). C'mon, grandpa. Sock it to him.

FOSTER. Because all this talk about you and me bein'

brothers and all just won't wash, lil ole chump. I'm the hangman, ya see?

JACKSON. Oh. I thought you were a prisoner, like me.

FOSTER. Yeah, I am. But they've given me that job, and I get a year knocked off my sentence for every man I hang. It's gravy for nothin'.

JACKSON. So, to atone for your crimes, they make you commit new ones?

FOSTER. Ahhh . . . c'mon now . . . you can't call them crimes; I'm only carrying out mah orders. And, anyway, crimes or not, they don't care. If you want to know what I think . . . they ain't Christians.

JACKSON. How many times have you hung a Blackman since you came here?

FOSTER. Well, like I said . . . I came in thirty years ago with seventy-five years on me. That was before I could work off my time like I do now . . . that started about twelve years ago. But when I tie the knot on you, son, I'll only have five more to go. You a smart youngster . . . figure it out for yourself.

JACKSON. Each man's life is worth a year to you.

FOSTER. Actually, somebody's else's life ain't worth nothin' to me . . . I just am able to cash it in for a year's worth . . . ya understand?

(JACKSON *shrinks away from him. The* GUARD *guides* FOSTER *toward the door.*)

JACKSON. So you're the grim reaper? . . . An old *negro*.

FOSTER (*from the doorway*). And you, mister . . . who do you think you is? (FOSTER *goes out.*)

(*Lights change.*)

GUARD'S VOICE (*off*). STAND BY FOR DRILL! . . . READY ON DECK FOR DRILL! . . . THREE MINUTES 'TIL DRILL! . . . STAND BY!

(CLEVELAND *and* HARRISON *enter.*)

HARRISON *(fiercely).* I want to throw the bomb.

CLEVELAND. No, Harrison. It's already been decided.

HARRISON. Hey, man . . . don't pull those rules and codes of bombers on me . . . you know it's bullshit as well as me. L, I beg you to let me throw it—you know how much it means to me.

CLEVELAND. No. We have our orders.

(Pause.)

I'm in the same shoes as you; I have to stay here while others are on the firing line. It's tough, but discipline must be maintained.

HARRISON. Who's gonna throw the first bomb?

JACKSON. I am. And Burk's gonna throw the second.

HARRISON. You?

JACKSON. Why d'ya sound like that? What's the matter . . . don't you trust me?

HARRISON. Experience is needed.

JACKSON. Experience? Hey, what kinda jive is that? . . . After you throw a bomb, baby, that's it . . . No one has ever had a second chance. It's not like if we had a time fuse or could use a high-powered rifle. That's why we bomber units in the Black Revolutionary Organization are listed as "Suicide Squads" and are composed of only true revolutionaries. It's . . .

HARRISON. A steady hand is needed.

JACKSON *(stretches out a hand).* Look! Does that look like it's shaking?

(HARRISON *looks away.*)

Steady as she goes. Don't you get shook, brother? When the time comes . . . it's goin'a be all over 'cept for the shoutin'. But do you think I'd cop out, if I had that mathafukker in front of me? Nawh, an' I ain't goin'a go fo that. And even if for some reason my arm might start shakin', I'd know a sure way of killin' the Grand Prefect.

CLEVELAND. What way?

JACKSON. I'd jump out in front of his car and we'd all go up. BOOOMMM!!! Just like that!

(HARRISON *paces about the cell.*)

CLEVELAND. No, man, that's not on the program. Your orders are to try to get away. The group needs you, and you must save your life, if you can.

JACKSON. Well . . . if that's how it goes down. I realize my great responsibility, brother. And I'm honored by it. I also promise to be worthy of it.

CLEVELAND. You, Harrison, will be in the street while Jack and Ken are waiting for the Grand Prefect's car. I want you to stroll up and down in front of our windows; we'll decide on the signal you're to give. Bonnie and I will wait here, ready to launch our manifesto when the moment comes. With luck we'll do the Grand Prefect in.

JACKSON (*excitedly*). Yeah, I'll do him in. And how good that will be if it comes off. But, he's really nothing, the Grand Prefect. We must strike higher.

CLEVELAND. The Grand Prefect to begin with. We have to get the whiteman's stooges first. We must cleanse our communities.

JACKSON. And what if we fail? Then, L, we must act like the Japanese.

CLEVELAND. Like the Japanese? What do you mean?

JACKSON. During the war the Japanese never surrendered. They killed themselves.

CLEVELAND. No, Jack, don't think of suicide. Even though we're classified as a high risk suicide unit . . . suicide is against the Black Revolutionary Codes. We must live, if we can, so that we can fight for the liberation of Black people.

JACKSON. But the reason I volunteered for this unit is because it is an absolute unit. There's no turning back here . . . we are absolute revolutionaries . . . and our commitment is based upon death.

CLEVELAND. Yeah . . . perhaps . . . yeah . . . but you shouldn't think of suicide.

JACKSON.   What should I think of, then?

CLEVELAND.   Of carrying on our work, of terrorism.

HARRISON (*from behind* JACKSON).   To commit suicide a
man must have a great love for himself. A true Black
Revolutionary cannot love himself. His life is the Black
people's.

JACKSON (*swings around*).   A true Black Revolutionary? Why
are you fucking with me like this? What have you got
against me?

HARRISON.   I don't like niggers who fuck around with revolution because they're bored.

CLEVELAND.   Harrison!

HARRISON (*rises to his feet and faces them*).   Yeah, it's hard
and brutal. And I'm brutal. But for me hatred is not just
a game. We haven't joined together to admire each other.
But to bring our people freedom, justice and self-determination. We have joined together *to get something done.*
To get something done for Black people . . . *by any means
necessary.*

(*A shrill, piercing police whistle shrieks.
Lights change.*)

GUARD'S VOICE (*coming nearer*).   FALL IN FOR DRILL!
. . . THAT MEANS PRONTO, GODDAMMIT! . . . FALL
IN FOR DRILL!

(BURK, BONNIE *and* SISSIE *enter. The*
REVOLUTIONARIES *line up, one behind
the other,* BONNIE *at the front,* SISSIE *behind her, the* MEN *behind them with*
MURRAY JACKSON *at the rear of the line.
Behind* BONNIE, *each marcher has his
right hand upon the right shoulder of
the one in front; and they march back
and forth across the stage in close lock-
step. The* GUARD *enters blowing his
whistle. The screens light up and show
scenes of firing squads, electric chairs,*

*gallows, gas chambers, guillotines, funer-
als, morgues, mass starvation, etc.)*

GUARD.   KEEP IN STEP, YA CLUMSY BASTARDS! . . .
   PICK 'EM UP 'N PUT 'EM DOWN! . . . SOUND OFF
   . . . 'N BRING IT ON DOWN FRONT! . . . I SAID
   DOWN FRONT!

BONNIE.   BONNIE MAE BROWN, SIR! . . . DOWN
   FRONT!

GUARD.   YA HARE ME! . . . I SAID DOWN FRONT!

SISSIE.   SISSIE ANN WILLIAMS, SIR! . . . DOWN
   FRONT!

GUARD.   RIGHT! . . . THAT'S THE WAY! . . . NOW
   DOWN FRONT LIKE I SAID . . . DOWN FRONT!

CLEVELAND.   ELTON "L" CLEVELAND, SIR! . . . DOWN
   FRONT!

GUARD.   'N AGAIN!

HARRISON.   HARRISON BANES, SIR! . . . DOWN FRONT!

GUARD.   LIKE I SAID!

BURK.   KENNETH BURK, SIR! . . . DOWN FRONT!

GUARD.   SHO 'NUF!

JACKSON.   MURRAY JACKSON, SIR! . . . DOWN FRONT!

GUARD.   'NUF SAID! . . . DOWN FRONT!

THE REVOLUTIONARIES *(together).*   DOWN FRONT!

GUARD.   WHAT CHOU SAY!

REVOLUTIONARIES.   DOWN FRONT!

GUARD.   AGAIN!

REVOLUTIONARIES.   DOWN FRONT!

GUARD.   SING FOR YOUR SUPPER . . . NIGGERS!

REVOLUTIONARIES.   DOWN FRONT, SIR! DOWN FRONT,
   SIR! DOWN FRONT, SIR!

GUARD.   WELL . . . ALL RITE DEN! . . . NOW GIT
   WIT' IT 'N DON'T MISS A BEAT!

*(GUARD marches them off, blowing
whistle. Lights go down. Images brighten
upon screens to show a few last stark
realities of late 20th century America,
then stage goes black.)*

Act II

*(In the dark there are sounds: footsteps,
words of command, clanging prison doors
and the hum of high voltage electric
wires and the whirr of well-oiled motors.
Lights up showing* SISSIE *downstage,
center, in a spot.* MURRAY JACKSON *sits
in his cell, unaware of* SISSIE.*)*

SISSIE *(out front).* I'm sorry . . . I'm sorry, brothers and sisters . . . Oh, please forgive me. Allah will bless you if you
have pity on one of his humblest children.

But it was the eyes . . . the electric eyes . . . I could feel
them on me as I stood on look-out. All the time I could
feel them . . . look at me . . . through me . . . as if I didn't
have no clothes on. They could see through my disguise
. . . could see my skin, brothers and sisters.

And when the car came up and nothin' happen . . . no
explosion . . . no screams or fighting . . . I knew the electric things had gotten them . . . and would get me . . . so
I ran. I ran. I deserted under fire . . . and ran and ran
. . . I found myself on 129th Street close to where I was
born . . . near Park Avenue . . . and I ran. Ran more. Tried
to run off into the river, brothers and sisters. Tried to jump
in the Harlem River and drown . . . But I couldn't . . . I
couldn't . . . there was barbed wire in front of me . . . and
it stretched north and south as far as I could see. And it
was so quiet . . . so *quiet.* No cars down the streets or the
East Side Highway or on Harlem River Drive . . . no
trains running overhead on the Park Avenue elevated . . .
no boats or tugs in the river . . . Just the steady electric
hum of the barbed wire that would kill me if I touched it.
And I was a deserter . . . and I wanted to throw myself on
the wire . . . but I couldn't. I couldn't. So I came here so
that you could give me the punishment I deserve . . .
Please . . . please execute me . . . give me the coward's
death I deserve, Black people. *(Crying.)* Please help me
. . . help me, please . . . execute me . . . now. I can't
stand this condition of living death dragging on into each

morning. I have failed my brothers and sisters . . . and I am unworthy and unrighteous in the sight of myself and my god, Allah, the righteous Black Spirit of our people.

(Light off SISSIE. *A noise.* JACKSON *is alert.* SMITH *enters, followed by the* GUARD. SMITH *is spick and span.)*

SMITH *(to the* GUARD). You can go.

*(*GUARD *exits.)*

(To JACKSON.) Good morning, or evening . . . or whatever it may be. You don't know me . . . now, do you? But I know you. *(Laughs.)* Quite a celebrity, aren't you? May I introduce myself?

*(*JACKSON *remains silent.)*

Oh, you don't feel like talking—yes, I understand. That's the effect of solitary confinement: seven days and nights. It gets you down, doesn't it? Your mind tends to wander sometimes, right? You may even feel that you're hallucinating . . . hummm? But that's all right as long as you're not hurting yourself . . . Ha ha . . . We've sorta fixed it so that you won't be hurting anyone else . . . *physically* . . . Well, your days of being entirely alone except for our gracious representative, the guard, are over. That's all over now. From now on you can have visitors. Your friends, perhaps? . . . We'd love to accommodate them . . . ha ha . . . And, of course, the press. The press especially. They are actually slavering to get at our young blood splattered Black Revolutionary . . . And in fact, you've had a visitor already—that old gentleman, Foster. He's kinda weird, isn't he? I thought that he might interest you . . . He's a very old acquaintance of mine. Yes, indeed, he is. But you must be happy over the change; it's good to see a human face again after a week's solitary confinement, right?

JACKSON. That depends on the face.

SMITH. Ah, that's good. If you're worrying about Foster's face . . . well, it won't be around here for long.

JACKSON. That's right . . . five more after me . . . then he gets out.

SMITH. Gets out? . . . Oh, ha ha ha . . . Of course, he told you that he'd be getting out . . . But he doesn't know what we know. You see, we know that he'll be our new executioner's first client.

JACKSON. But I thought . . .

SMITH. So does he . . . but, alas, his old head carries too many secrets . . . knowledge is dangerous, you know.

JACKSON (*violently*). You people are more evil than my wildest imaginings could fathom! . . .

SMITH (*mimics*). "You people are more evil than my wildest imaginings could fathom! . . ." (*Relaxed.*) Ha ha ha . . . your language is so quaint . . . so gauche . . . give some more samples . . . won't you, please?

JACKSON. You'll get nothin' from me but contempt!

SMITH. Splendid! . . . Ha ha ha . . . I see you know your own mind, my young friend. (*A short silence.*) So, unless I'm a fool, my face displeases you too?

JACKSON. Yes.

SMITH. That's too bad. Sorry about that, my young friend . . . ha ha . . . sorry about that. Still, I have hopes that you may change your mind. For one thing, the light here is poor; these basement cells make everything smell and look like shit . . . excuse the expression, but that is the reality we are confronted by. And then, too, you don't know me, do you? Sometimes a man's face puts one off at first, later, when one gets to know the man himself . . .

JACKSON. THAT'S ENOUGH! Who are you?

SMITH (*snaps to attention*). Smith here! . . . Chief of Security.

VOICE OVER LOUDSPEAKER. ATTENTION ON DECK! . . . ATTENTION! . . . STANDBY FOR INSPECTION!

SMITH. Yes, my young friend, it's me . . . ha ha . . . just ole Brother Smith.

LOUDSPEAKER. STANDBY FOR SMITH! . . . FOR (*Echo chamber effect.*) SMITHSMITHSMITHSMITHSMITH-SMITH . . .

JACKSON.   A Blackman . . . Chief of Security . . . the secret
police?

(Lights change; CLEVELAND *and* BURK
enter the cell.)

CLEVELAND.   There's no such place for any of us where
peace waits except death. All our paths lead to the same
end: the concentration camp, the prison cell, the gallows.

BURK.   Yeah, but you don't see the secret police as you see
the man you have to kill. You gotta imagine them. And,
lucky for me, I have no imagination where that's concerned. *(Brief, nervous laugh.)* Do you know, I've never
really believed in the secret police? Absurd, isn't it, for a
terrorist? I'll believe they exist only when I get my first
kick in the stomach. Not before.

CLEVELAND.   And when you're in prison? In prison you
can't help knowing, and seeing. There's no more shutting
your eyes to the facts.

BURK.   In prison you have no more decisions to make. What
a relief to feel that everything's decided for you. You ain't
got to tell yourself: "Now it's up to you, you must decide
on the moment when to strike." One thing I'm sure of now
is that I won't try and escape; for escaping, too, you got to
make decisions, you got to take the lead. If you don't try
to escape, the others keep the initiative—they do all the
work.

CLEVELAND.   Sometimes the work they do is—hanging you,
brother.

(Lights change; CLEVELAND *and* BURK
withdraw into the shadows.)

SMITH *(to* JACKSON*).*   Black people need security as well as
whites . . . wouldn't you say, my young man? Ha ha ha . . .

JACKSON.   You know what you can do with "my young man."
In other words you're saying that you're a flunky. A flunky
murderer for the whiteman.

SMITH.   My . . . my . . . your language just isn't inspiring.
But have it your own way. Still, if I were in your position,

I wouldn't be so cocky. You haven't been tortured, you
know . . . not yet, anyway. But maybe you'll learn your les-
son before too long. You know . . . one begins by wanting
justice—and one ends by setting up a security force . . .
secret police, in this case . . . to restore and protect justice,
of course . . . and guarantee law and order, naturally.
Anyhow, I'm not backing away from the truth, and let me
talk to you very frankly, young man. Oh, you don't like
that, do you? Let me say, brother, then.

JACKSON.   Brother? From you?

SMITH.   Let's not examine labels, shall we? Or get hung up
in semantics. You interest me. I'd like to help you get off.

JACKSON.   What do you mean?

SMITH.   Certainly, it's obvious. I can get you a pardon. I am
bringing you a chance for your life.

JACKSON.   Who asked you for it?

SMITH.   One doesn't ask for life, my friend. One's given it.
Have *you* never let anybody off?

(A short silence.)

Think hard.

(Lights change. BONNIE *and* CLEVELAND
enter.)

JACKSON *(anguish).*   Brothers . . . forgive me . . . I couldn't
do it . . .

*(*BONNIE *goes to him and clasps his hand.)*

BONNIE *(soothing).*   That's all right. Don't worry . . .

CLEVELAND.   What happened?

BONNIE *(to* JACKSON).   Don't take it so hard, Jack. Sometimes it's like that, you know; at the last minute everything goes wrong.

CLEVELAND.   No, I can't believe my ears.

BONNIE.   Leave him alone. You're not the only one, Jack.
Some of our old brothers couldn't bring it off the first time.

CLEVELAND.   Jack, were you . . . afraid?

JACKSON *(indignant)*. Afraid? Certainly not—and you haven't the right . . .

(HARRISON *enters*.)

CLEVELAND. THEN WHAT THE HELL DO I HAVE RIGHT TO?

JACKSON *(pleads)*. There were children in the Grand Prefect's car.

HARRISON. Yeah, the Grand Prefect's niece and nephew.

CLEVELAND. But our spies told us that the Grand Prefect would be by himself.

HARRISON. There was the Grand Prefect's ole lady too. Too many people, I guess, for our young poet. Good thing the police spies didn't notice anything.

(All stare at JACKSON *and back out of the light, except for* SMITH *who remains.)*

JACKSON *(to* SMITH*)*. Well, I don't want your pardon, and that's an end to it.

SMITH. Anyhow, please hear what I have to say. Appearances notwithstanding, I am not your enemy. I won't even say that your ideas are wrong. Except when they lead to murder.

JACKSON. I forbid you to use that word.

SMITH. Ah, your nerves are out of order, that's the trouble? *(Pauses.)* Quite honestly, I want to help you.

JACKSON. Help me?

SMITH. Yes. The Grand Prefect and I . . . how should I say it . . . we weren't exactly buddy buddy, you know?

JACKSON. Leave me alone. I'm ready to pay the price of what I've done. But I refuse to tolerate this familiarity on your part. Leave me in peace.

SMITH. The accusation you have to face . . .

JACKSON. That's wrong.

SMITH. I beg your pardon?

JACKSON. Accusation is not the word. I am a prisoner of war, not an accused person.

SMITH. Put it that way, if you prefer. Still, there's been

damage done, you must admit. Let's leave politics out of it and look at the human side. A man has been killed—and killed in a particularly horrible way.

JACKSON.   I threw the bomb at your tyranny, not at a man.

SMITH.   Perhaps, but a man got in the way. It was a living Black human being that your bomb blew to bits. And being the Blackman's policeman I'm concerned about crimes perpetrated against Blacks by Blacks . . .

JACKSON.   And what of crimes of whitemen against your Black brothers?

SMITH.   Let's not change the subject just now, please . . . It wasn't a pretty sight, let me tell you, my young friend. When they had pieced the body together, the head was missing. Completely disappeared. And as for the rest, an arm and a bit of leg were all that had escaped undamaged.

JACKSON.   I carried out a verdict.

SMITH.   Maybe you did. Nobody blames you for the verdict, son. What's in a verdict, as the saying goes. It's just a word that's all . . . and we don't want to hassle about words, do we? What you're accused of—sorry, I know you don't like that word—is, let's say, a sort of amateurishness, doing a messy job, in fact. The results, anyhow, were plain enough to see; there's no disputing *them*. Ask the Grand Madame Prefect. There was blood, you know, a lot of blood.

JACKSON.   Shut up, damn you!

SMITH.   Very well. All I want to say is that if you persist in talking about a "verdict" and asserting that it was the organization, and the organization alone that tried and executed the victim—that, in short, the Grand Prefect was killed not by a bomb but by an idea—well, in that case, you don't need a pardon. Say, suppose, however, we get down to brass tacks; suppose we say that it was you, Murray Jackson, who blew the Grand Prefect's head to bits —that puts a rather different complexion on the matter, doesn't it? Then undoubtedly you stand in need of pardon. And that's where I can be of aid, out of pure Black fellow feeling, I assure you. (*Smiles.*) That's how I'm built; I am not interested in ideas, I'm interested in human beings.

JACKSON (*furiously*).   But, damn it, I don't recognize your right or the right of your masters to sit in judgment of me.

You can kill me if you think fit, and that is the only right you have over my person. Oh, I can see what you're leading up to. You are trying to find a chink in my armor, you are hoping to make me feel ashamed of myself, burst into tears, repent of what you call my crime. Well, you won't get anywhere; what I am is no concern of yours. What concerns me is our hatred, mine and my brothers'. And you are welcome to it.

SMITH. That, too, is an idea, or rather, an obsession, young man.

JACKSON. Do you have to talk like that?

SMITH. But murder isn't just an idea; it is something that takes place. And, obviously, so do its consequences. Which are repentance for the crime, and punishment. Now we get down to the heart of the matter, and that in fact is why I joined the secret police. I like being at the heart of things. But you don't want to hear me talking about myself . . . *(Pauses. Then moves slowly toward* JACKSON.*)* All I wish to say is that you should not forget, or profess to forget, the Grand Prefect's head. If you took it into account, you would find that mere ideas lead nowhere. For instance, instead of feeling pleased with yourself, you'd be ashamed of what you did. And, when once you felt ashamed, you would want to live, in order to atone. So the great thing is that you decide to live.

JACKSON. And suppose I decided to live, what then?

SMITH. A pardon for you and for your brothers . . . and the two sisters.

JACKSON. I don't know what you're talking about.

SMITH. Yes . . . of course we know . . . we have recorded your group's every breath for months.

(Lights change.)

SISSIE *(from the shadows).* I can feel them . . . I can feel the machines watching and listening to us.

BONNIE *(in shadows).* Oh . . . stop scarin' yourself, sister. That electronic equipment of his can't reach us . . . nor stop us . . . You know that. We're too far away . . . That's why we work, live and are in the center of our people . . .

so we can be more effective in reaching Black people and
have protection from the beast.

SISSIE (*walks forward into light*).   But it was the eyes . . .
the electric eyes, brothers and sisters.

(*The screens show images of the areas
surrounding the theater, and the local
Black community: the people upon the
streets, in bars, in barber shops, attend-
ing meetings, of well-known local figures
photographed unsuspectedly, etc.*)

SISSIE.   I could feel the eyes on me. All the time I feel them
look at me . . . through me . . . as if I don't have no
clothes on. They can see me . . . *see me* . . . and I am
discovered.

(*Images out.* SISSIE *moves off. Lights
change.*)

JACKSON.   But why didn't you . . .
SMITH.   Stop you? Ha ha ha . . . stop you from what?
JACKSON.   The execution . . . the bomb . . . I . . .
SMITH.   How could I pardon you . . . if you had committed no crime. Ha ha ha . . . Besides . . . have you ever
really looked at the Grand Prefect? . . . I mean from up
close . . . say, as close as I stand to you?

(JACKSON *peers at* SMITH, *then backs
away.*)

JACKSON.   But it can't be.
SMITH.   But it is . . . ha ha . . . saves the Black taxpayers
money, doesn't it? Getting a Grand Prefect and a Chief of
Security in one head.
JACKSON.   But . . . but . . .

(*Successive images of* SMITH's *face appear upon the screens showing varied
expressions — wearing different official*

*headgear—policeman's cap, government
official's homburg, and bareheaded with
changing eye glasses and without them.)*

SMITH. The poor chap you murdered? . . . Oh, well, just
another double . . . some ignorant actor that took pleasure
in dressing up as me . . . ha ha ha . . . Those sweet little
Black children were doubles too. Their parents were able
to afford a second car and live in New Jersey from the
money they make by hiring their babies out . . . ha ha ha
. . . very shrewd people. They know that not even one of
those *dreadful* Black Revolutionaries would even touch a
kink of their little pickaninnies' naps . . . Ha ha ha . . .

*(JACKSON, hands over ears, rushes from
the cell area and staggers before the
screen images of SMITH, like an insect
defying a candle's flame. Lights change.
Images fade. Shapes move out of the
shadows. The REVOLUTIONARIES, except
for SISSIE, surround JACKSON. All are
gazing at him, who now looks up and
fixes his eyes on HARRISON.)*

JACKSON *(wildly).* I'd never imagined anything like that.
Children, children especially. Have you ever noticed children's eyes—that grave, intent look they often have? Somehow I never can face it. I have to look away . . . And, to
think, only a moment before I was so extremely happy,
standing at the corner of that little street, in a patch of
shadow. The moment I saw the car's lights winking in the
distance, my heart began to race. With joy, I can assure
you. And as the hum of the motor came nearer, my heart
beat faster and faster. Drumming inside of me like a drum.
I wanted to leap into the air. I was also laughing and
crying . . . laughing and crying with joy. And I kept on
saying: "Yes . . . yes . . ." Don't you understand? *(Averting his gaze from HARRISON, he relapses into his dejected
attitude.)* I ran forward. The car almost stopped to make
its turn in the narrow street. And then I saw them from

the light of the streetlamp, I saw the children. They weren't laughing, not them. Just staring into emptiness, and holding themselves very straight. They looked so sad and wise. Dressed in their Sunday go meetin' best, with their hands resting on their legs, like two little African statues framed in the windows on each side of the door. I didn't see the Grand Prefect or his woman, only them. I saw only them. If they had turned my way, I think I might have thrown the bomb—if only to put out that sad look of theirs. But they kept staring straight ahead. *(Raising his head, he looks at the others. Silence. Then, in a still lower voice.)* I can't explain what happened to me then. My arms went limp. My legs seemed to be giving way beneath me. And, a moment afterwards, it was too late. *(Another silence; he is staring at the floor.)* Bonnie, was I dreaming, or was there bells ringing then?

BONNIE.   No, brother, you didn't dream it.

(She lays her hand on his arm. JACKSON
*looks up and sees their eyes intent on
him.)*

JACKSON.   Yeah, look at me, brothers, look at me . . . But I'm no coward, L, I didn't flinch. Only I wasn't expecting them. And everything went too fast. Those two serious little black faces, and in my hand that thing of death. I'd have had to throw it at the *children*. Like that. Straight at them. No, I just couldn't bring myself to destroy black children . . . *(He scans their faces.)* In the old days when I used to go out driving on the freeway outside our town in California, I always drove like hell. I had a Jaguar then. I wasn't afraid of shit, man, nothin' except for running over a kid—that was my only fear. I . . . I could imagine a dull thump as my fender smashed a small head, and the thought of it sent shivers all over me. *(He is silent for some moments.)* Help me, brothers . . . *(Another silence.)* I wanted to kill myself just now. I came back only because I felt it was my duty; you are the only people who can judge me. I have to know whether I am right or wrong, and suffer the sentencing that you hand down. So here I am—say something, please.

(BONNIE *moves beside him, her hand brushing his shoulder. He looks round, then continues in a toneless voice.*)

This is what I mean. If you decide that those children—those Black children—must be killed, I will go to the theater where the Grand Prefect is sitting this very minute, The New Lafayette Theatre, and wait till they are coming out. Then I will take care of the situation by myself, without help; I'll throw the bomb and I can swear to you that I won't miss. So make your choice; I'll do whatever the group wants.

HARRISON. The group gave you orders to kill the Grand Prefect.

JACKSON. That's right. But I wasn't told to murder children.

CLEVELAND. Jack's right. That wasn't on the program.

HARRISON. His only duty was to obey his orders.

CLEVELAND. I'm in charge of operations and I'm to blame. I should have anticipated every unforeseen possibility so that everyone would know how to jump without the least hesitation. Well, we gotta decide whether we let this chance slip by, or tell Jack to wait outside the New Lafayette for them to come out. You, Ken, what do you think?

BURK. I don't know what to think. I guess I'd have done the same thing that Jack did. But I'm not that sure . . . my hands . . . I can't trust them always not to shake.

CLEVELAND. Bonnie? How about you?

BONNIE (*emphatically*). I'd done the same as Jack! I couldn't blow to bits young life that could have sprung from me.

BURK. What of the Grand Prefect and his woman . . . they were once children?

BONNIE. Don't confuse things, Brother Ken.

HARRISON. I wonder if you folks understand what this means? Two hard months gone. Two months of shadowing, of barely escaping with our asses—two wasted months!

Ahmed busted for no purpose. Chaka hanged for what? And we have to start all over again, do we? Weeks and weeks of terror without a break; of nights with no sleep, of plotting and scheming, before the day that that opportunity gives us the signal on our door. Have you all gone mad?

CLEVELAND. You know he'll be goin' to the theatre in two more days.

HARRISON. Two days in which we might get caught at any moment. I know that well as I know anything.

JACKSON *(starting to go)*. Well, that's that.

BONNIE. No, wait, brother. *(To* HARRISON.*)* You, Harrison, could you fire point black on a Black child? I don't have to ask you about a white one. But a Black child. With your eyes open?

HARRISON. I could, if it was ordered by the group.

BONNIE. You just shut your eyes now, why?

HARRISON. Huh? Did I shut my eyes?

BONNIE. Yeah, you shut them, brother.

HARRISON. Well, I know why . . . it was to picture . . . picture my answer so that I could make no mistake. I wanted only the true picture, sister.

BONNIE. Open your eyes, brother, and try and realize that the group would be torn apart if we allowed this to happen, even by accident. Open your eyes to the picture of innocent Black babies blown apart by *our* righteous bombs.

HARRISON. Sorry, but I don't have your tender heart; that kind of shit cuts no ice with *me* . . . Not until the day comes when we stop sentimentalizing about children will the revolution triumph. Yeah, they're Black kids, but they are on the other side. On the side of the whiteman.

BONNIE. Children have no side, fool! They are born into what they are born into. When they are men then they may choose what side . . .

HARRISON. We will be masters of the earth, even if we must destroy children, sister.

BONNIE. When the day comes when Black people see you destroy their children, the revolution will be hated by all Black people. As brother Mao said: "To treat a brother as an enemy is to go on the side of the enemy," brother. And to slaughter innocent Black children is to become the butchering whiteman.

HARRISON. If we love Black people enough to force our revolution on them, then we rescue Black people from themselves and from their enslavement.

BONNIE. And what if the Black people at large don't want the revolution? Suppose our people for whom you are fighting won't stand for the killing of their children, however wrong or lazy or Uncle Tomish they are. All Black people recognize Black children, whatever their father's allegiances. What then if they include you among the Mississippi sheriffs, and the Alabama highway patrol and the white citizens councils of America? What if they held your power of terror in awe second only to the Grand Prefect's himself, or, of course, his successor. What then, my brave Black brother? Would you turn on the Black people themselves then?

HARRISON. YES! If necessary. I would strike and strike and strike. And I would go on striking until they understood . . . Now, don't misunderstand me; I, too, love our people. But . . .

BONNIE. Love? You call that love? That's not how love shows itself.

HARRISON. WHO SAYS SO?

BONNIE. I say so.

HARRISON. You're a woman, and your idea of love is . . . well, let's say, unscientific.

BONNIE (*passionately*). In spite of what you think, brother, I have a very good idea of what shame means.

HARRISON. Only one time. Really, only one single time did I feel ashamed of myself. It was when I was beaten with the cat-o'-nine-tails in the concentration camp.

JACKSON. You were beaten?

HARRISON. Yeah, I was whipped. The cat—you know what that is, don't you? Reba . . . she was my soulmate . . . she was there beside me . . . even throwing herself in the way . . . her tears mixing with my blood as she supported me so I wouldn't fall at the whiteman's feet. She killed herself, as a protest. And the camp blew up in a revolt and more Blackmen died that day. But I . . . in spite of everything, I lived. So why should I be ashamed of anything, now?

CLEVELAND. Harrison, all of us love and respect you, brother. But whatever private reasons you may have for feeling as you do, I can't allow you to say that everything's permitted. Thousands of our brothers have died to prove that everything is *not* permitted.

HARRISON. Nothing that can serve our cause should be ruled out.

CLEVELAND (*angrily*). Is it permitted for one of us to join the police and play a double game, as Ennis suggested doing? Would *you* do it?

HARRISON. Yeah, if I felt it was necessary.

CLEVELAND. Harrison, we will forget what you've just said, for the sake of all that you have done for us and with us . . . Now, let's keep to the matter at hand. The question is whether, presently, we are to throw bombs at those two children.

HARRISON. Children! There you go again, always talking about children. Can't you realize what is at stake? Just because Jack couldn't bring himself to kill those two, thousands of Black children from the masses will go on dying of starvation for years to come. Have you ever seen children dying of starvation? I have. And to be killed by a bomb is a pleasant death compared with that. But Jack never saw children starving to death. He saw only the Grand Prefect's pair of innocent little puppies. What can you be thinking of? Not the future? Only of now? In that case then deal in charity and cure each petty suffering that meets your eye; but don't fuck around with the revolution, for its task is to cure *all* sufferings . . . present and to come.

BONNIE. Jack's ready to kill the Grand Prefect because his death may help to bring nearer the time when Black children will no longer die of hunger. That in itself is none too easy for him. But the death of the Grand Prefect's niece and nephew won't prevent any child from dying of hunger. Even in destruction there's a right way and a wrong way— and there are limits.

HARRISON (*vehemently*). There are no limits! The truth is that you don't believe in the revolution, any of you.

(*All, except* JACKSON, *react to this and surround* HARRISON.)

No, you don't believe in it. If you did believe in it sincerely, with all your hearts; if you felt sure that, by dint of our struggles and sacrifices, some day we shall build up a new Black nation, torn from the body of the whiteman that has consumed so much of our blood, a land of freedom, justice and self-determination that will spread out over the whole earth; and if you felt convinced that then and only then, freed from the whiteman and the slave's mind and religion, Blackmen will at last look up toward the heavens, a god in his own land—how, I ask you, could the deaths of two children be weighed in the balance against such a faith? Surely you would claim for yourselves the right to do anything and everything that might bring that great day nearer! So now, if you draw the line at killing these two children, well, it simply means you are not sure you have that right. So, I repeat, you do *not* believe in the revolution.

(*There is a short silence.* JACKSON, *too, joins them.*)

JACKSON. Harrison, I am ashamed of myself—yet I can't let you go on. I am ready to shed blood, so as to overthrow the whiteman. But, behind your words, I see the threat of another sort of oppression which, if ever it comes into power, will make of me a murderer—and what I want to be is a righteous Blackman, not a man of blood.

HARRISON. Provided justice, freedom and self-determination are achieved—even if it's achieved by assassins—what does it matter which you are, brother? You and I mean nothing to the total.

JACKSON. We are more than nothing, brother. If we are nothing then what are we killing for? If we are nothing then we should lie still like a filthy pig and allow the

whiteman to continue standing upon our heads. For you
it's pride, just pride, that makes you talk as you are talking now.

HARRISON.   My pride is my business. But Blackmen's pride,
their rebellion, the injustice that is done them—these are
the concern of all of us.

JACKSON.   Blackmen do not live by freedom, justice and
self-determination alone. We have survived this alien place
for five hundred years.

HARRISON.   When their bread and freedom are stolen, what
else have they to live by, brother?

JACKSON.   By justice, and, don't forget, by innocence.

HARRISON.   Innocence? Yeah, maybe I know what that
means. But I prefer to think that no Black man is innocent anymore . . . at least not to the facts of the white
beast. But I prefer to shut my eyes to innocence—and to
shut others' eyes to it, for the time being—so that one day
it may have a Third World meaning.

JACKSON.   Well, you must feel very sure that day is coming
if you repudiate everything that makes life worth living
today, on its account.

HARRISON.   I am certain that that day is coming.

JACKSON.   No, you can't be as sure as that . . . Before it can
be known which of us, you or me, is right, perhaps three
generations will have to be sacrificed; there will have
been more bloody wars, and no less bloody revolutions.
And by the time that all this blood has dried off the earth,
you and I will long since have turned to dust.

HARRISON.   Then others will come—other Blackmen—and I
salute them as my brothers.

JACKSON (*excitedly*).   Others, you say! Other Blackmen. Well,
you might be very right, brother. But those *I* love are the
men who are alive today, and walk this same earth. It's
they whom I salute, it is for them I am fighting and dying,
yes, for them I am ready to lay down my life. But I shall
not strike my brothers in the face for the sake of some
far-off city, which, for all I know, may not exist. I refuse
to add to the living injustice of the whiteman . . . that he
has spread all around me, in the hearts of some so-called
Black Revolutionaries, just for the sake of a dead justice.

(In a lower, but firmer voice.) Brothers, I want to speak to you quite frankly and to tell you something that any brother out on the corner would say if you asked him his opinion. Killing children is a crime against a man's honor. The spirit of the race would rebel and move against the hand that destroyed its children, as it is doing to the white-man now. And if one day the Black Revolution thinks to break with honor, well, I'm through with the Black Revolution. Remember what brother Jones said: "We are preaching a new virtue . . . ethics and aesthetics are one." Yes, brothers, a new virtue . . . a new ethic . . . a new Black morality, understand? If you decide that I must do it, well and good; I will go to the New Lafayette Theatre when they're due to come out—but I'll throw myself under the car wheels.

HARRISON. You fool! You fool! Honor is a luxury reserved for people who have limousines and chauffeurs.

JACKSON. No. It's the one wealth left to a poor Black man. You know it, and you also know that the revolution has its code of honor.

HARRISON. Honor to the whiteman?

JACKSON. No. It's far more involved than just with the whiteman. We should stop harping on the whiteman. He is not our reason for existing, is he? You know it, and you also know that the Black Revolution has its code of honor that it uses in regards to Black people. It's what we all are ready to die for. It's what made you hold your head up, Harrison, when they beat you; it's what made your woman, your Black woman, embrace you and lift you up so you would not fall at the whiteman's feet. And it's behind what you have been saying to us today.

HARRISON *(shrilly)*. Shut up! Don't you ever speak of that again, understand?

JACKSON *(angrily)*. Why must I keep quiet?

HARRISON. If you ever mention Reba again . . . I'll break your back.

CLEVELAND. Enough of this.

JACKSON. I took it lying down when you said I didn't believe in the revolution. Which was as good as telling me that I was ready to kill the Grand Prefect for nothing; that I was a common killer. I let you say that—and somehow I kept my hands off you—and now you talk of breaking *my* back!

CLEVELAND. Jack!

HARRISON. It's killing for nothing, sometimes, not to kill enough.

CLEVELAND. Harrison, none of us here agree with you. And we have made our decision.

HARRISON. Then I submit to the will of the group. But, let me tell you once again that there is no place in work like ours for chicken heartedness. No bullshit about it. We're killers, plain and simple, and we've chosen to be killers . . . Special killers . . . bombers! . . .

CLEVELAND. That's a lie. We are not murderers!

HARRISON. Not only do we murder . . . but our special way maims the flesh and shatters the senses . . . Think of it: gouged out eye sockets . . . exploded ear drums . . . limbs shredded from the body . . . WE ARE KILLERS, BROTHERS!

JACKSON (*screams, loses all self-control*). Stop the lies! I have chosen death so as to prevent murder from triumphing in the world. I've chosen to be innocent, to be righteous!

CLEVELAND. Jack! Harrison! That's all. The group has decided that the slaughter of these children would serve no purpose. We must start again from the beginning, and be ready for another try at it in two days from now.

HARRISON. And what if the children are with him again?

JACKSON. Then we will wait for another chance.

HARRISON. And supposing the Grand Prefect is with his woman?

JACKSON. *Her* . . . I will not spare.

(*Lights change, then down. And up again showing* JACKSON *in his cell with* SMITH.)

Her . . . I will not spare. *I will not spare.*

SMITH. Did I hear you right? . . . Who won't you spare?

JACKSON (*realization*). Oh . . . God . . . Oh most merciful Allah . . . strike me down where I stand.

SMITH. Now . . . now . . . don't allow your poet's nature to get the best of you.

JACKSON. But you said that you and the Grand Prefect were enemies.

SMITH. Not enemies, really . . . more like antagonists . . . two sides of the same coin, you might say. Both of us are determined to come up heads, always.

JACKSON. But what about the others our group has liquidated?

SMITH (*near hysterical laughter*). The supply of hungry actors is almost inexhaustible!

JACKSON (*after a pause, weary*). Have the others been arrested?

SMITH. Your friends? No. As a matter of fact they haven't. But if you decide to die, we shall arrest them. And that would be a shame, you see. They are so amusing . . . and useful . . . they keep us busy . . . they keep us prepared . . . what would we do with martial law if we had nobody to martial? . . . Ha ha ha . . . Yes, life would be much duller . . .

JACKSON. I wonder if I've really understood . . .

SMITH. Why, of course you have. Don't lose your temper—at least not yet. Think about it. Obviously from the standpoint of the idea—the ideal, if you would like to use that word—you cannot hand them over to us. But it doesn't matter . . . we already have them. If we want to reach out. But from a practical point of view you'd be doing them a service if you helped us to tie all the loose ends. You would be preventing them from getting into further trouble . . . and from suffering. Yes, and that's what I said . . . suffering, and by the same token, you'd be saving them from the gallows, and worse, if you are co-operative. And, best of all, you would regain your peace of mind and serve a necessary function in this life.

JACKSON. What do you mean?

SMITH. We'll get to that eventually. But, from whatever angle you look at it, you'd be doing the best thing, if you do things our way. Well?

JACKSON. My brothers will give you the answer before long.

SMITH. Another crime! Decidedly, it's a vocation! Very well,

I have had my say. And I confess I'm disappointed. It's all too obvious that you cling to your ideas like a leech; there's no pulling you off them.

JACKSON. You cannot separate me from my brothers.

SMITH. Well, so long then. (*He starts to go, then turns back.*) Why then did you spare the Grand Prefect's madame and her fake niece and nephew?

JACKSON. Who told you about that?

SMITH. I told you. We know everything . . . well, almost everything. You have been under surveillance before *you* even knew you would become a so-called Black Revolutionary. Your every breath has been recorded and filed away for future reference. Great revolutionaries you are . . . You should have listened to that little girl you have with you . . . Sister Sissie . . . But, tell me, why did you let them go?

JACKSON. That's none of your business.

SMITH (*laughs*). Ah, come off it . . . Well, let me tell you why. Your ideals can murder a Grand Prefect, but it hesitates at murdering women and children, if they are Black. That was a discovery you made, wasn't it? But let's go on. If your ideals won't allow you to murder Black children, how can they demand that you murder a Black Grand Prefect? You Black Revolutionaries are forever fantasizing about killing white people . . . but all I find evidence of is your willingness to destroy Blackmen.

No, don't answer *that*. I don't care one way or another. You will save your answers for the Grand Prefect's madame. Yes, tell Madame Prefect what is none of my business . . . but it is certainly hers.

JACKSON. The Grand Madame Prefect?

SMITH. Yes, she demands to see you. And my real reason for coming here was to make sure that that would be all right. It is. It may even cause you to think about some of your decisions. The Grand Madame Prefect is a very Christian lady. Yes, indeed, I've heard some people say that she makes a hobby of the soul. (*Laughs.*)

JACKSON. I refuse to see her . . . But . . . wait a minute . . . aren't you her husband?

SMITH. But she doesn't recognize me, dear fellow. She hasn't recognized me for years. She doesn't even recognize

her sons or daughters . . . or grand-nephews or nieces . . .
ha ha ha. Every so often one of my doubles is unfortunate
enough to meet a young hot-head like yourself . . . And
then she wears her black outfit for a while. Seems to be a
great pleasure for her . . . dragging out that musty black
uniform. And now it's your turn to suffer with her . . .
(Softly.) Be kind to her, young man, be patient as you
would with your own mother. Remember, some of you
even pretend to repent to her god . . . and some of you
lose your souls to the cross . . . Alas, it's all in how you
handle yourself . . . all in how you feel that day.

JACKSON. I'll have none of it!

SMITH. Oh, yes you will . . . you have no other choice. You
are guilty . . . so be guilty and accept the punishment
meted out by those who decide your guilt . . . And you
are not to tell the Madame Prefect our secrets . . . right?

JACKSON. And if I do?

SMITH. All your friends will die immediately, except for the
women. The two women, young Bonnie, especially, will be
taken to this very prison and first turned over to the
guards . . .

JACKSON. No! No!

SMITH. When my comrades are finished . . . then they will
be available to the prisoners . . . first to Foster . . . and
then we shall torture them slowly . . . Attaching live wires
to the sensitive and private parts of their bodies is a
method we refined in Vietnam, remember?

JACKSON. Oh . . . please . . . why are you doing this?

SMITH. Begging for mercy already? You see I must get
results. Madame Prefect commands. I'm sorry, but she
will not take no for an answer. And you do owe her
something. And not only that, since the incident, since her
husband's death, she has become—how shall I say it?—
more mentally unbalanced. It is a periodic condition, of
course, but she is getting more senile. So we thought it
better not to stop her. *(He waits.)* If you change your
mind, don't forget my proposal. I'll be seeing you soon . . .
I have some other things to discuss with you. *(Short silence,
he listens.)* Here she comes. You can't complain about
being neglected! But it all hangs together, doesn't it?

Imagine God—oh, pardon me—Allah, without prisons . . .
or prisoners . . . or guards. One would be lost without the
other.

(He exits laughing. Voices and words of
command off. The GRAND MADAME PRE-
FECT *enters. Pause.)*

JACKSON.   What do you want?
MADAME PREFECT *(lifts her veil)*.   Look!

*(*JACKSON *says nothing.)*

Do you know that many things die with a man?

JACKSON.   I know that.
MADAME *(in weary voice)*.   No, murderers and beasts do not
know that. If they did, how could they do nothing but kill?

(A short silence.)

JACKSON.   Okay, I've seen you. Now leave me alone.
MADAME.   No. I must look at your face.

*(*JACKSON *shrinks away. The* MADAME
moves beside him; she seems exhausted.)

I'm so lonely. I can't stay by myself any longer. In the
old days he'd be there when I was sad, he used to share
my sorrow—and I didn't mind it so much . . . then. But
now . . . No, I can't stand being alone and keeping quiet.
But who can I speak to? Nobody else *knows*. They pretend
to mourn. And perhaps they really care, for an hour or
two. Then they go off to eat, or drink—or to sleep. To
sleep really. In some way, I felt you must be like me. You
don't sleep, do you? I know that for sure. And who else
can I speak of the murder except to you, the murderer?
JACKSON.   What murder? All I know of is an act of justice.
MADAME.   The same voice! You have the same voice as his.

But, I guess, all men use the same voice when they speak of justice. He used to say "This is just," and no one had a right to question it. And yet perhaps you, too, are mistaken.

JACKSON. He was an incarnation of that supreme, unholy injustice under which the Blackman has been slaving and groaning for centuries and centuries. And in return for this . . . this Super Tom, *the Grand Prefect* of all the enslaved Blacks of northeastern America . . . this super Black vampire made in the devil's image was given privileges, rewards, and honors. But, as for me, even if I am mistaken, the wages I am due are imprisonment and death.

MADAME. Yes, young man, you are suffering. But he is dead, you killed him.

JACKSON. Did I?

MADAME. What? . . . Are you pleading innocence?

JACKSON (*remembers his role*). He died suddenly. He never knew what hit him. A death like that is nothing.

MADAME. Nothing? (*Lower voice.*) That's true. They took you away right afterwards. I'm told that you made speeches while the police officers were closing in on you. Yes, I can understand that. That must have helped you face what you are facing now. But it was different for me. I came sometime later, and I *saw*. I took all that I could collect. What a lot of blood there was. (*Pauses.*) I was wearing white . . . like an old nun.

JACKSON. Keep quiet.

MADAME. Why? I am telling the truth, only the truth. Do you know what he was doing two hours before he died? He was sleeping. In an armchair in front of the TV with his feet propped up on a hassock . . . as he did so often. He was sleeping, and you . . . you were waiting for him down in those mean streets. (*She is crying.*) Oh, help me now, please help me!

(*He stiffens and moves away.*)

You are young, so young, surely you can't be all wicked.

JACKSON. Wicked? I've never had time to be young, lady.

MADAME. Oh, why are you so hard, so cold? Do you never feel pity for yourself?

JACKSON. No.

MADAME. You're wrong. It's better that way. Yes, that's right, better . . . to see you as you are. And that too is my penalty. To see a dream that never was . . .

JACKSON. I am not a dream, you wife of a super nigger fantasy . . . The Grand Prefect . . . jailer of his people, consular of the whiteman's law . . . You went to bed, old slut . . . with the slavemaster's slave . . . the man who sold you into bondage . . . and I'm a dream . . . a . . . a dream of some poor Black lady's who kept quiet and had the slavemaster's children . . . and had the master's best nigger . . . fashioned in his own image . . . you were so quiet with your children.

MADAME. But it kept them alive, son . . . it kept them alive . . . alive . . . so that you could be here . . . the dream that is you could be here.

JACKSON. I am not a dream, I am a man . . . a Blackman . . . a righteous Blackman . . .

MADAME. And an assassin.

JACKSON. A bomber . . . one through whom the will of the Black people is launched and explodes as murders and terrorists . . . and deaths to the enemies of the Black people . . . whether they are Black or white.

MADAME (ironic). A righteous assassin . . . all you righteous bombers are mirror images of your fathers . . . My husband was exactly like you when . . .

JACKSON. We righteous bombers are the mirror of the future reality. We stand without souls . . . without hearts. The best of us have been invested with the spirits of the people . . . and we offer up ourselves to the people . . . No, Madame Prefect . . . we righteous bombers who began by looking into the single reflections of our fathers have shattered that surface and millions of splinters of Black recognition smile blackly back from the African frames . . . We righteous bombers, we righteous ones are the new, not something that we are killing and have killed.

MADAME. But your smug illusions do not stop my suffering. Why didn't you kill me with him, instead of sparing me?

JACKSON. I didn't spare you, mother . . . I've only given you the most difficult task, as usual.

MADAME. And you allowed me to live . . . how terribly you hate me.

JACKSON. It was not you I saved, but the children you had with you. That part of the future that you had with you.

MADAME. I know . . . But I don't like them much. *(Pauses.)* They were the Grand Prefect's favorites . . . not mine. Aren't they guilty, like us?

JACKSON. No.

MADAME. How can you be so sure? My grand-niece is an evil little Black bitch. When she's told to give something to the poor colored people, the poor Black people that she sees, she refuses, and spits from the limousine window at them. She won't go near them, except to spit upon them. Is she not unrighteous? Of course she is. And my poor husband was so fond of her; she was the light of his eyes. And he was very fond of Black people too, no matter what you might think. He used to drink and laugh with them. And now you've killed him! Surely you, too, are unrighteous. The world is bleak . . . a savage waste stretching before us until . . .

JACKSON. Stop the pity! You're wasting your time. You want to drain me of my soul and empty my Black heart of the rightness of my act. But you won't get to first base. So leave me alone.

MADAME. Won't you join with me in prayer, and repent? Then we would not be alone.

JACKSON. Let me get ready to die my own way. If I do not die . . . then I am a murderer.

MADAME. To die? You want to die? No. I forbid it. *(Goes to* JACKSON, *with rising emotion.)* It is your duty to accept being a murderer. You killed him, didn't you? Don't hesitate! . . . Well, didn't you? . . . Good! . . . I want to tell you that God is the only one who can justify your . . .

JACKSON. Whose God? Yours or mine?

MADAME. The God of our Holy Church.

JACKSON. What has the church to do with it? Besides . . . there is a new holiness in this land . . . the Black holiness of Allah.

MADAME.　The Holy Church serves a Master who too had experience in prison.

JACKSON.　The times are new. Don't forget your Church has given what it wanted from its Master's legacy.

MADAME.　What do you mean?

JACKSON.　The Church has kept for itself what it calls grace, and left for us something that is called charity.

MADAME.　Us? . . . What do you mean by *us*?

JACKSON *(with shrill exasperation)*.　Why, those of us that you hang. Those of us you help enslave. Us who die and are murdered and tortured under your white master's rule.

(A short silence.)

MADAME *(gently)*.　I am not your enemy, son.

JACKSON *(passionately)*.　Yes! Yes, you are! You are! And so are all your kind. You are the ghosts of all the niggers the whiteman knew you to be. You are more foul than a diseased whore . . . than anything that I can imagine or say. Look, you are forcing me like the syphilitic prostitute into this unnatural way of life . . . and death. I am a poet, not an assassin. I was never made to murder men who look like myself . . . who remind me of my father.

MADAME.　Please don't talk to me as if I were the enemy, son. Look. *(She holds her arms apart and steps forward)*. Now I am in your hands. You can do whatever you want with me. Here is my trust. *(Weeping.)* There's a man's blood between us. But, even though we went down from this world into the center of hell, we can still meet in God. Will you pray with me?

JACKSON.　Never. No, never. *(Goes toward her.)* The only thing I feel for you is pity; you have done something to me . . . this time. And now I would like you to understand something. I have never made any agreements with God, and never will. If in dying I can keep the vows . . . those I made to the living, my brothers, who are thinking of me this moment. And it would be betraying them to cop out with God.

MADAME.　What do you mean?

JACKSON *(excited)*.　Nothing. Nothing except that I shall soon be happy, very happy! An ordeal lies ahead of me, but I shall see it through. Then, when sentence has been pronounced and all is ready for the execution—ah, then, at the foot of the scaffold, I will turn my back on you and on this filthy world forever, and at last my heart will be filled with joy, joy of a love that was satisfied . . . Can you understand?

MADAME. There is no love where God is a stranger.

JACKSON. Yes, there is. Love for His people.

MADAME. His people are . . . the meek . . . the dull. One can pity them . . . or exterminate them . . . what else is there to do?

JACKSON. Die for them . . . or kill for them.

MADAME. Which is the same thing . . . in your case.

JACKSON. Yeah . . . the same.

MADAME. One always dies alone . . . or kills alone . . . Even when he believes he is a tool of the people. He died alone.

JACKSON. No, you're wrong, old lady. One can die with them. Those who love each other today must die together if they wish to be reunited. In life they are parted . . . by the whiteman . . . by the evil that the devil does to us . . . by crimes against our manhood. Living is agony for we Black people because the whiteman stands between us and life. We must remove this germ forever.

MADAME. God pulls the very universe together.

JACKSON. Not this universe. And the meetings which mean anything to me take place in this universe, on this world.

MADAME. This world is the meeting place of beasts, beasts who lap their tongues out licking everyone and everything, and never finding the flavors they desire.

JACKSON (*looks away*). Soon the truth will be clear to me.

MADAME. Yes.

JACKSON. But doesn't love exist in this world between the two people? Two people who have forgotten what love is or never knew what it might be but still love in spite of not knowing, loving in the tragedy of ignorance. Two people whose only bond is the ignorance of love. Can these people be bound together in their ignorance of love but not knowing of death?

MADAME.　A love whose only link is ignorance of itself. What kind of love is that?

JACKSON.　The only sort of love that the whiteman and you, his slave, allow us.

MADAME.　I loved the man you killed. And it wasn't ignorance that brought us together.

JACKSON.　I know. That is why I forgive you for the wrong that you and your kind have done me. You cannot perceive the degree of your misunderstanding. Now go, please. Please.

MADAME.　Yes, I'll go. I came here to reintroduce you to God, my son, but now I understand that you see yourself as our own judge. So save yourself, unaided. That is beyond all powers, even your own, save the Lord's. But God can do it, if you live. I will ask that you are allowed to live, my son.

JACKSON.　No! Don't do that! I beg of you, don't do that. Let me die—or else I will hate you, I'll despise and curse you forever.

MADAME.　I shall ask that you be allowed to live—you must have time to think of all that has happened. You must have lots of time.

JACKSON.　No, no! I won't let you. I won't let you! Don't!

(*She moves away. Lights change. Short silence, then images of* SMITH *appear on screens.* SMITH *enters.*)

JACKSON.　I am glad to see you.

SMITH.　You are? I must compliment you on your fine act.

JACKSON.　Act?

SMITH.　Yes . . . Well, it makes my heart beat fast your being glad to see me. But tell me why?

JACKSON.　Because I wanted something to hate again.

SMITH.　You did? . . . Tsk tsk tsk . . . Well, I've come for your answer.

JACKSON.　You have it.

SMITH (*different tone*).　No, you're wrong. Now, listen to me. The reason why I allowed the Madame Prefect to see you is because I can now publish a report of the meeting in

the papers. This report will say that a certain young man
known to his Black Revolutionary friends as Murray Jackson will have repented out of pity for the widow prefect
and betrayed them! Betrayed his brothers and sisters! They
will be screaming curses to your name as they are tortured,
executed and raped. They will spread the infamy of Murray Jackson across the revolutionary consciousness of
humanity . . . Your name will be spoken of to dwarf Bene-
dict Arnold's . . . to ridicule Judas' . . .

JACKSON. So be it! . . . I shall not betray them.

SMITH. Which is it better to be, man . . . Judas or Jesus!
. . . To live a life among men . . . or die like a dog for an
impossible dream?

JACKSON. To be a man . . . to uphold the truth of freedom
. . . justice . . . not a coward and traitor.

SMITH. Would you see your brothers and sisters die at one
swoop . . . all their visions and work extinguished by the
rope . . . at the same moment. Let them go on . . . one at
a time they will die . . . Who knows . . . they might even
advance your revolution . . . they might have time to
overcome me . . . Brother Jackson . . . if they are to die let
them have some lease on life . . . grant them this . . . for
this is your function to be from now on. The true harbinger
of death.

JACKSON. I don't understand what you are saying.

SMITH. You are our next hangman . . . our next executioner.

(JACKSON *backs away terrified.*)

JACKSON. This is not real . . . this cannot happen . . . Why
no one could believe this . . . or could they make it up.
Tell me I'm mad.

SMITH. Your friends will not believe anything . . . Why kill
them tomorrow. You hold the life of dear little Bonnie in
your hands for six more years . . . I swear to you . . . I'll
not touch her for six years, whatever she does . . . Give her
these years, brother, then it will be her time to go . . .

JACKSON. But Bonnie . . . Cleveland, Harrison and the rest
would never believe it. You don't know their love for me.
They'd die gladly for me and know I'd never betray them.

SMITH. But, brother . . . brotherhood wears thin as a worn blanket in the middle of a cool night . . . when it is measured by the rope. Think about it. I'll wait. (*Starts to leave.*) Take your time, young friend. Take your time. I'd hate to lose you. We shall have many long conversations in the years to come. And I've watched your chess game . . . yes, your game is well developed . . . especially that unorthodox opening you use. You learned to play in youth prison, didn't you? . . . Ha ha . . . no need to answer . . . our records are complete. So, just call when you want me.

JACKSON (*crying*). But you have an executioner.

SMITH. Have you forgotten that he will be your first client?

JACKSON (*mutters*). But seventy-five . . . seventy-five of my brothers and sisters.

SMITH. One hundred and fifty . . . One hundred and fifty, Murray Jackson . . . You see . . . we believe that you are twice the man that Foster ever was.

(SMITH *exits; his image continues upon the screens until the* GUARD *enters.*)

GUARD. LIGHTS OUT!

(*Lights off, except for the image that gradually dims.*)

I SAID LIGHTS OUT, DAMMIT! I AIN'T GONNA SAY IT AGAIN! ALL LIGHTS OUT!

(*Lights down.*)

ACT III

(*Under an eerie light* MURRAY JACKSON *prepares for the execution ritual. He slowly, ceremoniously dons his executioner's garb and tests his equipment: the rope, the white, sterile tape for mask-*

ing the victim's mouth, the leather thong
for tying the hands and binding the arms
next to the body. Simultaneously, as the
above action goes on, MURRAY JACKSON
and BONNIE *appear on the screens.)*

BONNIE. What's the matter, brother?
JACKSON. It's Harrison. We've fallen out. He doesn't like me.

(Pause.)

BONNIE. Harrison doesn't like anybody; that's how he is.
But he'll be glad when everything is through. Don't let it
make you sad, Jack.
JACKSON. But I *am* sad, sister. I want you all to love me.
When I joined the group I cut myself away from everything, and if my brothers turn against me, how can I
stand it? Time and again I feel they do not understand
me. Perhaps it's my fault. I know I'm often clumsy, I don't
say the right things, I . . .
BONNIE. They love you and they understand you. Only,
Harrison's different.
JACKSON. No. I can guess what he thinks; I heard somebody
say almost the same thing: "Jack's too shaky, too jive time
to be a revolutionary." I'd have them know that I'm not
at all weak. I imagine I seem to them as being not together,
dizzy very likely. But I believe in the revolution as
strongly as they do. Like them, I'm ready to give my life
up for the revolution. I, too, can be slick, silent, sharp,
when it's called for. Only, I'm still convinced that life is a
great thing, I'm in love with beauty, happiness. That's why
I hate the Black people's position here in America and the
world. The trouble is to make my brothers understand
this. Revolution, by all means. But revolution for the sake
of life—to give life a chance, if you see what I mean.
BONNIE *(impulsively).* Yes, I do! *(Short silence, in lower
voice.)* Only—what we're going to give isn't life, but death.
JACKSON. We? Oh, I see what you mean. But that's not the
same thing at all. When we kill, we're killing so as to build
up a Black world in where there will be no more killing.

We have to be murderers so that at last the innocent and righteous, and only they, will inherit the earth.

BONNIE.   And suppose it doesn't work out that way?

JACKSON.   How can you say such a thing? It's unthinkable. Then Harrison would be right—and we'd have to spit in the face of grace.

BONNIE.   I've had more experience than you in this work, and I know that nothing's so simple as you imagine. But you have faith, brother, and faith is what we need, all of us.

JACKSON.   Faith? No. Only one man had faith in that sense. Malcolm.

BONNIE.   Well, let's say then that you have a whole lotta soul, and you'll do your job, no matter what the cost. Why did you ask to throw the first bomb?

JACKSON.   When one's a terrorist one can talk of direct action without taking part in it?

BONNIE.   No.

JACKSON.   And one must be in the forefront, of course . . .

BONNIE *(musing).*   Yes, there's the forefront—and there's also the last moment. We all should think of that. That's where courage is at, and the selfless passion we all need . . . you, too, need.

JACKSON.   For a year now that has never left my thoughts; I've been living for that moment day by day, hour by hour. And I know now that I'd like to die on the spot, beside the Grand Prefect. To shed my blood to the last drop, or blaze up like napalm in the flash of the explosion and leave not an ash of me behind. Do you understand why I asked to throw the bomb? To die for an ideal—that's the only way of proving oneself worthy of it. It's our only justification.

BONNIE.   That's the death I, too, want.

JACKSON.   Yeah, the happiest end of all. Sometimes at night when I'm lying awake on the thin straw mattress that I sleep on, I'm worried by the thought that they have forced us into being murderers. But then I remind myself that I'm going to die, too, and everything's all right. I smile to myself like a child and go peacefully to sleep.

BONNIE.   That's how it should be, Jack. To kill, and to die on the spot. But, to my mind, there's a still greater happiness.

(Pause.)

The scaffold!

(As the scene plays upon the screen, down in the stage area, JACKSON continues to prepare himself for the execution ritual, until two black-clad GUARDS drag in FOSTER who struggles silently when JACKSON plunges a hypodermic into his arm which relaxes him. Then JACKSON prepares FOSTER for execution.)

JACKSON.   Yeah, yeah, the scaffold. Since martial law was first declared and the pacification began that long ago summer the penalty for terrorism and rebellion has been public hanging. Yeah, I, too, have thought of that. There's something missing about dying on the spot. While between the moment the bomb is thrown and the scaffold, there is an eternity, perhaps the only eternity a man can know.

BONNIE *(earnest)*.   And that's the thought which must help you through. We are paying more than we owe.

JACKSON.   What do you mean?

BONNIE.   We're forced to kill, aren't we? We deliberately sacrifice a life, a single life?

JACKSON.   Yes.

BONNIE.   But throwing the bomb and then climbing the scaffold—that's giving one's life *twice*. That way we pay more than we owe.

JACKSON.   Yeah, it's dying twice over. Thank you, Bonnie. There's nothing with which anyone can reproach us. Now, I'm sure of myself.

(A short silence.)

What is it, Bonnie? Why are you silent?

BONNIE. I'd like to help you in another way as well.
Only . . .

JACKSON. Only . . . what?

BONNIE. No, I'd better not . . .

JACKSON. Don't you trust me?

BONNIE. It's not that I don't trust *you*, darling; I don't trust
myself. Ever since one of our old brothers dropped a bomb
and died . . . I've been having . . . strange ideas. I have to
tell you about it sometime. And anyhow it's not for me to
tell you what will be so difficult.

JACKSON. But I like things that are difficult. Unless you have
a very low opinion of me, say what you have in mind,
sister.

BONNIE (*gazes at him*). I know. You're brave. That, in fact,
is what makes me anxious. You laugh, you work yourself
up, you go ahead and sacrifice yourself like you almost
enjoy it. But in a few hours' time you'll have to come out
of your dreams and face reality, and the terrible thing you
are to do. Perhaps it's best to speak of this beforehand—
so that you won't be taken by surprise, and flinch.

JACKSON. That's nonsense! I shall *not* flinch. But please
explain . . .

BONNIE. Throwing the bomb, the scaffold, dying twice
over—that's the easier part. Your heart will see you
through. But standing in the front line . . . (*She pauses,
scans him again and seems to hesitate.*) You'll be standing
in front, you'll see him . . .

JACKSON. Who'll I see?

BONNIE. The Grand Prefect.

JACKSON. Oh, only for a moment at most.

(SMITH's *image is superimposed over*
BONNIE *and* JACKSON's *upon the screen.*)

BONNIE. A moment during which you'll look at him. Oh,
Jack, it's best for you to know, to be forewarned! A man
is a man. Perhaps the Grand Prefect has gentle eyes . . .

(*Maniacal laughter and strange music
starts and surrounds them.*)

. . . perhaps you'll see him smiling to himself, scratching his ear. Perhaps—who knows?—you'll see a little scar on his cheek where he cut himself shaving. And, if he looks at you, at that moment . . .

JACKSON.   It's not he I'm killing. I'm killing the tyranny.

BONNIE.   That's quite true. And tyranny must be killed. I'll get the bomb ready and when I'm screwing in the fuse—that's the moment when it's touch and go, and one's nerves are taut—I'll feel a strange little thrill . . . of joy. But, then, I don't know the Grand Prefect; it wouldn't be anything so easy if while I was screwing in the fuse he were sitting in front of me, looking at me.

(SMITH *enters upon stage and watches*
JACKSON *complete his preparations for
the execution.*)

But you'll see him quite near, Jack, from only a yard or two away.

JACKSON (*vehemently*).   I shall *not* see him!

(*More laughter.*)

BONNIE.   Why? Will you shut your eyes?

JACKSON.   No. But, with Allah's aid, my hatred will surge up just in time, and blind me.

(*The* GUARD *enters on stage and silently
signals* JACKSON *that the time of execution has come. Images fade upon the
screen. Music and laughter down. With
the* GUARD *leading,* JACKSON, *the two
STRONG-ARM MEN on each side of* FOSTER
and SMITH *form a procession and march
silently off. Lights change and up on*
BONNIE *and* CLEVELAND *onstage.*)

CLEVELAND.   Try and get some rest, sister Bonnie.

BONNIE *(paces)*. My feet are numb.

CLEVELAND. C'mon, put this coat over you.

BONNIE *(still pacing)*. Time never ends . . . the night . . .
then sun comes up showing us our despair. L, this cold is
no good.

(HARRISON *and* BURK *enter. They greet
warmly.*)

Did you find out, Ken?

HARRISON. We think it's tonight. All the junior officers have
been ordered to report to their stations . . . They can watch
the execution on their televisions. The announcements
came over the air last night of a TV special this morning
. . . and you know what that means.

BURK. It's a requirement that all off-duty junior officers
watch when a Black Revolutionary is executed.

BONNIE. Are we going to . . .

CLEVELAND. Yes . . . we will turn the television on and
watch it too . . . when the time comes. But you don't
have to.

BONNIE. It's for dawn . . . this dawn.

CLEVELAND. There's still a chance, sister. It depends upon
the Chief of Security's decision.

HARRISON. It depends on the Security Chief. What if Jack
has asked for a pardon . . . what if . . .

BONNIE. He hasn't. He wouldn't.

HARRISON. Why did he see the Madame Prefect if it wasn't
to confess . . . if it wasn't to ask for a pardon? She's told
everybody that he's repented . . . become a fucken Christian, even. How do we know what went on? This very
moment he's probably writing our names down and handing them . . .

BONNIE. Shut up! You damn . . .

CLEVELAND. Brother! Sister! We cannot become hysterical
. . . we are professional revolutionaries . . . and we will not
break . . . understand, we will not!

BONNIE. We know what Jack said at the trial, and we have
the letter he smuggled out. Didn't he say that if he had
another life he would offer that too, he would spit in the

faces of the Black and white tyrants. Could the man who said that go on living . . . and . . . and repent . . . and ask for forgiveness like a dog? No, he will die . . . as we watch our television screen. Our Black and beautiful hero Jack is going to die because it is impossible for him to go back on what he's done . . . on what he is.

HARRISON. That's swell, baby, but he saw that Madame Prefect bitch.

BONNIE. He is the judge of what he had to do.

HARRISON. No. According to the code . . .

BONNIE. What code!

HARRISON. Our code . . . the code of the Black Revolutionary . . .

BONNIE. So you make up rules on the spot.

HARRISON. They may not be written down like the whiteman writes down everything but the truth in the alphabet he stole from our Arabic brothers in Africa before . . .

CLEVELAND. Please . . . please . . . no history.

HARRISON. It was his duty not to see her!

BONNIE. Our duty is to commit murder . . . nothing else . . . murder . . . pure and clean as death!

HARRISON. Let's not be subjective, sister.

BONNIE. Fuck you and that shit you spout out. We are human . . . Black Revolutionaries or not . . . My man is free! . . . Do you hear . . . Free! Jack is free . . . and don't you lick his corpse with your foul tongue coated with that bullshit you never put into practice . . . *(Ridicule.)* brother.

HARRISON. He's not free yet. In ten minutes, yeah . . . but not yet.

BONNIE. He's free, nigger! Now that death is holding his hand, he has the right to pull down his pants in the face of life . . . if he wants to. He owes nothing to life . . . and this piss poor life owes him nothin' but a kind burial. He is going to die, my brothers and there's nothing you can do about it or would if you could . . . Don't worry . . . you won't be cheated out of your circus.

CLEVELAND. Bonnie!

BONNIE. Why lie, niggers! Why hide behind the Black Revolution when it is your dry, flaking lips that wait to taste blood and bone splinters whether they belong to a

Grand Prefect . . . or a brother. Admit it, weak, selfish, cowardly nigger men . . . Murder is your last resort. You throwers of paper bombs and exploding bullshit. Your best you lead out into the monster's jaws and then desert him . . . your best! Jack is nothing. But a poor, scared nigger boy like yourselves . . . just an unambitious soul brother who scribbled poems . . . not a Malcolm . . . or Martin Luther King even . . . or a LeRoi . . . just a poor beaten Black boy who should have been busy giving me babies so that he would have someone to listen to his poems. That's all he was . . . and how he will end is part of the sport of defeat . . . a martyr to the God of Vengeance . . . a sacrifice to the God Assassination . . . a victim, my poor victim. Brothers, why shouldn't our poor little Black Revolutionary nigger poet repent and cry in the dark circle of the noose? He has committed the act. He has gotten his man. What more can he do? What other service can he do you, brothers? What? Nothing. He would only be good to father my children . . . and that stage of the revolution has passed already, right? So he will die . . . and you will believe in his death . . . and in the revolution . . . for men only die for the most profound reasons, right? And you will love his memory . . . and perhaps sing songs to his corpse and one day toast him . . . Toast his act that is nothing but stupidity and ignorance . . . Your love has a heavy price.

BURK. That's not right, sister. We always believed in him.

BONNIE. Did you? Well, maybe you did . . . So, I'm sorry. But it doesn't matter. We shall see the truth in a few minutes . . . in livid color . . . in our own home. But, Ken, my poor brother, why did you come back? I thought you had left us to work on revolutionary committees.

BURK. To take his place. When I heard what he'd said at the trial I cried I was so proud. You know his words by heart: "Black deaths by the millions will smother your animal breaths and you whitemen will fall and become fertilizer from which a new people will spring and grow, after the death of you beasts." When I heard that I shook all over, I could hardly stand . . .

CLEVELAND. So you raced back to die?

BURK. No, brother. I am here to serve.

BONNIE. "Whitemen will fall and become the fertilizer from which a new Black people will spring and grow." Yes, he said that. Very poetic.

BURK. Yes, he did. Bonnie . . . he had so much courage. And at the end he said . . . he said those words that sounded like the ghost of our African fathers echoing from across the seas and ages: "If my Black soul has caused me to be worthy of the duty placed upon me, of destroying violence and tyranny with all my manhood, may death take me, I throw my Black self into the teeth of history, and may it be a Black history, and may it judge me as merely a Blackman." I heard these words and returned to you to complete my duty.

BONNIE *(burying her face in her hands)*. It was truth he wanted above all else. But it was such a cruel path he chose to reach it.

BURK. Please don't cry, sister.

(Lights change. JACKSON enters, unnoticed by them, and goes to BONNIE, places his arms about her, attempting to comfort her.)

Remember what he asked—that none of us show anything except our revolutionary determination to go on. Oh, I understand him so well—now. How could I have doubted him before? I was miserable because I was a coward. And the coward me handed the bomb back to Cleveland. But I am a Jack too . . . and I take back my legacy . . . a righteous Black assassin . . .

BONNIE *(whispers)*. A righteous bomber . . . How sad.

(JACKSON nods.)

BURK. When I read that he was going to be executed . . . I couldn't help myself. I had to come as soon as possible and take my place beside him.

BONNIE. Who can take Jack's place tonight? Tonight he is alone with death, Ken.

BURK. We must keep him in our pride, as he keeps us by his example. Don't cry, sister.

BONNIE. But I'm not crying. I am not proud either.

HARRISON. Bonnie, forgive me. I want Jack to live. We need him.

BONNIE. But Jack does not want to live. And it's our duty to see him die.

CLEVELAND. Don't talk crazy, Bonnie.

BONNIE. But it's our duty, L. I know Jack. Only death will bring him peace. Please . . . let him die without our whimpers. Let it happen quickly . . . let it be quick.

HARRISON. Okay, L, I'm makin' it. C'mon, Ken. Let's make the rounds once more before it's time to turn on the TV.

BONNIE. Stop by Sister Sissie's watch station . . . and bring the little sister here with you.

HARRISON. Who will take the duty?

BONNIE. I don't give a damn if nobody does . . . I need her here with me.

(HARRISON *sighs and shrugs.*)

CLEVELAND. Yeah, you'd better make it if you're goin'a get back in time. But get back in time, okay?

(HARRISON *and* BURK *start to leave.* HARRISON *looks at* BONNIE.)

HARRISON. In a few minutes, sister, we will know everything . . . Take care of her, L.

(HARRISON *and* BURK *exit. Lights change.* CLEVELAND *moves away into the shadows, leaving* BONNIE *and* JACKSON.)

BONNIE. Yes . . . but why then are you so depressed? Not so long ago you looked so cheerful. Like a schoolboy going on vacation. But now . . .

JACKSON (*with bitterness.*) Today I know something I did not know before. You were right, Bonnie; it's not so simple as it seems. I thought it was quite easy to kill, provided one has courage and is lifted up by a dream. But now I've lost my wings. I have realized that hatred brings no happiness. I can see the poison in myself, and in the others, too. Murderous instincts, cowardice, injustice. I've got to kill—there are no two ways about it. But I shall see it through to the end. I shall go beyond hatred.

BONNIE. Beyond? There's nothing beyond.

JACKSON. Yeah. There's love.

BONNIE. Love? No, that's not what is needed, brother.

JACKSON. Oh, Bonnie, how can you say that? You of all people, you whose heart I know so well!

BONNIE. Too much blood, too much brutal violence—there's no escape for us. Those whose hearts are set on justice have no right to love. They're on their toes, as I am, holding their heads up, their eyes fixed on the heights. What room for love is there in such proud hearts? Love bows heads, gently, compassionately. We, Jack, are stiff-necked.

JACKSON. But we love our Black people.

BONNIE. Yes, we love them—in our own way. With a vast love that has nothing to support it; that brings only sadness. The Black people? We live so far away from them, shut up in our thoughts. And do they love us? Do they even guess we love them? No, they hold their tongues. And that silence, that deep silence.

JACKSON. But surely that's exactly what love means—sacrificing everything without expecting anything in return?

BONNIE. Perhaps. Yes, I know that love, an absolute, ideal love, a pure and solitary joy—and I feel it burning in my heart. Yet there are times when I wonder if love isn't something else; something more than a lonely voice, a monologue, and if there isn't sometimes a response. And then I see a picture floating up before my eyes. The sun is shining, pride dies from the heart, one bows one's head gently, almost shyly, and every barrier is down! Oh, Jack, if only we could forget, even for an hour, the ugliness and misery of this world we are in, and let ourselves go—at last! One little hour or so of thinking of ourselves, just you and me, for a change. Can you see what I mean?

JACKSON. Yeah, Bonnie, I can; it's what is called love—baby—in the simple, Black sense.

BONNIE. Yes, honey, you've guessed what I mean—but does that kind of love mean anything to you, really, darling? Do you love justice with that kind of love?

(JACKSON *is silent.*)

Do you love our Black people with that love—all tenderness and gentleness and self-forgetting?

(JACKSON *says nothing.*)

You see. (*She goes toward him—her voice low.*) And how about *me,* baby? Do you love me—as a lover?

JACKSON. No one will ever love you as I love you, woman.

BONNIE. I know. But wouldn't it be better to love—like an ordinary man?

JACKSON. I'm not an ordinary man. Whatever I am, I love you.

BONNIE. Do you love me more than freedom, justice and self-determination, more than the Black Revolutionary Organization?

JACKSON. For me, you, freedom and the rest, the organization are one. I don't make differences between you.

BONNIE. Yes. But do, please, answer me, brother. Do you love me all for yourself . . . selfishly . . . possessively? . . . Oh, you know what I mean! Would you love me if I were unrighteous?

JACKSON. If you were unrighteous and I could love you it wouldn't be you I loved.

BONNIE. That's no answer. Tell me only this; would you love me if I didn't belong to the organization?

JACKSON. Then what would you belong to, baby?

BONNIE. I remember the time when I was a student. I was pretty then. I used to spend hours walking around town, dreaming all kinds of silly daydreams. I was always laughing. Would you love me if I were like that now— carefree, sweet, like a young girl?

JACKSON (*hesitantly, in low voice*). I'm wanting to, oh damn, how I'm wanting to say yeah.

BONNIE (*eagerly*). Then say yes, honey—if you mean it, if

it's true. In spite of everything: of freedom, justice and self-determination, of our suffering Black people, of human slavery. Try and forget for a moment all the suffering—the hangman, the agony of little Black children, of Black men and women whipped until they die . . . the meat hanging from their bones.

JACKSON. Bonnie! Please, baby.

BONNIE. No, surely for once we can let our hearts take charge. I'm waiting for you to say the word, to tell me you want me—Bonnie, the living Black woman—and I mean more to you than this world, this fucked-up white world that is around our throats like a noose.

JACKSON (*brutally*). Shut up! My heart wants you, and you alone . . . But, a few minutes from now I'll need a clear head and a strong hand.

BONNIE. A few minutes from now. Oh, yes, I was forgetting. (*Laughs and sobs at once.*) No, darling, I'll do as you want. Don't be angry with me—I was talking nonsense. I promise to be sensible. I'm too tired, that's all. I, too, I couldn't have said—what I wanted you to say. I love you with the same love as yours: a love that's half frozen, because it's stuck in justice and raised in concentration camps . . . Summer, baby, do you remember what that's like, a real summer's day? But—no, it's a winter without end for us here. We don't belong to the world of living men. We are the righteous ones. Part spirits of beautiful Blackness, part dreadful ghosts of destruction and death. We are the righteous bombers. And outside there is sun and light; but not for us, never for us. Only the tomb and the concentration camp awaits us. (*Averts her eyes.*) May the pity of Allah shine on we the righteous.

JACKSON. Yeah, that's what we get out of this life, baby; love is . . . just not possible. But I will do what I must, and then at last there will be peace for you and me.

BONNIE. Peace? Oh, brother, you don't think that. When can we find peace?

JACKSON. Each of us will find peace soon . . . in his own way.

(*Lights change.* JACKSON *moves away,*

and CLEVELAND *enters and replaces* JACK-
SON.)

BONNIE.   Death. The hangman. Always death . . . L, L . . .
what are we going to do?

CLEVELAND.   Nothing, little sister. There's no other way.

BONNIE.   Don't talk like that. If death is the only way then
we are on the wrong path. The right one leads to life, to
sunlight . . . We can't only feel cold and then die.

CLEVELAND.   The path we are on, also, leads to life, sister.
To Black life. Black people will live, our children's children
will live. Remember what Jack used to say? "Black people
will seize the land of their dreams."

BONNIE.   Our children's children, always others—yes. But
Jack is in prison and the rope hangs down waiting. He is
facing it this very minute. Maybe he is already dead—so
that other Black people, after him, will go on, and live.
And, L, suppose . . . suppose that, after all, the others did
not live? Suppose he is dying for nothing?

CLEVELAND.   Shut up!

BONNIE.   Oh, it's so cold! And spring is here. I can see the
trees blooming out on 7th Avenue. He must be able to see
trees from his cell window.

CLEVELAND.   No. His cell is in the lower basement of the
prison. Security reasons.

BONNIE.   But if he gets a chance I know he would look at
the trees . . . and smell the changing of the air.

CLEVELAND.   Don't let your imagination get away from you,
Bonnie. And please try and stop shivering. Here, let me
put my coat around you . . . I'll hold you.

BONNIE.   I'm so cold I must be already dead. This life is
only a way of death, isn't it, brother? We will never feel
young again. With the first murder our youth ends forever.
And it is so sorrowful . . . our predicament. Here . . . we
are committed to murdering Black men. Blackmen . . . not
the whites we know we must destroy . . . but Blackmen
like ourselves. Oh, brother, I'm glad it is over . . . life is
such an evil game.

CLEVELAND.   Shhh . . . shhh . . . don't upset yourself anymore.

BONNIE. We throw a bomb and in the next instance everything in our existence and even our history has changed . . . A whole life time dissolved . . . and all that's left is death. Always death.

CLEVELAND. We are righteous Blackmen, sister. We do not fear death as the whiteman does. Each moment of our lives we build until the second of death. That way we meet death like heroes, fighting to the end.

BONNIE. You have gone about it too fast. You are no longer men . . . you have taken on the ways of the beast . . . and have become the monsters he has projected you to be.

CLEVELAND. But Black misery and injustice go fast as well. In today's world there's no time for patience and quiet progress. Our fathers had patience for four hundred years. Black people are in a hurry. And all the universe will step aside, if need be.

BONNIE. I know, Brother L. We have taken to our breasts all the sorrow of Black America. Jack took those sorrows and went out alone and did something . . . committed an act. That called for bravery. Yet I sometimes think that such pride will be punished.

CLEVELAND. It's Black pride, a pride we pay for with our lives. No one can do more. It's a pride to which we own entirely.

BONNIE. Are you sure that no one can do more? Sometimes when I hear what Harrison says I fear for the future. Others may replace us who might take our authority for killing; and will *not* pay with their lives. Only go on killing one after another Blackmen . . . for the savor of the kill.

CLEVELAND. Blackmen are not insane like the white beasts. And if we are our insanity takes human form . . . not animal.

BONNIE. We have long thought that the whites would exterminate us . . . and they have had some success. Is that why we only kill other Blacks at this stage, brother, not whitemen?

CLEVELAND. BONNIE!

BONNIE. Who knows? Do you make the decisions as who is to die? . . . No, you don't, do you? The orders come from a committee that none of us have ever seen . . . or know. And they give orders to kill only Blackmen, *brother*. Would they be so diabolical as to make up a committee of themselves and order us to destroy ourselves?

CLEVELAND. They? . . . What are you talking about, woman?

BONNIE. You know what I'm talking about. Wouldn't it be possible for the whites to be directing us?

CLEVELAND. Woman! How dare you! How dare you to blaspheme? You have lost your mind. The strain of your lover going to his death has been too much for you. You have lost the faith. I've never known you like this before . . . and would have never believed it. I wish I was dead rather than have heard what you just said. If I had a gun in my hand right now I'd lay it aside your head, sister, and put an end to your mad, miserable ravings.

BONNIE. Elton . . . L . . . I'm so cold, so cold. Hold me. And I'm thinking of him—and so many strange visions, dreams and images flood my mind, trying to block him out. I see him shivering . . . he's trying to hold himself upright, so not to be afraid. He seems to be dressed in black . . . Oh, L, it's so horrible . . . not the gray of the executed but the black . . . the black that the executioner wears. He's covered his head now . . . and he takes the rope in his hands and holds it tight to keep from shivering.

CLEVELAND. Are you no longer with me, sister?

BONNIE (*flings herself at him*). Oh, no, L, don't say that! I am here with you, whatever my mind holds I know that I am really here. That I am standing in the real world . . . in your arms. I will be with you to the end. I hate the world . . . the world the whiteman has created through destruction. And I know the only way to destroy the whiteman and his world is for us to be together. I cannot act any other way than together with my brothers. I was so happy when I began this adventure of world liberation . . . and it's so sad, sorrowful and lonely to keep it up. But continue I must. This life of death is the only life I have, brother. It's so horrible that it's beautiful . . . we are prisoners.

CLEVELAND. All Black people are prisoners . . . and all

America is a prison. But we will blow down the prison walls one day.

BONNIE. Yes, one day. Only give me the bomb to throw, or to plant. I shall walk through the flames and bodies laughing. I will not shiver then. It's easy to die . . . not live. And I will give my life to the death we serve. L . . . tell me, have you ever loved anyone? Really loved?

CLEVELAND. Yeah. It was so long that I've forgotten all about it.

BONNIE. How long?

CLEVELAND. Six years.

BONNIE. What happened?

CLEVELAND. She was white.

BONNIE. I see . . . Couldn't you have left the country, or done something?

CLEVELAND. When I found out what white means and what it means to be Black there was nothing I could do but live my life the way it has become.

BONNIE. How long have you been head of the organization for Harlem?

CLEVELAND. Three years. Now it's my only love.

BONNIE. Loving, that's strange . . . and to be loved, that's even more scary. No! We have too much work to do. It would be good to rest. But we have work to do. We haven't time to be in love with love because we love such things as freedom, justice, self-determination, liberation, righteousness . . . so many things other than people.

CLEVELAND. But we love Black people.

BONNIE. No, no . . . let's not go into that. For we would only find blind alleys and lies. We love what we love, that's all. There's nothing else. Keep on pushin', sister Bonnie. Keep the faith, brother L. *(She bursts into tears.)* But, for him, he is dead.

CLEVELAND *(takes her in his arms).* He'll be pardoned.

BONNIE. Oh, shut your mouth. You know that's impossible. You know that could not happen . . . It would be terrible. I can't see him in my mind anymore. He has escaped me. Perhaps he is walking to the gallows now. Oh, please turn on the television, L.

CLEVELAND. Are you sure you want to see this, Bonnie?

BONNIE. It is my duty! Isn't it my duty as a senior member of our revolutionary cell? *(He turns the television on.)* The picture isn't in focus yet . . . hurry, brother. I know the people will be there, standing silent as he approaches. I hope he's not cold like me . . . Hurry, L, get it. Do you know how men are hanged?

(Picture of an ANNOUNCER *comes into focus.)*

CLEVELAND. With a rope. Men are hanged by ropes . . . I can't, Bonnie.

(He turns it off.)

BONNIE *(wildly rushes him)*. And the hangman leaps onto his shoulder, his beautiful Black shoulders, right? His neck cracks, his feet jerk and dance. And they say Christian prayers over what's left of him.

CLEVELAND *(restraining her)*. And he finds happiness . . . peace and happiness, sister.

(She breaks away, and turns the television on.)

BONNIE. HAPPINESS!

CLEVELAND. To feel free that last second as you drop . . . just after feeling another man's hand upon you. *(He stands before the screen.)* Let's go away for a while, Bonnie . . . I can get forged passes and we can slip over to Jersey for a month.

BONNIE. Get out of the way.

CLEVELAND. We all need a rest. And I need you. I've loved you so long.

BONNIE. Get out of the way, brother.

(He does. The picture shows the procession to the gallows. There is no sound.)

CLEVELAND. I am your brother in revolution. But I need to be your man, as well.

BONNIE *(looks intently at the screen).* And all my brothers want to do nothing but love me . . . Between killing they want to love me.

(It is raining in the television picture. There is a patter of rain from offstage. Daylight is growing on the screen and on the outer area of the stage. Whispering.)

How I hate brotherhood, sometimes.

(HARRISON, BURK and SISSIE enter in rain gear. All stand watching the screen. BONNIE's knees sag; CLEVELAND supports her; SISSIE weeps.)

They have their heads covered . . . Both him . . . and the executioner. How strange . . . He looks so strange in gray . . . so small and shrunken . . . and frightened . . . And the executioner . . . Oh, how horrible . . . he looks like the Jack of my dreams . . . after he had put his hood on, Cleveland.

(SISSIE kneels and prays.)

CLEVELAND. Steady, sister. Steady . . . Jack has been through hell in the past month . . . they probably starved him . . . I'm so glad it'll be over soon.

(HARRISON steps forward and turns up the sound.)

TV ANNOUNCER *(Blackman with white voice).* Yes, folks . . . the procession is now at the foot of the gallow steps. Up to this point there have been no upsetting actions by the accused. These so-called Black Revolutionaries are cold, ruthless characters. They're fanatics, folks . . . and it's lucky that we are systematically wiping them out. Too bad we didn't get this monster before the unfortunate killing of that Black official up there in Harlem.

HARRISON. Wow, man . . . look how straight Jack is walkin'.

BURK. Yeah . . . that's a real man we're lookin' at . . . Man, I wouldn't have missed this for the world.

CLEVELAND. Let me turn it off, Bonnie.

BONNIE. No, I have to see. His death belongs to me . . . understand? . . . to me.

TV ANNOUNCER. They're reading the judgment of the court now, folks. Let's zoom in and catch this shot with our "right-there" lens.

VOICE FROM SCREEN (*white voice*). You have been tried by your approximate peers in the courts of lower Manhattan and found guilty of criminal acts against the state and city of New York, and for breaking the national anti-law and order codes. It is true that your jury was entirely white . . . but as you know Blackmen are not allowed any longer to serve on juries since their constitutional rights have been suspended . . . And the court finds you guilty and sentences you to death by hanging . . . And may God have mercy on your soul.

BONNIE. Oh, Jack . . . say something. Say something, Jack. Give the world words that we can create slogans which will inflame all revolutionaries of the world.

BURK. He can't say nothin', sister. They tape their mouths and drug them.

BONNIE. What beasts whitemen are . . . I can't look at any more.

HARRISON. Ahhh, please, don't turn it off, L.

ANNOUNCER. Like all the other Black Revolutionaries who are hanged this one doesn't seem like he's going to say anything, folks. But just before he left his cell he did give a speech: "I have given up my Black life, for Black people, and welcome death knowing that I am righteous in Blackness."

(SISSIE *begins chanting* "Allah Akbar.")

BONNIE. Did you hear that! Did you hear what the announcer said?

HARRISON. It's a good thing we kept it on.

CLEVELAND. Quick, Ken, write it down.

ANNOUNCER. And now the accused is walking up the steps

of the gallows . . . straight and certain. You have to admit
. . . these Black fellows have a certain style about them.
Someone from beyond the wall is singing an old time negro
spiritual . . . and . . . yes, and I can hear dogs barking from
way off . . . A soft rain is falling as dawn arrives. And the
accused is still climbing the long stairway to heaven or
hell . . . or wherever Black Revolutionaries go . . . supported by two red-hooded guards and followed by the
dreaded man in black. Remember, folks, that we will be
with you on instant replay of the actual hanging . . . just
seconds afterwards . . . and tonight we will bring you by
video tape the more stirring segments of this historic program.

And now they have reached the top. There are only
seconds before the military tribunal can intervene and give
a pardon. All eyes who are not on the accused now are
looking across the courtyard, waiting to see if that little
door will open and a messenger will come rushing out
bringing news of . . .

BONNIE. Turn it off! Turn it off!

CLEVELAND. Get ahold of yourself, sister.

(She turns the set off. SISSIE'*s wails rise.)*

HARRISON. Sissie! . . . cut out all that noise.

BURK. Let her pray, man.

HARRISON. But it gets to me, man. I don't want this broad
buggin' me while I'm trying to concentrate.

SISSIE. I can't stand it. I can't stand it here in the house of
the unrighteous. *(She rises and rushes off.)*

CLEVELAND. Now I want everybody to control themselves
. . . Remember who you are.

BONNIE. He's happy. There's nothing more to do but cry.

HARRISON. Are you crazy? Happy?

BONNIE. Didn't you see him? How calmly he walked? He
was happy in death. He is getting what he wanted. What
we all want.

BURK. But he was drugged, sister . . . he . . .

BONNIE *(screams).* Do not cry, brothers. He wouldn't have
it. Don't you realize this is a day of celebration.

(Bells begin ringing.)

> Do you hear the bells? It is over. All the revolutionaries of the world know what day this is. Jack is not a murderer but a man of important deeds. A revolutionary. And what confirmed it was a terrible crash that we didn't hear. But the bells tell us about it. And he was so young. L.

CLEVELAND.   Yeah?

BONNIE.   You're my friend, my brother? Take me away for a while. Take me to Jersey . . . and play my man . . . and I'll be your woman.

CLEVELAND.   Whatever you say, sister.

BONNIE.   And when we return . . . give me the bomb . . . the next bomb.

(All stare at her.)

> Give it to me. I want to throw it. I want to be the first to throw.

CLEVELAND.   You know it's against our policy for women to be on the direct firing line. You can be a lookout like Sissie.

BONNIE.   A woman! You say I'm a woman after this?

BURK.   Let her have it, L.

HARRISON.   Give it to her.

CLEVELAND.   It was your turn, Harrison.

HARRISON.   Say yeah, man. She's the one.

BONNIE.   It is mine, isn't it? And I can throw it. And after that . . .

CLEVELAND.   Okay. Okay. It's yours, but first Jersey, okay?

BONNIE.   Yes, yes, anything. Anything! Jack! One dawn not so long from now I will join you on TV . . . and the same rope . . . the same rope will bind us forever . . . Oh, the sun is out, brothers, it is spring . . . and how suddenly happy I am.

Sister
Son / ji

---

by Sonia Sanchez

CHARACTERS:

SISTER SON/JI—dressed in shapeless blk/burlap dress, blk/leotards & stockings; gray /natural wig—is made to look in her fifties.

(Scene: *The stage is dark except for a light directed on the middle of the stage where there is a dressing/room/table/ with drawers/and chair—a noise is heard offstage—more like a deep/guttural/laugh mixed with the sound of two/slow/dragging feet—as a figure moves and stops, back to the audience, the stage lightens.*)

Time: *Age and now and never again.*

SISTER SON/JI (*as she turns around, the faint sound of music is heard*).

not yet. turn off that god/damn music. this is not my music/day. i'll tell u when to play music to soothe my savage sounds. this is my quiet time. my time for reading or thinking thoughts that shd be thought. (*Pause.*) now after all that talk, what deep thoughts shd i think today. Shall they be deeper than the sounds of my blk/today or shall they be louder than the sounds of my white/yesterdays. (*Moves to the dressing/table and sits in the chair.*) Standing is for young people. i ain't young no mo. My young days have gone, they passed me by so fast that i didn't even have a chance to see them. What did i do with them? What did i say to them? do i still remember them? Shd i remember them? hold on Sister Son/ji—today is tuesday. Wed. is yr/day for remembering. tuesday is for reading and thinking thoughts of change.

Hold on! hold on for what? am i not old? older than the mississippi hills i settled near. Ain't time and i made a truce so that i am time

a blk/version of past/ago & now/time.

no, if i want to i shall remember.

rememberings are for the old.

What else is left them? My family is gone. all my beautiful children are buried here in mississippi.

Chausiku. Mtume. Baraka. Mungu./brave warriors. DEAD.

Yes. rememberings are for the near/dead/dying.

for death is made up of past/ actions/deeds and thoughts. *(Rises.)*

So. fuck the hold/ ons.

today. i shall be a remembered Sister Son/ji. today i shall be what i was/shd have been and never can be again. today i shall bring back yesterday as it can never be today.

as it shd be tomorrow.

(She drags her chair back to the dressing table and opens the drawer—her movements are still slow-oldish—she takes off her gray/wig and puts on a straightened/ blk/wig—stands and puts on a wide belt, a long necklace and a bracelet on her right ankle. as she sits and begins to remove the make/up of old age from her face her movements quicken and become more active. a recording of Sammy Davis Jr. singing "This is my beloved" is heard and she joins in——)

SISTER SON/JI. "strange spice from the south, honey from
the dew drifting, imagine this in one perfect one and this
is my beloved. And when he moves and when he talks to
me, music—ah-ah-mystery——"

(Hums the rest as she takes off all the
make/up and puts on some lipstick. when
she stands again she is young—a young/
negro/woman of 18 or 19. she picks up a
note/book and begins to run across the
stage.)

SISTER SON/JI. i'm coming nesbitt. i'm coming. Hey.
thought i'd never catch u—how are u? *(Looks down for she*
has that shyness of very young women who are unsure/
uncertain of themselves and she stretches out her hand
and begins to walk—a lover's walk.) yeah. i'm glad today
is friday too. that place is a mad/house. hunter college
indeed. do u know nesbitt that that ole/bitch in my political theory course couldn't remember my name and there
are only 12 of us in the class—only 3 negroes—as different
as day and night and she called out Miss Jones, Miss Smith,
Miss Thomas and each time she looked at the three of us
and couldn't remember who was who. Ain't that a drag?
But she remembered the ofays' names/faces and they all
look alike honey. *(Turns & faces him.)* you know what i
did? u know what i did nesbitt? i stood up, picked up my
note/book and headed for the door and u know she asked
where i was going and i said out of here—away from u
because u don't even know my name unless i raise my
hand when u spit out three/blk/names—and she became
that flustered/red/whiteness that ofays become, and said
but u see it's just that—and i finished it for her—i sd it's
just that we all look alike. yeah. well damn this class (i
wanted to say fuck this class honey but she might have
had a heart/attack/rt/there in class) i said damn this class.
i'm a human being to be remembered just like all the
other human beings in this class. and with that i walked
out. *(Is smiling as she turns her head.)* what did u say? am
i going back? no honey. how/why shd i return? she showed

me no respect. none of the negroes in that class was being respected as the individuals we are—just three/big/blk/ masses of blk/womanhood. that is not rt. can't be. (*Stops walking.*)

Uh-huh. i'll lose the credit for that course but i'll appeal when i'm a senior and u know what i'll write on that paper. i'll write the reason i lost these three credits is due to discrimination. yes. that's what i'll say and . . .

oh

honey. yes. it might have been foolish but it was right. after all at some point a person's got to stand up for herself just a little and . . . oh. u have a surprise. what? there? that's yrs? boss. o it's boss. (*Jumps up & down.*) Nesbitt yr/father is the nicest man. what a beautiful car. now u can drive up from Howard on weekends. yes. i'd like that. Let's go for a ride. u know upstate N.Y. is pretty this time of yr. where we headed for?

Yes. i do love u nesbitt. i've told u so many times but i'm scared to do it because i might get pregnant; i'm scared of the act. i guess u're right in saying that i'm against it becuz it has not been sanctioned by church/marriage and . . .

i'm trembling nesbitt.

i

feel the cold air on my thighs. how shall i move my love; i keep missing the beat of yr/fast/movements.

is it time to

go already? that's rt. we do have to go to yr/father's/ dance. how do i look?

any different? i thought not. i'm ready to go.

(*Softly.*) nesbitt do u think after a first love each succeeding love is a repetition?

(*The stage darkens and* son/ji *moves to the dressing/table and sits. Then a tape of Malcolm's voice is heard and* son/ji *adds a long skirt, removes the straightened/wig and puts on large/hoop/earrings.*)

SISTER SON/JI.   racist? brothers & sisters. he is not the racist
here in white/america. he is a beautiful/blk/man who talks
about separation cuz we must move there. no more fucking
SIT/ins—toilet/ins—EAT/ins—just like he says—the time
for ins is over and the time for outs is here. out of this
sadistic/masochistic/society that screams its paleface over
the world. the time for blk/nationhood is here. (*Gets up &
moves forward.*)

    Listen. listen. did u hear those blk/words
of that beautiful/blk/warrior/prince—Did u see his flashing
eyes and did u hear his dagger/words. cuz if u did then u
will know as i have come to know. u will change—u will
pick up yr/roots and become yr/self again—u will come
home to blk/ness for he has looked blk/people in the eye
and said

    welcome home. yr/beautiful/blkness/awaits u.
here's my hand brother/sister—welcome. Home. (*Stage
lightens.*)

    brother Williams. this blk/power/conference is
outa sight. i ain't never seen so many heavee/blk/people
together. i am learning too much. this morning i heard a
sister talk about blk/women supporting their blk/men, listening to their men, sacrificing, working while blk/men
take care of bizness, having warriors and young sisters. i
shall leave this conference brother with her words on my
lips. i will talk to sisters abt loving their blk/men and
letting them move in tall/straight/lines toward our freedom. yes i will preach blk/love/respect between blk/men
and women for that will be the core/basis of our future
in white/america.

    But. why do u have to split man. u've
been out all this week to meetings. can't we have some
time together. the child is in bed. and i don't feel like
reading. it's just 11 PM. can't we talk/touch. we hardly
talk any more. i'm afraid that one day we'll have nothing
to say to each other.

    yes. i know u're tired. i know that the
brothers are always on yr/case where u're organizing; and
u need to unwind from the week but i want to unwind
with u. i want to have a glass of wine with u and move

into yr/arms; i want to feel u moving inside of me. we haven't made love in weeks man and my body feels dead, unalive. i want to talk abt our past/future—if we have one in this ass/hole country. Don't go. Stay home with me and let us start building true/blk/lives—let our family be a family built on mutual love and respect. Don't leave me man i've been by myself for weeks. we need time together. blk/people gots to spend all their spare time together or they'll fall into the same traps their fathers and mothers fell into when they went their separate ways and one called it retaining their manhood while the other called it just plain /don't/care/about/family/hood. a man is a man in a house where a woman/children cry out for a man's presence—where young warriors can observe their father's ways and grow older in them—where young sisters can receive the smiles of their fathers and carry their smiles to their future husbands. Is there time for all this drinking—going from bar to bar. Shouldn't we be getting ourselves together—strengthening our minds, bodies and souls away from drugs, weed, whiskey and going out on Saturday nites. alone. what is it all about or is the rhetoric apart from the actual being/doing? What is it all about if the doings do not match the words?

(Stage becomes dark with only a spot-
light on SISTER SON/JI's *face and since*
she is constantly moving on the stage,
sometimes she is not seen too clearly.)

SISTER SON/JI *(is crooning softly).* hee. haa. haa. THE HONKIES ARE COMING TO TOWN TODAY. HOORAY. HOORAY. HOORAY.

        THE CRACKERS ARE COMING TO TOWN TODAY. TODAY. TODAY. HOORAY.

                where are u man? hee hee. hee. the shadow knows. we are our brother's keepers. we must have an undying love for each other. it's 5 AM in the morning.

            i am scared of voices moving in my head.

ring-around-the-honkies-a   pocketful-of-
gunskerboomkerboomwehavenopains.

the child is moving
inside of me. where are you? Man yr/son moves against this
silence. he kicks against my silence.

Aaaaaah. Aaaaaah.
Aaaaaah. oh. i must keep walking. man, come fast. come
faster than the speed of bullets—faster than the speed of
lightning and when u come we'll see it's SUPER-BLOOD.
HEE. HEE. HAA. FOOLED U DIDN'T IT? Ahhh—go
way. go way voices that send me spinning into nothingness.
Ah. aah. aaaah. aaaaah. Aaaaaah. aAaaAaah. Aaaaah.
Aaaaaah. AaAaah. AaaaaaaaaaaaaaaaaaaaH. (SISTER SON/JI
falls on her knees and chants.)

What is my name o blk/prince in what house do
i walk while i smell yr/distant smells
how have i come into this land
by what caravan did i cross the
desert of yr/blk/body?

(SISTER SON/JI *finally moves to the dress-*
ing/table. her walk is slower. almost old-
ish. she rests her head. then the sound
of drums is heard mixed with a Coltrane
sound. SISTER SON/JI *puts her hands over*
her ears to drown out the sounds but
they grow louder and she lifts her head,
removes her jewelry, removes the long
skirt, puts on a gun and belt, ties a ker-
chief around her head and puts a baby/
carrier on her back. the music subsides.)

SISTER SON/JI. do u think they will really attack us? what
abt world opinion? no, i hadn't noticed that they had a
new administration. newer and better fascist pigs. So we
must send all the children away. will i help take them?
Yes. but will i have enough time to get back and help.
good. Ahh—u think it'll be a long/drawn/out fight. are we
well prepared mume?—come children. Malika-Nakawa-

Damisi, Mungu, Mjumbe, Mtume, Baraka. come. the trucks
are ready to take us on our trip. make sure u have yr/
lunches and canteens. make sure u have yr/identification
tags, where is our drummer?

Mwenge play us yr/songs as
we leave.

i shall return soon mume. i shall return soon. *(The
sounds of guns/helicopters are heard.)*

So the war is be-
coming unpopular. and many devils are refusing to fight
us. good. mume. can we trust the devils who have come
to fight on our side? the women and i don't mind the
male/devils here but the female/devils who have followed
them. they shd not be allowed here. what happens to them
when the one they are following is killed. It will become a
problem if we don't send them packing. rt. away.

Ah. that
sounds like a heavy attack. It is. women. sisters. Let us
sing the killing/song for our men. let us scream the words
of dying as we turn/move against the enemy. (SISTER
SON/JI *moves as she chants.)*

OOOOU—WAH
OOOOU—WAH
OOOU—OOOU—OOOU—WAH—WAH—WAH—
OOOU—OOOU—OOOU—WAH—WAH—WAH—
EEYE—YO
EEYE—YO
EEYE—EEYE—EEYE—YO—YO—
EEYE—EEYE—EEYE—YO—YO—

Is it true that Mungu is here? But. he is only thirteen. a
child. He's still a child mume. He's as tall as u mume but
he's still a boy. send him back. all the other warriors are
fifteen. are we—do we need soldiers that badly. Mume.
please send him back. he's just a boy. he's just my little
boy.

he's not so tall stretched out on the ground. the bullets have taken away his height. Mungu. Mungu. Mungu.
can u hear me?

do my words go in and out yr/bullet/holes

till they finally rest inside u? Mungu. Mungu. Mungu. My
first warrior. i love u my little one even as u stare yr/death
stare. SCREAM-HEY-SCREAM-HEY.

Yes. u. death. i'm
calling yr/name. why not me? Stay away from my family.
i've given u one son—one warrior for yr/apprenticeship.
git stepping death for our tomorrows will be full of life/
living/births.

if he keeps the devil/woman then he shd be
made to leave. Yes. he must go. Mume. tell me what are
all these deaths for, with more likely to come? so he can
feel sorry for a devil/woman and bring her whiteness
among all this BLK/NESS.

he feels sorry for her. and
what abt our teachings. have we forgotten so soon that we
hate devils. that we are in a death/struggle with the
beasts. if she's so good. so liberal. send her back to her own
kind. Let her liberalize them. Let her become a camp
follower to the hatred that chokes white/america. yes i wd
vote to send yr/partner to certain death if he tries to keep
her.

these mississippi hills will not give up our dead. my
son/our son did not die for integration. u must still remember those ago/yrs when we had our blk/white period. they
died for the right of blk/children to run on their own land
and let their bodies explode with the sheer joy of living.
of being blk/and many children have died and these brown
hills and red gullies will not give up our dead.

and neither
will i.

(The sounds of guns, planes are heard.
sister son/ji *moves slowly to the dress-*
ing/room table. the war/sounds decrease
and a sound like Coltrane mixed with
drums begin slowly, tiredly. she puts on
the gray/haired/wig, takes off the gun &
baby/carrier—and puts on the make/up
of all the yrs she has gathered. then she

*turns around in the chair and stares at
the audience.)*

SISTER SON/JI.   Death is a five o'clock door forever changing
  time. And wars end. Sometimes too late. i am here. still in
  mississippi. Near the graves of my past. We are at peace.
  the state supports me and others like me and i have all
  the time i want to do what all old/dying people do.
  Nothing. but i have my memories. *(Rises.)* Yes. hee. hee.
  i have my sweet/astringent memories becuz we dared to
  pick up the day and shake its tail until it became evening.
  a time for us. blk/ness. blk/people. Anybody can grab the
  day and make it stop. can u my friends? or may be it's
  better if i ask:

  will you?

The Black Bird

(Al Tair Aswad)

A One-Act Play

by Marvin X
(Bismillah-
r-rahmani-r-rahim)

CHARACTERS:

A BROTHER, about 26
1st SISTER, 6
2nd SISTER, 7
3 DANCERS in black

(Setting: A room in the Black community. There is a table near the only window (SR) with a typewriter on it; a bed, refrigerator, stove, wash basin, and dresser drawer complete the room. On the wall is a large poster-size picture of the Honorable Elijah Muhammad, Messenger of Allah. The BROTHER is typing. He senses someone watching him, so he turns and looks in the direction of the door (SL) which is partially opened.)

BROTHER.   Hi! (We hear childish laughter.) As-Salaam-Alai-kum. (BROTHER laughs.)
VOICE.   What you doin?
BROTHER.   Typin.
VOICE.   What you typin?
BROTHER.   Somethin.
VOICE.   You know how to type?
BROTHER.   Yeah.
VOICE.   Who taught you how to type?
BROTHER.   The white man.
VOICE.   He did?
BROTHER.   Yeah. (BROTHER goes to the door.) What you doin?
VOICE.   Playin.

BROTHER. Where you live?
VOICE. Down the hall. This your room?
BROTHER. Yeah.
VOICE. What's your name?
BROTHER. Just call me brother.
VOICE. You my brother?
BROTHER. Yeah.
VOICE. You really my brother?
BROTHER. Yeah.
VOICE. Naw you ain't!
BROTHER. Yes I am.
VOICE. You really my brother? (BROTHER *nods.*) Ooooouuuuu,
 I'm gonna tell my sister you said you my brother.

(BROTHER *stretches and returns to the
typewriter. After a few moments two
little* BLACK GIRLS, *maybe 6 and 7, run
into the room.*)

1ST SISTER. Brother, tell her you her brother!
BROTHER. I'm your brother.
2ND SISTER. How you get to be my brother? You ain't none
 a my brother.
BROTHER. Yes I am.
2ND SISTER. Well how you get to be my brother?
BROTHER. Your daddy's my daddy!
2ND SISTER. My daddy ain't your daddy!
BROTHER. Yes he is.
2ND SISTER. How my daddy get to be your daddy?
BROTHER. We all got the same Father.
2ND SISTER. What's yo daddy's name?
BROTHER. Allah.
2ND SISTER. Who?
BROTHER. Allah.
2ND SISTER. See, that ain't my daddy's name. My daddy's
 name ain't no Allah.
BROTHER. Well, what's your daddy's name?
2ND SISTER. Thomas Jefferson Jones.
BROTHER. Really?
2ND SISTER. Yeah.

BROTHER. That ain't your daddy's name.

2ND SISTER. It is too.

BROTHER. Naw it ain't.

2ND SISTER. Yes it is. (*To her sister who is checking out the room, mostly staring at the picture of the Messenger.*) Tell him that's our daddy's name.

1ST SISTER. That's his old name.

BROTHER. No, that's not his name.

2ND SISTER. Well what's his name then—tell me what's his name?

BROTHER. His name ain't Thomas Jefferson Jones. Thomas Jefferson Jones is a white man's name. Your daddy ain't white, is he?

2ND SISTER. Naw, he ain't white!

BROTHER. Better be glad.

1ST SISTER. He cullud!

BROTHER. Don't say cullud, Sister, say Black.

1ST SISTER. Naw, he ain't Black—he's cullud.

BROTHER. He's Black, little Sister. He ain't cullud. Black ain't no color—it just is—it always was. Be glad you Black. We all Black. Black is the best. White wish they was Black. God is Black!

1ST SISTER. He is?

2ND SISTER. God ain't Black.

BROTHER. Yes He is.

2ND SISTER. How you know?

BROTHER. The Bible told me so!

2ND SISTER. God ain't no Black.

BROTHER. He ain't white—that's for sure!

1ST SISTER. Who is he? (*Pointing to the Messenger.*)

BROTHER. He's the Honorable Elijah Muhammad, Messenger of Allah.

1ST SISTER. Who?

BROTHER. The Messenger of Allah—God. He's the leader of our people—the Black people. The white folks have a leader and we have a leader. They have a president—Nixon—and we have a president, Elijah Muhammad.

1ST SISTER. He's our president?

BROTHER. Yeah.

2ND SISTER. He ain't no president.

BROTHER. Yes he is.

2ND SISTER. How he get to be president—He don't live in the white house.

BROTHER. He lives in the Black House.

1ST SISTER. The Black House! I ain't never heard of the Black House.

BROTHER. The president of the white people lives in the white house—the leader of Black people lives in the Black House.

2ND SISTER. Where is the Black House at?

BROTHER. In Chicago.

1ST SISTER. You been to the Black House?

BROTHER. Yeah.

2ND SISTER. You see the Black president?

BROTHER. No—he was busy.

2ND SISTER. What kinna house he got?

BROTHER. A Black House.

1ST SISTER. Is it pretty?

BROTHER. Yeah.

1ST SISTER. And he's our president?

BROTHER. Yeah. So when somebody come to your house and ask your mama who's she gonna vote for—you tell her to say we already got our president—the Honorable Elijah Muhammad. Okay?

1ST SISTER. Okay.

BROTHER. Let me hear you say: The Honorable Elijah Muhammad, Messenger of Allah.

1ST SISTER. The Honorable Elijah Ma-ham-mat, Messenger of Allie.

BROTHER. Al Lah, Sister. Say: Allah.

1ST SISTER. Allah.

BROTHER. Say: Muhammad—not Mahammet. Say it real soft.

1ST SISTER. Muhammad.

BROTHER. Right. Say Allah.

1ST SISTER. Allah.

BROTHER. Right.

2ND SISTER. Who is Allah?

BROTHER. Allah is God, The Only God—Allah is the Black Man—Allah is your daddy!

2ND SISTER.   My daddy's name ain't no Allah.

BROTHER.   His name sure ain't no Thomas Jefferson Jones. That's the devil's name.

2ND SISTER.   The devil?

BROTHER.   The white man.

1ST SISTER.   The white man is the devil?

BROTHER.   Yes, he's the devil.

2ND SISTER.   I thought the devil was red?

BROTHER.   Naw, Sister, the devil is white—when he gets mad, he turns red.

1ST SISTER.   White people is the devil?

BROTHER.   Yeah, Sister.

2ND SISTER.   I thought the devil was in the ground.

BROTHER.   Naw, Sister, the devil ain't in the ground—he's *on* the ground.

1ST SISTER.   Where do he be at?

BROTHER.   He's all around. He lives in the white house.

2ND SISTER.   The president lives in the white house.

BROTHER.   The devil lives in the white house.

1ST SISTER.   Is the president a devil?

BROTHER.   He's the main devil—he's devil number one! Is your teacher white?

1ST SISTER.   Mine is—hers is cullud.

BROTHER.   Don't say cullud—say Black.

1ST SISTER.   Hers is Black. Mine is white.

BROTHER.   Your teacher is the devil.

1ST SISTER.   She is?????????? I ain't goin to dat old school no mo. Shoot!

BROTHER.   Is the man at the grocery store white?

2ND SISTER.   Yeah.

1ST SISTER.   He's the devil!

BROTHER.   Right. Is the policeman white?

1ST SISTER.   He's the devil.

BROTHER.   Right.

2ND SISTER.   The mailman is white.

1ST SISTER.   He's the devil.

BROTHER.   Right. So you gotta watch them devils, now, you hear?

1ST AND 2ND SISTERS.   Yeah.

BROTHER.   Where do the devil live?

1ST AND 2ND SISTERS. In the white house.

BROTHER. Right. Who is Allah?

1ST SISTER. My Daddy.

BROTHER. Right.

2ND SISTER. Allah is the Black man!

BROTHER. Right. Thomas Jefferson Jones is a devil name. Your daddy ain't no devil is he?

1ST SISTER. Naw, he ain't no devil—don't be callin my daddy no devil.

2ND SISTER. My daddy's Black.

BROTHER. Be glad you Black, hear?

1ST SISTER. I am.

2ND SISTER. Black is the Best.

BROTHER. Where is God?

1ST SISTER. In heaven.

BROTHER. Where is heaven?

1ST SISTER. Up in the sky.

BROTHER. That's a big white lie!

1ST SISTER. That's what my Sunday school teacher—

BROTHER. That's a big white lie.

2ND SISTER. That's what my mama—

BROTHER. That's a big white lie. Sisters, heaven is on earth! Say: Heaven is on earth.

1ST AND 2ND SISTERS. Heaven is on earth.

BROTHER. Say: The white man's heaven is the Black man's hell.

1ST AND 2ND SISTERS. The white man's heaven is the Black man's hell.

BROTHER. I want you to remember now, heaven is on earth and hell is on earth—God is on earth and the devil is on earth. Remember that. We in hell now, little sisters, you know that?

1ST SISTER. We is?

BROTHER. That's right. In hell you work all day and don't have no pay. Don't your daddy work all day?

1ST SISTER. Yeah.

BROTHER. Do your daddy ever have any money?

2ND SISTER. Sometimes.

BROTHER. Right—in hell people have money sometimes— most times they don't have nothing. In hell the people

suffer day and night, they don't never get no peace. The
people is always sick and tired in hell. Don't yo mama
and daddy be sick and tired all the time?

1ST SISTER.   Yeah.

BROTHER.   That's hell. Your daddy, soon as he come in from
work, he eat, sit in front of the TV and go to sleep. Right?

1ST SISTER.   Yeah.

BROTHER.   He's going through hell. In hell the people fight
all the time, and cuss and shoot each other. Don't yo mama
and daddy be fightin all the time?

1ST SISTER.   Yeah.

2ND SISTER.   How you know all that?

BROTHER.   I know everything, Sister. Allah knows everything. Well, Sisters, I gotta finish my typing. Tell you
what, you all want to hear a story before you go?

1ST SISTER.   Yeah, tell us a story bout the devil.

BROTHER.   Naw, we ain't got time for the devil, Sister—just
make sure you know who the devil is, and you tell the
other little kids who the devil is—when you see the devil
coming down the street, or if you see the devil on TV, you
tell the other kids, "Look, here comes the devil! there's the
devil." All right?

1ST AND 2ND SISTERS.   Okay.

BROTHER.   Well, this story is about Allah's children. Sometimes we get lost from our home and Allah has to come and
find us. Once upon a time, there was a Black bird. (*As*
BROTHER *begins the story,* DANCERS *appear on stage. There
is flute music. The* DANCERS *suggest the story* BROTHER *is
telling.*) The Black bird lived in a cage, and the cage door
was always open, but the little bird wouldn't come out. He
loved the cage, he had been in it so long. Other birds
would fly into the white house and beg the little bird to
come out, but he wouldn't. Sad, the other birds would fly
away home to paradise, their hearts white with anger and
sorrow for their lost brother who loved the cage. "He is so
hard-headed," the other birds said on their way home, "but
we will get him out, we will get him out . . ." He was a
smart bird. Nobody could tell him anything—except his
master. He could sing too. When the master sang, the little
bird sang. He knew all of the master's songs by heart. He

didn't like to sing bird-songs. From all around, people came to see him do tricks. The little bird knew a lot of tricks the master had trained him to do when visitors came to the white house. He was a good house pet. The little bird was so good his master always left his cage door open; he knew the little bird had forgotten what freedom was. "Come, fly away to freedom with us," the other birds would say. But the little bird didn't want to go for self! "I like being in a cage," he said. "You birds are the crazy ones—get away from me!!!!" For days and days, the Black bird would sit in the cage looking at himself in the mirror. "He is such a beautiful Black bird," all the visitors said. "Yes," the master said, "I have a good bird." To himself, the master said, "This little Black fool has made me rich doing tricks and he's too dumb to fly away to freedom— what a stupid bird!" The master would feed the bird crumbs from his table. The little bird loved the crumbs so much he wouldn't eat anything else, not even when the other birds sneaked into the master's house and offered the little bird some righteous soulfood. One day the master's house caught on fire. Nobody knew how the fire started, not even the little Black bird. The master fought hard to put the fire out, but there were too many flames, so he ran outside, leaving the little Black bird behind. The flames grew bigger and bigger, but the little Black bird just sat in his cage. Maybe he was waiting for his master to return . . . Then, suddenly, a friendly bird flew into the burning white house. "Black bird!" he yelled, "don't you know the house is on fire??? Hurry—come fly away with me." "But I love my cage," the Black bird cried, "I want to stay!" "You want to burn," said the friendly bird. The friendly bird went into the cage, grabbed the Black bird and flew away from the burning house. "Bye," the Black bird yelled as he passed his master who was crying in the yard. "Bye, Master," the little bird called out again—he was on his way home. *(The* DANCERS *exit.)*

1ST SISTER. Ouuuuuuu, that was a good story.

BROTHER. Yeah, that's the story of the Black bird, Sisters. Don't ya'all be no Black bird, now, hear?

1ST SISTER. I ain't gon be no Black bird!

2ND SISTER.   Huh, me either—that Black bird was crazy.

BROTHER.   Yeah, he sure was. Well, I'll tell ya'all another story, sometime, but I gotta finish typing now. As-Salaam-Alaikum.

1ST SISTER.   What?

BROTHER.   As-Salaam-Alaikum—that means peace be unto you. You say: Wa-Alaikum-Salaam.

1ST AND 2ND SISTERS.   Wa-laikum-salaam. *(The* SISTERS *exit.)*

BROTHER *(performs ablution and recites the following prayer, facing the East).*

In the name of Allah,
The Beneficent, The Merciful,
Allah is He besides whom there is no God, the Ever-Living, the Self-subsisting, by whom all things subsist; slumber does not overtake Him nor sleep; whatever is in the heavens and whatever is in the earth is His; who is he that can intercede with Him but by His permission? He knows what is before them and what is behind them and they cannot comprehend anything out of His knowledge except what He pleases; His knowledge extends over the heavens and the earth, and the preservation of them both tires Him not and He is the Most High, the Great.

The Man Who Trusted the Devil Twice

by *Herbert Stokes*

Time: Present Friday
Place: Office

CHARACTERS:

PRINCIPAL
1st GUARD
2nd GUARD
JOHN—son
MIDDLE AGE NEGRO
1st BOY
2nd BOY

(The scene opens up with a MAN *sitting
at a desk in an office. A young* MAN
*about 19 or 20 dressed in a military uni-
form walks in the office. He is carrying
a rifle and a military gun belt, with a
pistol. The* PRINCIPAL, *who is dressed in
a suit and tie, rises from his seat and
salutes the* MILITARY MAN.)*

1st MILITARY MAN. You have been given new orders from
your commanding officer.

PRINCIPAL. Okay, what are they?

1st MILITARY. Before I tell you, I want to tell you some
new news. You have been promoted.

PRINCIPAL *(very excited).* Oh wow! Tell me what have I
been promoted to?

1st MILITARY. You will become our new executor, but will
still act as principal of this school. You will continue teach-

ing the administration how to brainwash the students. You will continue instructing brainwashery until every boy and girl thinks that white people are good. We have to keep telling them that they are Negroes. They must never think they are Black. They must be taught that blackness is a Dirty Disgraceful ugly thing. They must be taught that if anyone calls them black to take it as an insult.

PRINCIPAL. Don't worry! I have been making sure that they will never be taught their true history. Don't forget I have been doing this job for five years. A matter of fact, I follow my father's footsteps. My family has been doing this for three generations.

1ST MILITARY. Well that's nice. But I don't have any time to listen to your family and their misfortune. I mean well getting to the point about your new job. The mayor don't want to have any more of that riot shit going on in his city. So he wants you to exterminate all the radical students you have in your school.

PRINCIPAL. You mean he wants me to kill them? Who?

1ST MILITARY. That's right, kill them. The ones you wrote him about. The ones that you said wouldn't salute the flag. The ones that have them Afros, and the ones that write on the bathroom walls Black Power. He said that these boys could start something. And cause big problems.

PRINCIPAL. Look I'm grateful for the promotions, but I'm not a killer.

1ST MILITARY. Well I'm sorry but you don't have any choice. You have been given your orders. Either you obey or you disobey. And you know the punishment for disobeying.

PRINCIPAL. But how can I kill these boys? I might reveal myself.

1ST MILITARY. Don't worry! He's aware of that.

PRINCIPAL. But by revealing myself, I will reveal the organization.

1ST MILITARY. Oh, don't worry! He'll have you watched. He sees any mistakes, he'll be forced to have you killed.

PRINCIPAL. He won't kill me. He needs me. And if he did kill me, how would he explain my death to the school and the students?

1ST MILITARY.   What school? What students? There wouldn't
be any school!

PRINCIPAL.   You mean he would . . .

1ST MILITARY (*cutting in*).   That's right. He would burn the
whole school—students and all! So what's your decision?

PRINCIPAL.   Like you said, I have no choice. When do I
start?

1ST MILITARY.   You will have until Monday when the school
opens up.

PRINCIPAL.   Can you tell me how I am supposed to do this?

1ST MILITARY.   Sure. When the bell rings in the morning—
the late bell, that is—you will call the boys to your office.
Me and my assistant will already be in your office. We
will hide in your closet. Oh yes, I almost forgot. We heard
that your son hasn't been going to his history class.

PRINCIPAL.   Yes, I know. I've been talking to him about it.
It won't happen anymore.

1ST MILITARY.   I hope not. We wouldn't want your son to
get mixed up with these other boys. Now would we? (*All
of a sudden there is a loud gun shot outside the school.
A* BOY *rushes in the building. He knocks on the principal's
door. The* MILITARY MAN *hides in the principal's closet.*)

PRINCIPAL.   Come in.

(*A* BOY *rushes in, dressed in regular
school clothes.*)

BOY.   Sir! Mr. Wine Berry! The history teacher has just been
shot!

PRINCIPAL.   Did anyone see who did it?

BOY.   Yes, it was your son. Some people saw him running.

PRINCIPAL (THE PRINCIPAL *sits back in his seat. Very loud*).
NO! NO! NO! They're lying. It couldn't have been my
son. NO!

(*The* BOY *leaves the room. The* MILITARY
MAN *comes out of the closet.*)

1ST MILITARY.   I am sorry, but you know what's got to be
done.

PRINCIPAL (THE PRINCIPAL *gets on his knees and begins begging to the* MAN). Please! Oh please! Not my son. But you can help me. Look, you don't have to tell the mayor. Oh please, don't tell him. I'll do anything. Oh please.

1ST GUARD. There might be one thing you can do.

PRINCIPAL. Anything?

1ST GUARD. You can sign this contract saying you will do everything we say at any cost. And you will of course send your son out of the state. (*Putting the contract on his desk.*) If you agree, will you please sign here?

PRINCIPAL (*hesitating*). I have no alternative. But you would have to give me time. I haven't any way of knowing where my son is.

1ST GUARD. Sorry, that's your problem.

PRINCIPAL. Oh please, just a little bit—a half hour. All right?

1ST GUARD. All right. A half hour. But don't forget your other job. (*The* GUARD *leaves.*)

PRINCIPAL (*talking to himself*). Why, son, why in the hell you have to do something like this? Why?

(BOY *enters.*)

BOY. Because I'm tired, Father.

PRINCIPAL. John, where have you been? Why did you do this?

JOHN. Where have I been, Father? I've been running, Father, but I'm not going to run anymore.

PRINCIPAL. But why did you do it? Why did you kill him? What did he ever do to you?

JOHN. I killed him because he was white. I killed him because I hated his guts. And I will continue killing them until they are all dead.

PRINCIPAL. Tell me, son, how do you expect to kill all these white people by yourself?

JOHN. I'm not, Father. They're four of us. We plan to kill every white teacher and every Black white-minded teacher and principal in this school.

PRINCIPAL. What you mean? I'm your father. Would you? After all, what makes you think I'm white-minded?

JOHN. Don't lie, Dad. We already know about you and

your so-called organization. Why, Dad? Why did you want to harm my friend? And even your own son?

PRINCIPAL. But son, I was only doing it for you. I wanted you to have some of the things that I didn't have. I wanted you to be a big man some day.

JOHN. A man? You wanted me to be a slave, a Tom, and a murderer to my own people. You wanted me to be just like you—a punk and a fag.

PRINCIPAL (*stands up and grabs the* BOY *by his shirt collar*). Don't you ever talk to me like that again you dirty little . . .

JOHN (*taking out a gun and putting it in his father's belly*). Get off me, Dad, or I'll kill you.

PRINCIPAL (*laughing*). You won't kill me. You never had a gun in your life. You don't even know how to use it.

SON. That's just why you'd better be careful.

(*Two* BOYS *rush in with rifles.*)

FIRST BOY. John, there's a guard coming up the school steps.

PRINCIPAL. That must be . . .

JOHN. Who, Dad? Is he your boss? (*Pointing to the closet.*) Come on. Let's hide in here.

GUARD (*walking in the office*). I just left the boss's office, and he told me that your son and them boys that you were having trouble with are to be killed immediately.

PRINCIPAL. You told him? Why? You knew what he was going to do. You knew he would have them killed. Why?

GUARD. Because I'm white and I don't give a shit about any niggers.

PRINCIPAL. But I thought you were my friend.

GUARD (*laughing*). You thought wrong. As usual. As far as I'm concerned, you could have sat somewhere and died. The only reason you wasn't killed was because the mayor needed you to brainwash these young-minded boys. And you was stupid enough to do it. Listen, nigger, as soon as we find your son and his gang, I'm going to take the pleasure of killing you myself.

PRINCIPAL. But you can't kill me. I'm the only Negro brain-washer you've got.

GUARD. Are you crazy, nigger? We have a whole tin full of
them. A matter of fact, the television is our most effective
machine. It's probably the quickest way of brainwashing
niggers. But what makes it funny? Have your own niggers
who are already brainwashed. Brainwash the rest of you!
So see, nigger, what makes you think we need you?

PRINCIPAL. But who will you use as a brainwasher if you
kill me?

GUARD. Simple. We'll use an ordinary man. A white man.
Can't you see we only use you as a front? See? As you
know, all the students that came here were pretty smart.
If we used a white man as a brainwasher, they might have
gotten hip to it. But if we used a nigger man like them,
they wouldn't think nothing about it. So we used you.

PRINCIPAL. But if you kill me, how will you explain my
death?

GUARD. What explain? Who do we have to explain it to?
Just like I told the mayor, if you give a nigger a little
something, they think you have to explain something to
them. Listen nigger! You get this straight. Us white people
don't have to explain nothing to you niggers. We never
did and we never will.

PRINCIPAL. But if you kill me, it might start another riot.

GUARD. A riot over you? Shit! If I was a nigger, I wouldn't
risk my life saving a man like you. But if they were that
stupid, it wouldn't work. All the mayor has to do is to send
for a couple of R.G.'s and the niggers would run back into
their ghettos. Look, I ain't got time to talk to you anymore. I'm going to help the men find your son and them
boys.

PRINCIPAL (THE GUARD *begins to walk out the door when suddenly* THE PRINCIPAL *shouts out*). Wait a minute! Suppose I told you I know where they are. Would you kill me
then?

GUARD (*smiling*). Oh no! Of course not. Hey! Mack, come
here.

(*Another* GUARD *comes in carrying a rifle.*)

GUARD 2. Where are they?

PRINCIPAL.   You promise not to kill me? Cross your heart
and hope to die?

GUARD (*crossing his heart*).   Okay, where are they?

PRINCIPAL.   They're in the room over there.

GUARD 2.   All right, come on out or we'll start shooting.

VOICE.   Go ahead! We're not afraid to die.

PRINCIPAL (*runs over and grabs* GUARD).   NO! Wait.

GUARD 2.   Get out of my way nigger! (*Bang bang. He shoots
him.*)

PRINCIPAL (*grabbing his heart*).   You prom——

GUARD.   Why did you kill him? I wanted to kill him.

GUARD 2.   What are you talking about? What difference
does it make who does it? (*While they are talking,* JOHN
comes out of the room and kills them both.)

(*After he kills the two* MEN, JOHN *walks
over to his father and lifts his head up.*)

PRINCIPAL.   Sorry, son, I woke up too late.

Y BOY.   Bullshit! The same old Negroish line. I woke up too
late. These motherfuckers been asleep for more than 300
years and then when it's time to die they wake up. But I'll
bet you one damn thing, if they keep on sleeping, I'm
going to kill them and wake them all up.

JOHN.   Come on! Get their guns and let's go. The war has
just started.

Y BOY.   I'm hip.

(*But just as the* BOYS *begin to leave
about 5 more* MEN *come in with guns.*)

I MAN.   Where the hell do you think you're going? We got
your ass now. Drop them damn guns and put your hands
up against the wall. (*They begin searching the* BOYS.) Now,
since it's even, we're going to beat your black asses. (*They
beat the* BOYS *with their guns and rifles until they fall to
the ground.*)

(*The scene closes with the* BOYS *being
dragged off by the big bad* FAGS.)

SCENE 2

Place: Court room
Time: Present

CHARACTERS:

WHITE
JUDGE

(Big fat, white, bald-headed MAN *dressed in clown suit with round dots. The* PEOPLE *walk in, everyone rises except the two* BOYS *being prosecuted. Next to the* JUDGE *is a tall dark* NEGRO MAN *dressed in a clown suit.)*

TOM. Will everyone please rise.
JOHN. We will not rise and especially for a punk in a clown suit.
TOM. Why you son of a bitch . . . *(Walks over to the boys and points at them.)* Stand up or I'll blow your damn head off.
JOHN. Go ahead like I said before. We're not scared to die.
JUDGE. No. Hold it. Don't kill them. It would just make it easier for them. After they are found guilty and when I sentence them, they're going to wish they were dead. But first they must get a fair trial.
1ST BOY. Fair trial! You know, you really are a beast. How can you sit there and tell us we're guilty before we've even started the trial, and then tell us we must get a fair trial. You don't know the meaning of fair. No! I take that back. You have your own meaning of fair. I learned that when your trained animals attacked me—us—and tried to kill us.
JUDGE. Try! Don't you think if they wanted to kill you, they could have easily done it?
1ST BOY. I tell you what you do, judge. You come from behind that desk, and I'll beat your ass myself.
JUDGE. Why you little punk. I dare you to threaten me.
1ST BOY. I dare you to come from behind that desk and call me a punk.

JUDGE (JUDGE *grabs the* NEGRO GUARD *that is standing next to him*).   Kill him!

(*But before the* GUARD *gets his gun out,
a large group of* BLACK PEOPLE *rush in
with guns, sticks, etc.*)

JUDGE.   What is this? Who are these people? Guards! Guards! Get these people out of here!

VOICE.   That's right, judge. You said it right. We are people, and we people come here to protect our brothers. And to show you white people that we're not going to die any longer from some stupid shit like you and that Negro who thinks he should protect you.

TOM.   Who, me?

JOHN.   That's right, you motherfucker. And don't come with pity shit. It's too late. We ain't got no time.

1ST BOY.   Let's go. We have a lot of brothers to free.

(*A* NEGRO *falls on the floor.*)

TOM.   Oh please, let me come with you.

In New England Winter

(#2 of *The Twentieth Century Cycle*)

by Ed Bullins

THE PEOPLE:

1960   CLIFF DAWSON, large, husky, going to fat but still appealing to his many girlfriends. A hint of a subdued swagger and worldliness remains. He is light complexioned, brown, not yellow. 29 years old.

STEVE BENSON, Cliff's half-brother. Darker than Cliff, brooding and a thinker. 24 years old.

CHUCKIE, a follower. Quiet most of the time unless he is familiar with the situation. A dull, not yet pathetic person who already suspects that he will discover death some night in the street or in a prison cell. 27 years old.

BUMMIE, a bully but loyal. Medium height and athletic build. 27 years.

1955   *Liz's place.*

LIZ, a very dark girl, black, in fact, with fine features and oriental casted eyes. She is thin to the degree of emaciation but extremely sensual. In a quiet way she is free of many social restraints, hiding behind her profanity and her professed insanity. She draws men to her in numbers, some as friends, more as adorers, mainly as lovers, though her fellow women either love, hate or are frightened by her. She is seldom ignored. 18 years old.

OSCAR, Liz's brother-in-law. A long shaggy haired criminal in vagabond's dress. A rope ties his patched, baggy trousers. He wears combat boots, hoping to get into the kind of fight where he can use them. 24 years old.

CARRIE, a thin girl who smiles often out of drunkenness. She is light brown, a shade darker than her husband, Oscar. She is also Liz's sister. 17 years old.

CROOK, small and puffy from a lot of hard, cheap drink, poor kidneys, liver and stomach. His eyes are too close together and they are glassy. He is the two-bit con man, hustler type and talker, but also is a watcher and waiter. 30 years.

The Prologue

We picked Chuck up at noon and drove with brood hanging close to our bodies blended with the sweat. The '53 burped reliability in its infirmity; its windows accepted the grit which peppered my face, and Indian summer rode with us across the city, a spent brave, a savage to the last, causing me visions of winter in New England. . . .

In New England winter we played gin rummy and groped nudely under the patched quilt. While we each read the other's thoughts erroneously, I chanted Whitman as she curled in a corner with Superman and Mickey Spillane. We shrilled from the moment's gratification under the quilt; it was our bond of permanence in the cold times.

"Steve?"
"Yeah, Cliff," I said.
"Feel, okay?"
"Sure."
"How 'bout you, Chuck?" Cliff asked.
"Great, man."
The car turned off Spring and then in and about some side streets before heading again south on Broad. Chuck was a hell of a driver; I was glad he was at the wheel even though I don't dig him. Just maybe, just maybe, with Chuck, I might get back to winter and New England. . . .

We danced to something called Be-bop around the pot-bellied stove in my single set of pajamas, ate like gluttons from her lone pot, and drank a daily jug of muscatel from our mayonnaise jar. The jar was cherished; the common spittle was as personal as we dared be. We loathed to bathe to wash the other's funk away; each ate their fish-ends and black-eyed

*peas and drank when they could, but all nourishment was a
trifle compared to our daily fare, for we fed with gusto upon
the other's store of dream . . .*

"Well . . . this is the place, Steve," Cliff said.

"We're here," Chuck filled in.

"Yeah . . . I know," I said.

"Sure she'll kick over," Cliff asked Chuck.

"If it don't, we's got a long run."

Cliff and I got out on the street side, adjusting our sun
glasses and stretching confidently. We walked around the
corner and climbed narrow stairs to the finance co's office;
the rest were at lunch like I had planned. I walked to the
counter; Cliff, certain, trailed my heels.

The blonde had been in my freshman class in high school.
Our distance had prevented her from knowing me, but I did
catch her once staring around me, staring as I stare at the
silhouette of my shadow.

"Good afternoon, sir . . ." She smiled as she had learned,
fastening her stare upon my glasses' frame. "May I help you?"

"Yes, you may . . ." She seemed so fragile standing in
my gun's way, awaiting its punishment. "Don't say anything
. . . just don't give me any trouble and don't say a word."

We tied them; I twisted the ropes about the blonde's wrists
so she would never forget. Cliff gathered the money easily
and locked it in his briefcase; it was all finished in seven
minutes. The best job was over and done; it was finished and
I was done, all over and done . . .

*Ice grows upon window panes in New England winter.
The dread of it entering our world caused her nightmares;
but, I didn't dare claim these, so I awoke her and soothed
her chatters with the jar. And afterwards, we promised ourselves that somehow we would find a stop for haunting yes-
terdays and tomorrows which waited to be refused.*

*Our futures loomed bitter and less bearable than the snow-
drifts blocking the alleys below; but our fears seared, raging
about our souls, fanning a combustion of brutality. As my
manhood leaked away upon the wintry streets by day, she*

cemented together my backbone under the patched quilt
through the long long icy nights. . . .

There were thirteen hundred four dollars and thirty-two
cents for my share after we counted the money at Cliff's
place.

"You're a genius, Steve," Cliff raved, congratulating himself for teaming with me.

"He sure is . . ." Chuck said.

"Well you guys know what to do . . . just don't flash your
rolls . . . and keep your goddamn mouths shut!"

"Sure, Steve."

"Yeah, man . . . you knows we ain't no punks."

I patted my wallet, making its bulge less awkward, and
adjusted my glasses.

"I'll see you guys," I said.

"Okay, Steve," Cliff said, "call when you want me."

"Forget it . . . I won't be calling . . . ever."

"What d'ya mean," Chuck asked.

"I'm through . . . that's what I mean . . . don't ever expect
to see me again . . . and if you do bump into me, just act
like ya never knew me."

Cliff usually knew how to take me. "Well . . . then take
care, Professor." He offered his hand; I gripped it harder
than I should; but it might be the last time I ever saw my
brother.

"Thanks, Cliff," I said.

"Got any plans," Chuck said.

"Yeah . . . a couple . . . a couple of very simple ones," I
said as I stepped out of the door and shut it tightly.

Yeah, two very simple ones, I thought, as I stepped out
into dying autumn's hate.

Two very simple ones: pray for winter and head north.

(There are two playing areas: CLIFF'S
room, a modestly furnished room with
three doors—one, to a closet, the others,
to the bath and stairs. And LIZ's apart-

ment: cheap, bare but for necessities,
and LIZ's *lived-a-lot look about it.)*

1. Now . . . THIS IS THE PLAN

(At rise: CLIFF's *room.* CLIFF, BUMMIE,
STEVE *and* CHUCKIE *sit on the bed and in*
chairs. Modern Jazz of the late fifties and
early sixties, maybe Miles Davis or Can-
nonball or Nate Adderly.)
(There are intervals after Scenes 2 and 5.)

BUMMIE. It's too goddamn hot to do anything . . . even
fuck.

STEVE *(stares at* CLIFF*).* So you're going out tonight?

CHUCKIE. Awww, Steve. Ain't nothin' gonna happen if Cliff
takes his . . .

STEVE. I was talking to Cliff.

CLIFF. Chuckie didn't mean nothin', Steve. Besides . . . he's
right.

BUMMIE. Chuckie right?

CHUCKIE. Nawh, man . . . I was just . . .

STEVE. All of us, especially you and me, Cliff, have to be
sharp for the scene we gonna make tomorrow. We're not
kids . . .

CLIFF. I know that!

BUMMIE. Hey . . . why don't we get started?

STEVE. I said we're not kids, anymore. We're not knocking
over a candy store like in our junior flip days. This . . .

CLIFF. Yeah, I know as much about the job as you do,
Steve.

BUMMIE *(under his breath).* That goddamn Chuckie . . .

STEVE. Then you know how important it is to have everything perfect?

CHUCKIE. But we been rehearsing for days.

BUMMIE. Shut up, Chuckie . . . let's get . . .

CHUCKIE. Lissen, man!

STEVE. Yeah, and we gonna rehearse tonight. A dress rehearsal.

CHUCKIE. I ain't gonna take anymore . . .

CLIFF. Quiet! Everybody!

(Pause.)

Steve . . . you still going through with it, huh?

STEVE. What do you think?

CLIFF. What about tonight?

STEVE. The rehearsal and everything else.

CHUCKIE. Awww . . . sheet.

STEVE. Just like we planned.

BUMMIE. Well, man . . . you guys don't need me.

STEVE. Get into your costume, Chuckie . . . And you help him, Bummie.

BUMMIE. Look Steve!

CLIFF. Bummie!

CHUCKIE. Aww, man, it's too hot to wear all that stuff. *(Appeals to* CLIFF.*)* Aww, man, do I got to do that?

(Pause. Sounds of music and traffic come through the window. A neon sign goes on outside and casts colored shadows.)

STEVE. Yeah.

CHUCKIE *(protesting)*. Look, man, I don't like this . . . I ain't funny or nothin' like that.

BUMMIE. Ain't nobody said you was . . . you coppin' out?

CLIFF. He don't have to dress up, do he, Steve?

CHUCKIE. I ain't gonna take no more of your shit, Bummie!

BUMMIE. I ain't gonna help this mathafukker, man!

STEVE. That's what I said, Cliff. I want a sense of realism brought into this room.

CLIFF. Ain't we real enough? Ain't this heat real enough for you?

STEVE. We can't rely upon distorted senses of reality to . . .

CLIFF. Okay, Professor . . . can the textbook speeches. *(Abrupt.)* Chuckie, go get ready.

BUMMIE. But, man . . .

CLIFF. You too, Bummie.

CHUCKIE. Cliff, you not gonna make me . . .

STEVE. Chuckie! . . . We're waiting.

(CHUCKIE *mutters, picks up a small suit-
case and enters the bathroom.* BUMMIE
follows, muttering.)

STEVE.   Why do you keep them around, Cliff?

CLIFF.   Chuckie? . . . Bummie? . . . They're good boys,
that's why. Chuckie's one of my best boys, and we need
a good driver for this job.

STEVE.   Good boy . . . Good flunky . . .

CLIFF (*correcting*).   Good driver.

STEVE.   Good flunky driver.

CLIFF.   Suit yourself, Steve. Suit yourself.

STEVE.   And Bummie?

CLIFF.   That's your department, ain't it, brother? . . . Guns
and things?

STEVE.   It didn't have to be Bummie. He's your boy.

CLIFF.   That was a long time ago, Steve.

STEVE (*intense*).   No . . . it was yesterday . . . *yesterday.*

CLIFF.   But you know how good he is . . . we need him.
And we all grew up together, didn't we? We all fought
each other. Bummie didn't hassle no more than you . . .
He's even aimed at us on occasion . . . just like . . .

STEVE.   At me, not you!

CLIFF (*insincere*).   Ha ha . . . it's still in the family.

STEVE (*disgust*).   A fool . . . a thug . . . and two . . .

CLIFF.   Well, we have different tastes, brother, don't we?

STEVE.   That nigger knocked me down, put his foot on my
chest and aimed a .38 at my head.

CLIFF.   It's over.

STEVE.   Cops and niggers . . . that's what it was.

CLIFF.   It was a long time ago.

STEVE.   In his monkey mind he was playin' white cop . . .
and I was just a nigger he could . . .

CLIFF.   Let it ride, Steve. It's waited this long.

STEVE.   Let it ride? . . . Yeah . . . let it ride.

CLIFF.   Steve?

STEVE.   Humm . . .?

CLIFF.   We are only half brothers but what do you think
makes us so different and still be brothers?

STEVE (*joking*).   Our mother.

CLIFF.   Huh?
STEVE.   Forget it.

(CLIFF *lifts his beer.*)

Do you have to drink so much?
CLIFF.   It's good for fighting off my distorted sense of reality.

(*Silence. Music plays.* STEVE *looks at his watch and walks to the window.*)

You still think about Liz, don't you?
STEVE.   Liz? . . . Yeah.
CLIFF.   That's been a long time too, Steve.
STEVE.   Less long.
CLIFF.   But you're about as far away from it as you can get.
STEVE (*regret*).   You know . . . I think about her all the time.
    (*Reminiscing.*) It's snowing up there now. Snowing . . .
    Big white white flakes. Snow. Silent like death must be.
CLIFF.   Our deaths will be roaring hot.
STEVE.   The dying will . . . not the death . . .
CLIFF.   Red and orange and blue . . .
STEVE.   Death must be still and black and deep.
CLIFF.   . . . with white heat reaching all around us.
STEVE.   Deathly cold.
CLIFF.   Hell is a safe place for black boys.
STEVE.   And Christians.
CLIFF.   But private.
STEVE.   Well . . . it's hot enough here. I don't even know
    what I'm doing here . . . This place . . . heat, smog, cars,
    Freeways . . . in January. I don't even know wha . . .
CLIFF.   For me when a broad is out of sight . . . you know
    how the saying says, man . . . The only time I worry about
    a broad is when I can't get another one.
STEVE.   Which is hardly ever, right, Cliff?
CLIFF.   And you like that cold ass New England.
STEVE.   I'm not so crazy about the place.
CLIFF.   That's why you doin' this job, ain't it? . . . so you
    can get back up there. How you say it? "I need some
    travelin' money."

STEVE.   Yeah, so I can go and see my woman. What's the matter with that? I'm not like you. I don't have a different broad for every day of the month.

CLIFF *(casual.)*   Oh . . . I strike out sometimes . . . Like tonight, for instance . . . *(Chuckles.)* I had to go and make a date with my ole faithful . . .

STEVE.   Sandy?

CLIFF.   Who else? *Sandra.*

(Pause. STEVE *changes position. He saunters about and looks out front as if he were looking for someone beyond the window.* CLIFF *finishes his beer, snuffs out his cigarette and goes for another drink.)*

STEVE.   Are you gonna marry her?

CLIFF.   Sandy?

STEVE.   Yeah, Sandra.

CLIFF.   Are you joking?

STEVE.   You think so? You been using her all these years and treating her like a puppy . . . I thought you might marry her.

CLIFF *(annoyed).*   Awww . . . Come off that bullshit, man! Have you been marryin' all those bitches you been fuckin' around with?

STEVE.   But they don't mean nothin' to me . . . they're just fillin' in time.

CLIFF.   Oh, that's the new name for it.

STEVE.   Sandy loves you. You like her . . . You'd . . .

CLIFF.   Look . . . you know better than to even ask me somethin' like am I gonna get married.

STEVE.   Lou was a good while ago.

CLIFF.   If it was a thousand years it would be like this morning . . . I sat in a cell . . . I sat in a cell one day draggin' its behind after the other . . . waitin' to get out . . . waitin' to see her, to touch her . . . smell and taste her.

STEVE.   But you were in prison for years, Cliff.

CLIFF.   So? *(Mocking.)* And I was in prison for years . . . Hahh! . . . She didn't even send me a letter to tell me . . .

I got home and found you had moved into the bedroom
. . . she and my baby gone . . . and you . . . the master
bedroom, *brother*.

STEVE. How can you expect someone to wait for you forever when you're in the slammers? You were sent up for
murder.

CLIFF. It wasn't but for five years. I was out in three and
then some.

STEVE. She only did what was human.

CLIFF (*ridicule*). Human?

STEVE. You're not easy to live with, you know. And she had
your kid to take care of after you were gone.

CLIFF. Human . . . you call leavin' me up there and takin'
my son human?

STEVE. You know how Lou is. You know she'll never take
relief.

CLIFF. But she took my blood . . . And then what did she
do?

STEVE. She did what she had to do . . . I know . . . I was
there.

CLIFF. What did she do then?

STEVE. She had that other baby . . . but . . .

CLIFF (*accusing*). You were there . . . *brother* . . . you were
there. Was that necessary?

STEVE. She got lonely. That guy started comin' around . . .
She was a grown woman . . . what could I say to her?

CLIFF. You could have cut his throat . . . you could have
cut his nuts off . . . that's what I would have done in
your place.

STEVE. Cliff!

CLIFF (*hate*). You won't even tell me his name . . . you
bastard!

STEVE (*softer*). Cliff.

CLIFF. Does he have a name, Steve?

STEVE. It's been a long time, Cliff.

CLIFF. You should have reminded her of where I was an
. . . and why I was there.

STEVE. You didn't kill that boy Red because of her . . . It
was . . .

CLIFF. Oh, shut up, Steve!

STEVE (*angry*). Like she did . . . like Lou did because you beat the sound out of her?

CLIFF. You're all knowledge you learned from some books you borrowed from the library and never returned.

STEVE. You won't listen . . . you want to hear everything except the reason why you think everything happens to you!

CLIFF. You're the always filled second seat in the second row of some second-rate night course.

STEVE. Attacking me won't get you your wife and son back.

CLIFF. Then if I talk pretty to you, brother, dear . . . you might whistle for them and they might come trotting back?

STEVE. Can't we talk sense sometime?

CLIFF (*angry*). I know why I killed a man . . . and she knows why I was in that jail and she has a debt that she hasn't even begun to pay off to me yet.

STEVE. And will it be paid?

CLIFF. You're fuckin' "A" right it will, Steve . . . Fuckin' "A" . . . in blood . . . in blood . . .

(*Expressionless,* STEVE *looks at him for a
while then turns to the bathroom door.*)

STEVE. CHUCKIE . . . BUMMIE . . . get the hell out of here!

(*The door cracks.*)

CHUCKIE (*mutters*). Just wait a minute . . . We'll be out.

STEVE. We've waited long enough . . . c'mon!

(CHUCKIE *enters followed by* BUMMIE;
CHUCKIE *wears a dress and pink female
mask with blond wig. As* CHUCKIE *moves
into the room,* BUMMIE *shoves him, causing him to stumble.*)

CHUCKIE. Sonna a bitch!

(CHUCKIE *turns and shoves* BUMMIE *in*

the chest. BUMMIE *falls back; angered, he regains his balance and rushes* CHUCKIE, *launching a haymaker that misses. In fear,* CHUCKIE *pushes out a weak jab that connects upon* BUMMIE's *nose, squirting blood in several directions. As they both realize their shock and predicament,* STEVE *and* CLIFF *grab them and wrestle them to different sides of the room.)*

BUMMIE. LET ME GO! GODDAMMIT! . . . CLIFF . . . LET ME GO SO I CAN KILL HIM!

CLIFF. Come on, Bummie, babe. Forget it.

BUMMIE. Forget hell! I'm gonna kill that mathafukker! . . . Turn me loose so I can kill that sonna bitch.

(STEVE *has released* CHUCKIE.)

CHUCKIE *(calm and confident).* That's okay, Cliff . . . let him go if he's that much a fool.

BUMMIE *(scared, his nose bleeding profusely).* I'm gonna kill you . . . you black mathafukker!

STEVE. Take him in the bathroom so he can clean up, Cliff!

CLIFF *(pulls* BUMMIE *half-heartedly toward the bathroom).* C'mon . . . Bummie . . . you need some cold compresses on that nose. It might be broke.

BUMMIE *(half-heartedly resisting).* Mathafukker! I'm gonna take this out of your ass, Chuckie!

CHUCKIE. Yeah, man . . . yeah . . . I know . . . You gonna do numbers and shit cucumbers . . . I know.

(CLIFF *maneuvers* BUMMIE *into the bathroom; the door slams. Sound of water from faucets and muffled cursing.* STEVE *laughs.)*

STEVE. You better straighten your wig, man.

CHUCKIE *(distracted by noises in bathroom).* Yeah . . .

yeah . . . (CHUCKIE *looks in mirror and fixes his mask and wig.*)

STEVE.　And, Chuckie . . .

CHUCKIE *(engrossed)*.　Ahuh?

STEVE.　Your seams could stand straightening.

(CLIFF *comes out of the bathroom.*)

CHUCKIE *(perceiving)*.　Hey, wait a minute, man . . . look . . .

(CLIFF *and* STEVE *laugh.*)

CLIFF.　Ha ha . . . ole bad Bummie the Bruiser walked into a one man windmill.

STEVE.　Man . . . ha ha . . . man, I wouldn't have missed this for anything.

(They laugh more.)

CLIFF.　Did you see the look on Bummie's face?

STEVE.　Yeah . . . pure shock and terror . . . ha ha . . .

CLIFF.　Wait till I tell everybody . . . Bummie's rep will be lower than whale shit . . . ha ha ha . . .

CHUCKIE *(muffled behind the mask)*.　Hey, you guys . . . don't laugh at me.

CLIFF.　Bummie . . . smashed by a little blond girl.

STEVE *(smiles)*.　It's okay, Chuckie. You look just fine.

CLIFF *(laughs)*.　Yeah . . . you look so sweet, honey.

CHUCKIE *(turns)*.　Awww, man . . . I ain't goin' for this.

STEVE.　C'mon . . . take your places. Knock it off, Cliff. And turn off that radio.

CLIFF.　It's a good station, Steve. And maybe girlie here will want to kick up her legs and dance some.

CHUCKIE.　Fuck you, Cliff! (CHUCKIE *moves toward* CLIFF.)

CLIFF *(mimics John Wayne)*.　Now look'a here, boy . . . don't get carried away cause you smashed Bummie with a sucker punch. I'm still twice the man that both of you are together . . . if you don't believe it . . . I'll turn you over mah knee, young lady.

STEVE.　Lighten up, Cliff.

CHUCKIE.   Just stop laughin' at me . . . that's all.

STEVE.   Let's go you guys. This is our last night.

CLIFF.   Okay . . . okay . . . but that girlie sure looks nice.
Ha ha ha . . . You gonna let me take you out tonight,
baby?

(CHUCKIE *mutters a curse. He turns off
the radio. They move into place;* CHUCKIE
pulls out the table and stands behind it.
CLIFF *and* STEVE *walk into the closet.*)

CLIFF.   Man, I don't like walkin' into this closet . . . it's too
much like jail.

STEVE.   Get in place and concentrate on the character.

CLIFF.   Sure is funky.

(*The door is shut. Pause. The closet door
opens.* STEVE *steps out, followed by*
CLIFF; *they wear black sunglasses, and
guns are in their hands.*)

STEVE (*to* CHUCKIE).   All right, Miss. Don't say anything and
keep your hands where I can see them.

(*He moves around the table and takes*
CHUCKIE *by the arms and maneuvers
him to the center of the room.* CLIFF
*walks around them and pantomimes the
action of someone taking money from a
safe, stuffing it in a briefcase.*)

Okay, Miss. Now lay down on the floor and put your arms
behind you. C'mon, now! I ain't gonna hurt you if you do
like I say. Lay down like I said!

(CHUCKIE *lays down on his stomach and
puts his hands behind his back. Quickly,*
STEVE *ties his hands with a nylon cord
taken from his pocket. To* CLIFF.)

Okay?

(CLIFF *nods and closes his briefcase.*)

Then go.

(CLIFF *walks around the front of the table, out of the sight of* CHUCKIE, *takes off his sunglasses and walks into the closet.* STEVE *kneels beside* CHUCKIE *and twists the rope about his wrists until he gasps.*)

CHUCKIE.   Hey, not so hard, man.

STEVE.   Don't get out of character, stupid!

CHUCKIE.   Hey man, I'm not stupid . . . I ain't gonna take that shit from nobody.

(STEVE *stands.*)

STEVE (*angry*).   Come back in here, Cliff!

CLIFF (*enters*).   What's happenin'?

STEVE (*sullen*).   Nothin' . . . nobody's fault but my own.

CHUCKIE.   Hey, Cliff, your brother here hurt my arms with that rope and then he . . .

STEVE.   I'm sorry, Chuckie . . . I didn't know I was twisting the ropes so hard.

CLIFF.   Better be careful about that tomorrow, Steve, or that little bitch will be screaming her lungs out.

STEVE.   Yeah . . . yeah . . . I know . . . C'mon . . . let's take it back to where you exit.

(*They get back into position.*)

CLIFF.   You want me to be over here?

STEVE.   Yeah . . . we'll take it from where you're over there.

CHUCKIE.   Hey, you guys, hurry up! My arms are beginning to ache.

STEVE.   Shut up, Chuckie!

CHUCKIE.   Hey, Steve, you can go fuck yourself for . . .

CLIFF. Steve said shut up, Chuckie . . . You want me to
kick your head around like a football? Just shut up . . .
Steve's the boss on this job . . . and you do what he says.
CHUCKIE. Awwww . . . man . . . I'm sorry. I . . .
CLIFF. Shut up so we can get out of here.

(CHUCKIE *quiets.*)

Okay . . . little brother. It's your show.
STEVE. Well . . . let's take it from where you shut your bag.
Then I'll give you your cue, okay?

(CLIFF *pantomimes the action of someone taking money from a safe, stuffing it
in a briefcase.*)

STEVE. Cut!
CLIFF. Now what?
CHUCKIE. Man . . . this ain't no fun down here.
STEVE. I thought somethin' was wrong.
CHUCKIE. What's wrong?
STEVE. This is supposed to be a dress rehearsal, ain't it?
CLIFF. Yeah . . . but . . .
STEVE. Well, where's your briefcase?
CLIFF. Briefcase? Man, it's in the closet . . . I forgot . . . it
ain't that important.
STEVE. Everything's important. Get the briefcase.
CLIFF. Awww . . . sheet . . . (*He goes into the closet and
comes back carrying a large black briefcase.*) Is this okay,
Professor?
STEVE. Looks just fine . . . now fill it up.
CLIFF. The cost of this thing goes on my expense account
you know?
STEVE. Yeah, I know.
CHUCKIE (*whines*). Hey, man, it's really gettin' miserable
down here.
CLIFF. Too bad I ain't fillin' it with real money right now
. . . instead of . . .
STEVE. Places!
CHUCKIE. I'm in place already, man.

STEVE. Okay, Cliff.

(CLIFF *pantomimes the action of someone taking money from a safe and stuffs
it in his briefcase.*)

Okay, Miss. Now lay down on the floor . . .
CHUCKIE. I'm already . . .
STEVE. Okay, skip that part! (*He pantomimes the action of
tying* CHUCKIE. *To* CLIFF.) Okay?

(CLIFF *nods and closes his briefcase.*)

Then go.

(CLIFF *walks around the front of the
table, out of the sight of* CHUCKIE, *takes
off his sunglasses and walks into the
closet.* STEVE *kneels beside* CHUCKIE *and
twists the ropes about his wrists.*)

Now, Miss, I'm going to leave you like this. No gag.
Nothin' . . . I don't want you gettin' choked before your
boss comes back from lunch. But if I hear any noise out of
you before five minutes . . . I'm going to come back here
and stomp that nice face of yours . . . Understand?

(CHUCKIE *nods.* STEVE *stands, walks
around the table and enters the closet.*)

CHUCKIE. Hey, Cliff . . . Steve . . . How bout gettin' me
loose? Hey!

(BUMMIE *emerges from the bathroom
with a wet towel held to his nose and a
switchblade knife in his hand.*)

BUMMIE. You goddamn mathafukker . . .
CHUCKIE (*apprehensive*). Hey, man . . . I'm tied . . .

(STEVE *and* CLIFF *enter from the closet.*)

CLIFF. What you gonna do, Bummie . . . carve up the
    fatted calf?

CHUCKIE. I'm gonna cut this mathafukker's throat.

STEVE. But his hands are tied, killer.

BUMMIE. I don't care . . . I'm gonna cut his eyes out and
    send them home to his mama . . .

CHUCKIE (*scared*). Hey . . . get this crazy sonna bitch away
    from me . . . he's gonna kill me.

CLIFF. Nawh . . . I don't think he's gonna kill ya, Chuckie.

STEVE. Cut you up some, maybe . . . but not kill ya.

CHUCKIE. Well . . . don't just stand there . . . keep him
    away from me!

BUMMIE (*bending over* CHUCKIE). Shut up, mathafukker! It
    ain't gonna do you no good to holler.

CLIFF (*soft*). Bummie.

CHUCKIE. Pleez, you guys . . .

CLIFF (*threatening*). Bummie!

STEVE. The man said Bummie, Bummie.

BUMMIE. You guys keep out of this . . . this is between me
    and Chuckie.

CLIFF. Put the knife on the table, Bummie.

BUMMIE (*belligerent*). Who's gonna make me?

STEVE. On the table, Bummie.

BUMMIE (*doubtful*). Don't try and stop me.

CLIFF. You lookin' to die . . . friend.

STEVE. Slow.

BUMMIE. He's got it comin'.

CLIFF. The table.

(BUMMIE *puts the knife on the table; he
raises his foot above* CHUCKIE's *face.*)

BUMMIE. I should step on your head, punk!

CLIFF. Why don't you go get some beer, Bummie?

STEVE (*untying* CHUCKIE). Wait until I get Chuckie loose . . .
    he can go with you.

CHUCKIE. Hey . . . man . . . you shouldn't tie up a guy
    helpless like that. Anything could happen to him.

2. In New England Winter

*LIZ's place. LIZ, OSCAR and CARRIE sit
about the kitchen table. Joe Williams
sings "Goin' to Chicago" over the drug
store radio. And Count Basie plays
through the remainder of the scene.)*

LIZ. Look how it's snowin' . . . regular goddamn blizzard.
Look at it, Carrie.

OSCAR. She don't want to see no snow . . . warm blooded
as she is.

CARRIE. Yeah, you can keep your snow, Liz. I wish I was
back in Florida.

LIZ. Then why the fuck you up here? Why the hell ain't
you back there pickin' cotton?

CARRIE. Cotton? Woman, you know we ain't never picked
nobody's cotton. We left Florida when we was babies.

OSCAR. Ha ha . . . she can't stand nothin' like that cotton
choppin' . . . Daddy's little girl's too tender. *(He touches her
knee and runs his hand beneath her skirt.)*

CARRIE *(moves away)*. Stop it, Oscar.

OSCAR *(pulls her arm)*. What you mean, woman? I can do
anything I want to you . . . you my wife, ain't cha?

CARRIE. Don't be messin' with me in front of people, man.

OSCAR. Liz ain't people.

LIZ. Yeah, we got a real heavy snowfall. It's pilin' up an'
blowin' across Hoyle Street . . . and pilin' up snow in that
damn Duke's yard.

OSCAR *(kisses CARRIE)*. Ain't you my woman?

CARRIE. Stop it, Oscar. I'm goin' home if you keep that up.
Don't do that in front of people.

OSCAR. You goin' home? . . . You mean all the way across
the landing to the other side of the hall?

LIZ. When we was little girls, Carrie and me . . . we didn't
even know what snow was . . . when we was down there
in Florida. West Palm Beach didn't even have a lick of
snow. I remember the mangoes that I fed Carrie . . . and
the sapodillas . . . and the kumquats. Someday I'm goin'

back there and just sit in the sun and stick my feet in the
sand and look out into the water.

OSCAR. You my wife and woman, and don't you forget that.
And I can touch you whenever I feel like it.

CARRIE (*annoyed*). Oscar, you shouldn't do things like that
around people . . . How about if Crook was here, or if
Steve wasn't sleepin' in the bedroom?

OSCAR. Well Crook ain't here. He's got to get that jug of
muscatel and climb these here five flights with it. He's got
to drag his little short draggy ass through the snow. And
Steve don't get up until the sun goes down.

LIZ. Steve's lived in snow all his life. All his life. I guess
that's why he's so cold most of the time. A cold, hard northern black bastard . . . Ha ha . . . he'd be mad if he heard
me call him black, more than my callin' him bastard . . .
I do that all the time. Don't like that first word none, but
he sure likes me cause I'm black. Said to me . . . "The
blacker the berry . . . the sweeter the juice." Sounded like
some whiteman . . . cause I'm the blackest girl he's ever
been with . . . his mamma didn't want him to fool round
with no real black girls . . . leastwise that's what he said.
Said his mamma said for him to find a light skinned girl
. . . "To put some color in the family." . . . But I'm black
as sin . . . and that's why he loves me so much. No danger
of me lightenin' up his family none. (*Sighs.*) Yeah, he's cold
as snow and as brown as a coconut. Hummp . . . listen to
me . . . soundin' like my auntie. But I love him . . . but
he's so wild and crazy. Wild like only a northern nigger
can be wild. All of it inside, mostly, and cold and sharp
and slick like ice. But I love him cause I need him. He's
hot underneath and he makes me . . .

CARRIE. What you hummin' like that for and starin' out that
window for, Liz? You watchin' for Duke?

LIZ. Duke? That fuckin' man? Nawh, girl, my man is right
through that door in the bedroom, sleepin'.

OSCAR. When's Steve gettin' up? I want him to help us out
on this jug of wine that Crook's bringin'.

LIZ. Sheet . . . he's helped you too much already. He ain't
no damn wino like you and Carrie!

OSCAR. No wino! . . . That's how I met him . . . he was lookin' for a drink . . . and I showed him . . .

CARRIE. Listen to mamma . . . protectin' her little boy.

OSCAR. That's right . . . showed him where to go.

CARRIE. You better make a man of him . . . not a little sleepy boy. Send him back as a man, sister.

OSCAR. Next thing I knew I had introduced him to my sister-in-law. Ha ha ha . . . ha ha ha . . .

LIZ. He's not my child. He's my man . . . and he sleeps all day and loves me half the night . . . not runnin' the street. We black like the night . . . 'cause the night's our home. We're children of the black god of night.

OSCAR. Ha ha ha . . . and who would have thought it . . . they're shackin'. And me responsible for it.

CARRIE. Livin' up to their ears in the snow . . . in the black night . . . hee hee ha ha . . .

OSCAR *(joyous)*. Up to their coat tails.

LIZ. We gonna have a baby, one day . . . Our own baby.

OSCAR. Who else's? . . . Your own black baby.

LIZ. Yes, that's right . . . *black*. Thin and dark like me. Smart and quiet and mean like his daddy.

CARRIE. How you know it's goin'a be a boy?

LIZ. And we'll take our baby sleddin' in the snow and skatin' across the ice. We'll take our baby swimmin' in the warm Florida waters . . . and splashin' in the California Pacific. He'll be with us in the mountains and camp with us in the desert. The world is ours: thus sayest my black lord and master, Steve . . . And Steve's mine and our baby's. If our baby's made yet, and if he's not made already then we'll make him tonight . . . or tomorrow night . . . or while the snow falls and we drink muscatel and I sing to him and he reads to me and we love. Oh, we must love quick . . . quick and hot and hard . . . for they might come for him . . . they might come to steal him away. Steal his blackness . . . steal his spirit and soul . . . steal his manhood and make him not mine . . . nor his son's to be . . .

OSCAR. Ha . . . ha ha . . . woman, since the last time you got out of the nuthouse, Liz, you . . .

CARRIE. Shut up, Oscar!

OSCAR. Awww, baby, everybody knows about Liz . . . this is a small town.

CARRIE. How long's Steve been a deserter, Liz?

LIZ. Huh?

OSCAR. You heard what she said.

LIZ. No, I can't hear a goddamn thing! (*Shouts.*) You bastards have made me lose my hearing! Do you hear? I can't hear a fuckin' thing because of you . . . because of you . . . my own goddamn family!

(*Lights lowered and colored.* CROOK *enters holding a large bag and is silhouetted in the doorway.*)

CARRIE and OSCAR. How long's Steve been a deserter?

LIZ (*fear*). Don't say that . . . don't say it!

CARRIE. Why, Liz? You mean for us not to say what's true?

OSCAR. He's been gone for over thirty days, Liz . . . thirty days . . . and a guy's gone over the hill from the navy for that long's a deserter, right?

LIZ. He's mine . . . and he's not goin' back. He's my man . . . the father of my baby. (*Terror.*) Who'll be with me at night if he goes?

CROOK (*from the shadows*). I'll look after you at night, Liz.

LIZ. No, you won't . . . no one will but Steve. He's my man . . . my black man.

CROOK. I'll be with you at night, Liz. (*Chuckles*). And I'm just a nice brown skinned.

LIZ (*anguish, brushes at the invisible cobwebs*). No . . . no . . . that's not what I mean . . . ohhh, you know that's not what I mean. He's mine . . . and I'm his . . . I'm his queen!

CROOK (*laughing ridicule*). His queen?

LIZ. Yes, his queen. He said so . . . he said I was his queen . . . his sorceress queen of the snow land . . .

(*They laugh maniacally.*)

OSCAR (*sarcastic*). Steve . . . the poet.

CARRIE (*ridicule*). Steve . . . the phoney.

CROOK *(from the shadows).* I'll be with you to keep you warm in the black nights ahead.

OSCAR. I wonder when that little short-ass Crook is goin'a get back with the wine?

CROOK. I'll tear away the shadows, Liz. I'll shield you from pain.

LIZ. Yes . . . pain.

CARRIE. Oh, he'll be here . . . in enough time to get us all drunk. Relax, there ain't nothin' to do except get drunk on a day like this, anyway. That's probably him comin' up the steps now.

LIZ. Steve talks so poetic. Bad poetic, he says. If he goes I don't know what I'll do. I don't know how I can go it alone.

CROOK. You won't be alone. You'll just make it with me, baby . . . like you always make it with the next guy who comes along. I'm next, right? You hip to that? . . . When he's gone, it's me and the night and the snow. And it can't be too soon.

LIZ. It is dark and cold and loneliness is all around.

CROOK. My warm body next to yours . . . my hot meat inside you.

(Lights up gradually. CROOK *steps into the room.)*

CARRIE. Yeah . . . I thought so. It's him. Hi, Crook.

OSCAR. It took you long enough. What'chou do, little thief; squeeze them grapes on the way.

CROOK. Yeah, man, between my big toes.

*(*CARRIE *goes for glasses.* CROOK *takes a gallon jug of muscatel out of the bag.)*

How you don', Liz? You got the blues today lookin' out that window like that at the snow?

LIZ. Hello, Crook. Nawh, I'm all right.

CROOK. Nawh, you're not.

OSCAR. How you know how my sister-in-law is, buzzard pickin's?

CROOK. Oh, I know a lot about Liz, I know a lot, Oscar.

CARRIE *(passes glasses around)*. What do you know? You don't know shit about my sister, man.

CROOK. Relax . . . relax, Oscar's woman.

OSCAR. Ha ha ha . . . look at little Crook Crook. The dwarf slickster, that's him. Havin' kitchen debates with the ladies. That's your speed, ain't it, short and sly?

CROOK. If you know then you know, friend of mine.

OSCAR *(to the GIRLS)*. He got his style from old John Garfield movies . . . ha ha . . . and hasn't changed it in fifteen years . . .

LIZ. Oscar . . . leave Crook alone.

CARRIE *(bitter)*. Nawh, he shouldn't . . . that sawed off little nigger ain't no good.

CROOK *(teasing)*. I went and got the wine, didn't I?

CARRIE. Fuck that.

CROOK. Drunk already and only after half a glass.

CARRIE. Fuck you!

CROOK. Sure sign of a drunk.

LIZ. Stop it, Carrie.

OSCAR. You know, short and square . . . there might be something in what she's sayin'.

CROOK. Poor Crook.

LIZ. Leave him alone.

OSCAR. Awww, he's a good nigger . . . me and him done did a lot of good jail time together.

CROOK. Good Crook.

CARRIE. He ain't shit.

LIZ. Crook and Carrie and me grew up together, Oscar.

CROOK. Ole, faithful Crook.

CARRIE. He still ain't shit . . . nigger tried to rape me when I was eleven.

CROOK. This young lady has a fine memory. Would have gotten it too 'cept for Liz seein' me playin' with her baby sister and runnin' up and down the street screamin' for her mamma.

OSCAR. But that nigger can steal . . . whewww. Steal your eyeballs out while you lookin' at him with them . . . if you let him.

CARRIE. Leastwise . . . Oscar ain't been to jail for no petty thieving.

LIZ *(ridicule)*. No, indeed, he ain't.

CROOK. Defend Crook to the last.

OSCAR. What's so bad about what I been to jail for?

LIZ. You just ain't no good, Oscar.

CROOK *(serious)*. That's right, Oscar. You ain't no good.

OSCAR *(to* CROOK*)*. If you wasn't my good friend, big shorty, I'd make you take that back.

LIZ. Would you cut him, Oscar?

CARRIE. Liz . . . you know he would.

OSCAR. Sure I would . . . you know me, sister-in-law. Don't you?

LIZ. Yeah, I know you, butcher. You done cut thirteen boys.

OSCAR. Fourteen . . . Richie Sanchez didn't go to the hospital or press charges.

CROOK. Yeah . . . Richie's a good boy.

LIZ. You act like an animal, Oscar.

OSCAR. I don't do nothin' so bad, Liz. When some guy bothers me I cut him. That's all. It's for the Por-ta-gee in me.

CARRIE. Oscar's dad's a black Portuguese fisherman . . . there's a lot of them up here. You know how they are, don't cha?

OSCAR. Nawh, baby . . . don't tell that lie. He was no fisherman . . . just a drunk . . . but he was black and Por-ta-gee all right . . . leastwise that's what he said . . . A mean bastard. Couldn't hardly speak no English . . . ha ha ha . . . hardly spoke anyway cause he was drunk all the time . . . Ha ha ha . . . just would say to me "Git out the way." Just that . . . and kick me if I wasn't gittin' fast enough.

CROOK. We can shed a tear . . . if it'd make you feel better.

LIZ. And his son's a drunken beast who beats my sister.

OSCAR *(fondles and coos to* CARRIE*)*. Baby needs some beatin' sometime . . . all babies do, right? Liz, your boy in the bedroom there knocks you up side your head when he gets ready, don't he?

CROOK. Sho does and he better watch how he treats our women.

LIZ. Our what, Crook?

OSCAR. Yeah, I've cut fourteen cats and I'm goin' cut some more. I'm a young man . . . this state ain't got no capital punishment. Even if I kill somebody the most I'll get is seven to fourteen years. Be eligible for parole in seven years and be out. I'd still be a young cat . . . and I'd have my reputation . . . my rep. I'd really have a rep. Just like Philly Billy . . . or One-eyed Slim . . .

CROOK. Or that stomp-down bitch Brown Betty.

OSCAR. I'd have a rep, Liz. How you like that?

LIZ. My sister married to a murderer.

CARRIE (*getting drunk*). Yeah, married to a crazy nigger . . . ha ha ha . . . but I loves him. You my man, ain't cha, Big O?

OSCAR. Sho is, baby.

CROOK. Here, Liz, have another drink.

LIZ. Thanks, Crook. I sure wish Steve would get up.

CROOK. Don't worry bout bein' lonely, Liz. I'm here . . . been here a long time . . . waitin' . . . waitin' for you to come my way. And I'll be around for a while to come . . .

3. SHAKE MARILYN MONROE!

(*Liz's place. A fold-away spring and mattress has been produced, and* CARRIE *is curled at one end, in a fetal position.* STEVE *and* CROOK *dance the popular shuffling style dance of the day, on opposite sides of the table.* OSCAR *sits at the table singing loudly and clinking a fork on the bottles, glasses, ashtrays, etc.* LIZ *stands by the door scowling, her arms folded.*)

OSCAR. SHAKE MARILYN MONROE!

CROOK (*claps*). YEAH!

OSCAR. SHAKE MARILYN MONROE!

CROOK (*claps*). YEAH!

OSCAR. SHAKE THAT DIRTY BIG WHOAH!

CROOK *(claps)*.　YEAH!

OSCAR.　SHAKE THAT DIRTY BIG WHOAH!

CROOK *(claps)*.　YEAH!

(STEVE stumbles over to the table and lifts his glass. OSCAR and CROOK continue.)

LIZ.　Steve! I told you not to get drunk.

(He stares at her and takes a big drink.)

I'm sick of this shit! Every night you get up you start in drinkin'. It's bad enough havin' a family of winos . . . but you don't have to join them.

OSCAR.　A FAMILY THAT WINES TOGETHER . . .

CROOK.　. . . DINES TOGETHER.

(They laugh.)

OSCAR.　Hey, man . . . dig this . . . A family that stays together . . .

CROOK.　. . . LAYS TOGETHER . . .

(They laugh.)

STEVE *(moves toward LIZ)*.　C'mon, baby. Why don't you have a drink with me?

(She moves into the doorway.)

LIZ.　Oh, Steve. Leave me alone!

CROOK *(mocks, in a falsetto voice)*.　Ohhh, Stephen. Leave me alone.

STEVE.　But, baby.

OSCAR *(in a "Kingfish" dialect)*.　But, baby.

CROOK.　Baby? . . . Ha ha ha ha . . .

(LIZ flees down the stairs. CROOK turns up the radio.)

Hey, man, you hear what they playin' . . . "The Slop." You know how to do it, man?

STEVE. Nawh, man, I don't want to dance no more.

CROOK. Sure you do, Steve . . . Hey, Oscar . . . fix things so my man here can express his self. Let's make it easy for the young man.

OSCAR (*an "Andy" dialect*). Why sho, Mr. Crook . . . (*Sprinkles salt on the linoleum.*) . . . How's that?

CROOK. Why I couldn't have done better me own self, buddy buddy. It'll surely slide this young lad right into tomorrow, I haven't a doubt. (*To* STEVE.) Yeah, man, go on do "The Slop." Go ahead now.

(*Drunk,* STEVE *hears the music and dances, shuffling his feet upon the salt.*)

OSCAR. He ain't half-bad.

CROOK. Could stand some practice.

OSCAR. Yeah . . . takes time to . . .

CROOK. Hey, Oscar.

OSCAR. What?

CROOK. Let's take a walk . . . I got somethin' to tell you.

(*They swallow their drinks, watch* STEVE *a moment more and exit. At some point on the way downstairs they begin singing "Shake Marilyn Monroe" while* STEVE *continues dancing to the radio.*)

4. BRENDA'S BOYS

(CLIFF's *room. He and* STEVE *sit waiting, occasionally wiping their sweat away with hands and handkerchiefs. The radio plays.*)

CLIFF. Relax, Steve . . . relax.

STEVE. Damn . . . what's takin' those fools so long?

CLIFF. They just left. You'll get your beer.

STEVE. Beer is just what we don't need.

CLIFF. As hot as it is?

STEVE. We got to be sharp tomorrow . . . heat or no heat.

CLIFF. We're not only going to be sharp tomorrow . . .
we're gonna be cool . . . and slick . . . and quick . . .

STEVE. And dead if we don't pay attention to details!

CLIFF. Details . . . details . . . fuck details, Steve. Fuck 'em!
We could pull this job anytime we want . . . All we got
to do is get up off our asses and walk in there and take
what we want.

STEVE. Some may do it that way, Cliff . . . we don't.

CLIFF. Anyone of us . . . me, you, Bummie or even Chuckie
could do it. Tomorrow . . . I could pull that job my own
self just as easy as . . .

STEVE. Why don't you?

(Pause.)

CLIFF. I thought we was in this together.

(Pause.)

    Well . . . ain't we, Steve?

(STEVE walks to the window.)

STEVE. Why does it get so damn hot here in the summer?

(Pause.)

CLIFF. Well . . . ain't we, Steve?

(STEVE's back is turned to CLIFF.)

STEVE. Yeah . . . I guess we are . . . now.

(Pause.)

CLIFF *(opens beer).* This is the last of the beer until
Chuckie and Bummie get back . . . halfies?

STEVE *(chuckles).* Halfies? . . . Sounds like we're kids again.

CLIFF. Yeah . . . don't it?

STEVE. Nawh . . . drink it all. It's too hot to drink or think or anything . . . Ya know . . . New England's summers aren't like this.

CLIFF. How would you know? You only spent a winter up there.

STEVE. I just know . . . that's all.

(Pause.)

CLIFF. Damn . . . they're sho takin' their time. I wonder if . . .

STEVE. Sure are.

CLIFF. Chuckie really hates rehearsing like you want him to. Maybe he took off.

STEVE. Not even Chuckie's that stupid.

CLIFF. Nawh, I guess not. But they know I got somethin' to do tonight.

STEVE *(sits upon bed).* You got somethin' to do every night, brother.

CLIFF *(cynical).* Do I, brother?

STEVE. Yeah . . . you should be studyin' how to take care of business.

CLIFF. No kiddin'? . . . You're really not jokin'?

STEVE. Be serious for once!

CLIFF. Like you?

STEVE. Why not?

CLIFF *(ridicule).* I'm not a machine, *brother.*

STEVE. You really hate me, don't you? I can hear it every time you say "brother."

CLIFF *(startled).* Wha . . . did you say?

(Pause. STEVE *doesn't look at him, but stretches out on the bed, upon his back.)*

Did I hear you right, Steve?

STEVE. Is it like a machine to plan an action to the last detail?

CLIFF. Why did you say that, Steve?

STEVE. Is it like a machine to complete successfully what you begin?

CLIFF. But I am your *brother* . . . and you're almost the last of the family. *(Sincerely.)* Look, buddy . . . I'd give my life for you.

STEVE. Cliff and Steve . . . born of one Brenda King and two very unlike and disappearing spirits . . . sometimes called runaway fathers.

CLIFF. I'm not just talkin' about how you plan jobs, Steve. It's how you live . . . that's the part you can keep. Your bein' on time or you'll have a heart attack. Your keepin' to the schedules you make . . . whether it's takin' some bullshit night course, gettin' your hair cut a certain time ah month . . . or waitin' for years to go see the woman you love . . . 'cause . . .

STEVE. You know it all, don't you?

CLIFF. What makes you think you got to get yourself ready to meet her?

STEVE. It's not her! I got to get myself ready to meet the future, Cliff. Don't you see?

CLIFF. The future is with us right now, brother. We drown in our future each breath we take. Its phoney promises leak into our brains and turns them to shit!

STEVE. Come off it, Cliff. It's because of not planning that our futures are always so bleak.

CLIFF. They are?

STEVE. How else?

(Pause.)

CLIFF. You've got a lot to learn in some areas, Steve.

STEVE. Like with women?

CLIFF. Yeah . . . that too.

STEVE. You've had a lot of experience, why don't you teach this young dog some new turns?

CLIFF. You've always hated my being older than you, haven't ya?

(STEVE *turns away.*)

STEVE (*annoyed*). I can't even get into a conversation with you that sticks to the point.

CLIFF. Can I help it if my ole man came first?

(STEVE *turns and stares at him.*)

STEVE. What's wrong with you, man? Has all that drinkin' an' whorin' messed with your mind?

CLIFF. You would like that, wouldn't you, brother Steve? Then you could feel pity for me . . . like that poor dumb animal . . . what's her name?

STEVE (*bewildered*). Poor? . . . Dumb? . . . Animal? . . .

CLIFF. Yeah . . . whojamahgiggy . . . The one you're breakin' your ass to get back to . . . up in the frozen north.

STEVE. It's no wonder that Lou left you.

CLIFF. What went on between me and my wife ain't none of your business.

STEVE. Listen to yourself sometimes . . . all that poor girl wanted was some peace.

CLIFF. Is that what you told her when you were stayin' in my house while I was in jail?

STEVE. Do you think I'd tell her somethin' like that?

CLIFF. Yeah!

STEVE. Well, you're right. That's what I told her and more.

CLIFF. Like I'm the bastard of the family . . . Brenda King's first big mistake. Her love child.

STEVE. What are you talkin' about? Lou knew about that . . . why would she . . .

CLIFF. You've never liked me, Steve. I don't know why . . . I love you and mom. (*Sincere.*) Really . . . I dig you, little brother.

STEVE (*angry*). I've got your "little brother" swingin'.

CLIFF. Wha . . . huh? Are you afraid to feel? Can't you feel anything for me?

STEVE. No self-pity, please.

CLIFF. I'm talkin' about you and me, man. Brothers!

STEVE. No, I can't feel . . . don't want to if I could. That's for you, big boss. Me . . . I don't have feelings, emotions, sympathy, tenderness, compassion . . . none of it.

CLIFF. What's wrong with you?

STEVE. I don't need it . . . it slows you up. I wouldn't have any of that sickness in me if I didn't have to deal with people like you.

CLIFF. All we poor losers, huh?

STEVE. Awww, come off that crappy shit, man. *Losers*. Stop pitying yourself. We're brothers . . . we know . . .

CLIFF. You've never gotten used to the idea that some other man besides your ole man made it with Brenda.

STEVE. You used to call "Brenda" mom.

CLIFF. You hated me for havin' Brenda all to myself five whole years before you did.

STEVE. Look . . . if you keep talkin' this sick shit I'm goin'a call the job off. You're not talkin' responsible, Cliff.

CLIFF (*simpers*). Responsible!

STEVE. Is somethin' wrong with you or somethin'?

CLIFF. Can't you tell? You've known me for quite a while.

(*Noise of* CHUCKIE *and* BUMMIE *returning: footsteps on the stairs and argument.*)

Yeah . . . there's somethin' wrong with me. I feel. Mostly I feel good. I have emotions. Mostly I'm so emotional that I have to drink myself to sleep after I become exhausted by a woman. And I don't give a damn who knows I feel or have the emotions of a man . . .

STEVE. A fourteen year old!

CLIFF. I don't have my head tied-up by a tape measure. Why are you so tight, brother? Do you doubt yourself?

STEVE. You know I always win, Cliff. Does that sound like doubt?

CLIFF. You don't win them all.

STEVE. One day even mom will like me more than you.

CLIFF. Wha . . .? What's goin' on in . . .

STEVE. I live to win, Cliff.

CLIFF. Why do you have need to win? Win what? From who?

STEVE (*joking*). From your mamma . . . you bastard.

CLIFF. I can't break through, can I?

(CHUCKIE *and* BUMMIE *enter, muttering and glaring at each other.*)

STEVE. They're here with your beer. C'mon, one more run-through and you can go back to bein' just plain ole Cliff. My big brother.

(*The brothers look at each other a long moment.*)

> 5. GIT OUTTA TOWN . . . GIT OUTTA TOWN . . .
> YOU CLOWN . . .

(*Liz's place.* STEVE *and* CARRIE *sprawl across the small bed, drunkenly, snoring, each in the other's arms.* CROOK *and* OSCAR *stand over them.*)

CROOK. See, Oscar. See, man. Just like I said. Just like I told ya.
OSCAR. The little mathafukker.
CROOK (*shakes* STEVE). Hey, punk! Hey!

(STEVE *stirs.* OSCAR *pushes* CROOK *aside and prods* STEVE *in the side with his combat boot.*)

OSCAR. Get up . . . you black sonna bitch!

(STEVE *opens his eyes; he is drunk and doesn't see the two men, but leans over and kisses* CARRIE *on her cheek.* OSCAR *grabs him by the collar and drags him from the couch.*)

Are you crazy! Are you crazy, mathafukker! That's my wife!

(STEVE *looks up groggily from the floor.*)

STEVE *(bewildered)*.   Oscar . . .

OSCAR.   Git up, mathafukker. Get up! I don't want to kick you yet. Get up so I can beat yo ass!

(It is apparent that OSCAR *is putting on a show for* CROOK's *benefit.)*

STEVE.   What's the matter?

OSCAR.   Don't ask me what's the matter when I find you in bed with my wife.

STEVE.   In bed . . . your wife? Carrie?

OSCAR.   Get up, mathafukker!

STEVE *(rising)*.   Wait a minute, Oscar. I don't know . . .

OSCAR *(raises hands in a fighter's stance)*.   C'mon, you black sonna bitch! I'm gonna beat your ass today.

*(*CROOK *takes a bone-handled switch-blade out of his pocket and opens it with a snap. He offers it to* OSCAR. STEVE *sees the knife and is wary;* OSCAR *and* CROOK *are between him and the door.* OSCAR *waves knife away.)*

Nawh . . . nawh . . . this is gonna be a fair fight. Put that knife away, Crook. I'm gonna beat this little mathafukker with my hands.

STEVE *(groggy, pleads)*.   Now . . . Oscar . . . look, man, I'm sorry. I didn't do anything with your ole lady, man.

OSCAR.   Are you gonna fight, man?

STEVE *(whines)*.   Awww . . . please, man. I just fell asleep on the couch and I guess she did too. Please, Oscar. I didn't do anything wrong.

OSCAR *(slaps him)*.   You punk ass mathafukker . . . you gonna fight?

*(*STEVE *drops his head and backs off.)*

(turns on the still sleeping CARRIE*)*. Bitch! Get your funky ass offa that couch.

(He pulls her to her feet violently. She awakes shuddering and he slaps her viciously several times.)

CARRIE.   Oscar . . . Oscar! What's wrong?
OSCAR *(pulls her to the door).*   Shut the fuck up, bitch!
CARRIE.   Oscar, please!

(They exit. Noise of them crossing landing and the opening and slamming of a door.)

CROOK *(saunters out).*   See you later, Steve. *(He turns in doorway.)* Hey, Steve.

(STEVE stares at him.)

   Hey, man, when you goin' back to the service?

(Silence.)

   I think it's best if you went back and cleared up your business. Don't you agree? It would make it easy on everybody . . . especially Liz. You want the best for Liz, don't you? Don't you? . . . Not talkin' anymore, huh? Well . . . you know what the man sez about actions shoutin' at ya, huh?
   I think you better leave soon, boss. In fact, I'm tellin' you . . . ha ha . . . you know what the sheriff said to the man in the black hat? . . . Ha ha . . . I mean like tonight, bossman.

(He exits. His footsteps descend the stairs. STEVE sits on the bed with his head lowered. Lights dim and the harsh hallway glare spills into the room. Music comes up: Fats Domino sings "Blue Monday." Sound of someone slowly climbing the stairs.)

6. What Difference Does It Make?

(Music comes up: Big Joe Turner sings.
LIZ *stands in doorway a moment, looking*
over the scene. Her figure, outlined, is
thin and sensual. STEVE *notices her*
shadow falling across his feet, looks up.)

STEVE. I'm sorry . . . I'm sorry, baby.

LIZ. You always are, Steve. Always sorry as hell.

STEVE. I didn't do nothin'.

LIZ *(moves into room)*. What difference does it make? I met
   Crook outside and by then the story goes that you had
   been caught by Oscar astride his wife . . . my sister . . .
   and that the only thing that kept Oscar from cuttin' you
   to pieces was Crook holdin' him back. What difference
   does it make? Huh? This is a small town, Steve . . . Is there
   much worse than that?

STEVE. Liz . . . I didn't even touch her. I didn't even touch
   her, baby. She . . .

LIZ. Don't tell me a goddamn thing about it! I don't want
   to hear about you and my sister.

STEVE. Liz . . . please. You don't think . . .

LIZ *(anguish)*. Shut up! Stop it! I don't want to hear . . . I
   don't want to hear. You can give her all the babies you
   want.

STEVE. Babies?

LIZ. I don't care . . . I don't care . . . It doesn't matter to
   me, you see, it don't matter. You see it doesn't matter,
   Steve. I'll still be his aunt. Yes, his aunt. Aunt Liz. And I
   can take him for strolls in the park. Don't you see? It
   doesn't matter that he isn't mine but Carrie's.

STEVE. Liz!

LIZ. He'll still be yours . . . he'll still be yours, darling . . .
   ha ha . . . so between the two of you then he'll be mine
   as well. I hope he has your build . . .

STEVE *(pleads)*. Liz, listen.

LIZ. . . . and Carrie's looks . . . though she's fast losing
   them drinkin' all that wine. Mamma would have a lot to

say to Carrie if mamma wasn't such a chippy herself. You
know what mamma do, man? She's a party girl . . . *(Snapping her fingers and struts.)* . . . yeah . . . mamma . . . mah
little ole mamma . . . still partying to this day. *(Strong
southern accent.)* Lives down in Hartford . . . heee heee
I'm sho glad. It could be worse . . . she might be livin'
here. She might want to touch my baby . . . our baby,
Duke.

STEVE *(bewildered).* Liz?

LIZ *(cradles and rocks baby in her arms).* He's so big,
darling. So big and handsome . . . like you, Duke . . . like
you. He's so *beautiful* . . . blond hair just like yours . . .
blond and golden like the sun. Ohhh . . . poor mamma's
baby . . . if your hair just doesn't turn dark . . . *(Grimaces
and shivers.)* . . . dark and ugly . . . if it doesn't darken in
the summer sun. If it remains so beautiful . . . that is all
I ask . . .

STEVE. Liz . . . can't you see me? Can't you recognize me?

LIZ. And our baby's skin . . . so soft so pale . . . blond hair
. . . soft as snow . . . skin . . . pale as yours, Duke . . . pale
as yours, darling. And we must keep our baby that way . . .

STEVE. But what about *our* baby, Liz? Yours and mine . . .
what about *our* baby?

LIZ. We must keep him in the New England winter . . .
away from the sun . . . away from the heat and light . . .
we must guard him . . .

STEVE *(crying).* Madness . . . madness and death and loneliness . . .

LIZ. . . . eyes blue as our cold cold sky . . .

STEVE. Madness madness madness . . . God, I can't take
this . . . I can't live this out. It can't be *this* way. This isn't
it . . . there must be order . . . perfection . . . there must
be form . . . there must be reason and absolutes . . .
There can't be only madness and reaching out and never
touching the sides . . . everyone can be felt, can't they?
There *has* to be something for me besides this emptiness
. . . this living death . . . this white coldness . . .

LIZ. Our baby . . . our baby, Duke . . . our baby like the
winter's face . . .

*(The door across the landing bursts open
and* CARRIE *rushes in.)*

CARRIE *(still drunk).*   I came as soon as I could, Steve . . .
I came as soon as I could.

LIZ *(hums and rocks).*   Carrie . . . we have a baby . . . a
boy child.

CARRIE.   Steve! Crook's gone to get the police and the shore
patrol . . . Oscar knows it and told me before he went to
sleep. They're comin' for you, Steve! They'll arrest you
for desertion . . . they'll get you and I'll never see you
again.

STEVE *(dressing hurriedly).*   Oh, God! Oh, goddamn!

LIZ *(apprehensive).*   Where are you going, Duke? Where
are you going? You're not going out in the snow, are you?

*(*OSCAR *enters.)*

STEVE.   Carrie . . . something's wrong with Liz. Take care
of her, please.

CARRIE.   Hurry, Steve. Hurry! Don't let them get you.

(Outside, sound of cars' doors slamming.
OSCAR *comes up behind* CARRIE *and
punches her, knocking her on the bed.)*

No, Oscar. No! Please don't!

*(*OSCAR *begins choking her but* STEVE
*breaks a chair across his back, flooring
him.)*

LIZ *(screams in agony).*   NO, DUKE . . . NO . . . NO . . .
DON'T LEAVE ME! . . . DON'T LEAVE US TO DIE!

*(*STEVE *runs out the door and down the
stairs.)*

DUKE . . . DUKE . . . COME BACK . . . DON'T LEAVE!

*(Sound of a brief, violent struggle on
stairs below. Silence.)*

Ohhhh . . . it's so lonely, baby. It's so cold.

CARRIE *(helps* OSCAR*).* Oscar . . . Oscar . . . c'mon . . . let
me help you.

OSCAR. That sneak got me . . . I should have cut him, Carrie. I should have killed him. He was the one . . .

CARRIE. Yes, I know . . . I know, Oscar. I'm here, baby,
and I'll help you.

OSCAR. Did Crook bring 'em? . . . Did they get him?

CARRIE. Yeah, Oscar . . . yeah. They got him.

OSCAR. Good! . . . but I should have killed the mathafukker!
. . . Ouch! Be careful! That sonna bitch really nailed me.

CARRIE. I love you, Oscar. Please don't beat me no mo'.

*(They exit. Lights down; stairwell light
casts light through doorway.* LIZ *still
stands rocking and humming.* CROOK
stands in doorway.)

CROOK. Liz.

LIZ. That you, Duke? Is that you?

CROOK. Nawh, baby . . . it's Steve.

LIZ. Steve?

CROOK. Yeah, don't you remember, baby? Remember,
Steve?

LIZ *(recalls).* Steve? . . . Oh, yes! . . . Steve . . . Please come
in, Steve . . . I'm so in need of company. Steve . . I've
been waiting for you . . .

CROOK. Yeah, I know.

LIZ. Come in, Steve. Come in. As soon as I put the baby
to bed I'll be with you. *(Dances and hums.)* Steve?

CROOK. Yeah, Liz.

LIZ. You won't leave me, will ya?

CROOK. Nawh, baby. Nawh. I ain't gonna leave . . . not for
a long time. (CROOK *shuts the door.)*

7. HEADIN' NORTH

(CLIFF's *room*. CLIFF *has phone to his ear.* STEVE, BUMMIE *and* CHUCKIE *lounge about the room. "Do the Twist" by Chubby Checker comes softly from the radio.* CLIFF *hangs up phone.*)

CLIFF. It's busy . . . must really be the party line this time.
STEVE. What you gonna tell her this time, brother?
CLIFF (*scratching himself*). Nothin' . . . not a damn thing, brother.
BUMMIE. He don't have to tell the bitch anything, Steve.
STEVE. Who was talkin' to you, big mouth!
BUMMIE. What did you call me?
CHUCKIE. Are we finished for tonight, man?
STEVE. Yeah . . . that's it. Tomorrow should go off like an exercise.
BUMMIE. I asked you what did you call me, Steve.

(STEVE *seems to ignore him.*)

CHUCKIE. Sho should . . . much as we practiced.
STEVE (*stands*). Our rehearsals were necessary . . . practice . . .
CLIFF. Makes perfect!

(BUMMIE *gets up and faces* STEVE. *They eye each other;* CLIFF *and* CHUCKIE *are aware of what is happening.*)

STEVE. I wasn't going to say that!
BUMMIE. What was you going to say, Steve . . . that I'm a big mouth?
CLIFF. Whatever anyone was going to say I've heard it already. So forget it.
STEVE. Watch yourself, Bummie. Remember I still owe you somethin'.
BUMMIE. I paid that debt, friend. Or don't you remember

. . . we're *old* friends. We've been sharin' things for a long time.

CHUCKIE. Well, look . . . I'm goin'. I'll see you tomorrow.

CLIFF. Me too . . . why don't you studs clear out? I'm already two hours late for my date.

STEVE. Hold up, Cliff. I have somethin' to tell you.

BUMMIE. What have you got on your mind, Steve?

STEVE. Still a big mouth, huh? And nosey too.

CLIFF. Let it wait, man. This chick, Sandy, is goin'a give me a lot of static.

STEVE. Hang on . . . it won't take long.

BUMMIE. Are you gonna tell him somethin' he really don't know, Steve? You know you could tell him a lot of things.

STEVE. What's buggin' you, man?

CHUCKIE. Do I got to wait too?

STEVE. Nawh . . . we'll see you tomorrow, Chuck.

CHUCKIE. Yeah . . . well, okay. See you then.

(BUMMIE *holds* CHUCKIE's *arm.*)

BUMMIE. Hold on, Chuckie. We got somethin' to talk about . . . all of us.

CLIFF. What now, Bummie?

BUMMIE. I want everybody to hear this . . . 'specially Steve. And you, Cliff.

STEVE (*threat*). You better know what you're sayin'.

BUMMIE. What I'm sayin' is how are things really goin' down tomorrow?

CLIFF. What ya mean? Steve's had us up here practicing for two weeks.

CHUCKIE. Yeah, man . . . if . . .

BUMMIE. Shut up! I don't mean playin' games but how things are between us . . . (*Pointing them out.*) between you and me and him.

STEVE. We're listenin'.

BUMMIE. We pullin' the biggest job of our lives so far, right?

CLIFF. Right.

BUMMIE. If anything goes wrong we got five to life, or a pine box . . . right?

CHUCKIE.   Ahuh?

STEVE.   You're not gettin' yellow are you, Bummie?

BUMMIE.   You would like that, wouldn't you? No, this is Bummie you're talkin' to and who's talkin' to you . . . don't get me mixed up with yourself.

CLIFF.   We're waitin', Bummie.

BUMMIE.   Okay . . . okay . . . let me say this. There're things between us. Things that happened years ago and should be cleared up before we step out of this room and put our lives in each other's hands.

CHUCKIE.   Yeah, man . . . that's right.

STEVE.   Quiet, Chuckie. Let him finish.

BUMMIE.   There's somethin' between some of us . . . somethin' . . .

STEVE.   What's between us?

CLIFF.   Let him finish, Steve!

BUMMIE.   You know! . . . You know what's between us! And I want it out in the open.

STEVE.   You're talkin' too much, Bummie.

BUMMIE.   No . . . not enough! You know what I'm talkin' about. Don't you?

STEVE.   Yeah . . . I know. (STEVE *picks up the knife from the table and plunges it in* BUMMIE's *throat.*)

CLIFF.   Steve!

(BUMMIE *writhes upon the floor, gagging on his blood.*)

CHUCKIE.   Goddamn . . . ohhh . . . goddamn.

(BUMMIE *dies.* CHUCKIE *goes into the bathroom and is sick.*)

CLIFF.   Steve . . . Steve . . . do you know what you've done?

STEVE.   Yeah . . . I know . . . I know. Now Bummie and me are even.

CLIFF (*incredulous*).   But it was for nothing. Steve . . . I knew . . .

STEVE.   We're even, I said.

CLIFF.   I knew, man. I knew about you and Lou and Bummie.

STEVE (*anguish*). We're even! Bummie and me are even now. I paid him back! No more cops and niggers . . . I paid him back for everything.

CLIFF. No, no . . . Steve. No. Look what you've done . . . look . . . and for no reason.

STEVE. I had my reasons!

CLIFF. But Lou wrote me in prison, Steve. My wife wrote me that she loved you and that her second baby was yours.

STEVE (*disbelief*). You knew?

CLIFF. She told me that she had given in to Bummie so that you would hate her. She drove you away from her because of me being your brother.

STEVE. I never hated her . . . never. But Bummie knew about me and her and he would have told you.

CLIFF. She knew Bummie pretty well . . . that's why she told me. She knew how I felt about you . . . and asked me not to blame you.

STEVE. You knew . . . all this time.

CLIFF. I couldn't tell you.

(CHUCKIE *enters*.)

CHUCKIE. I gotta get out of here, man. I got to go.

CLIFF. No, Chuckie. Nawh.

CHUCKIE. But, man, this is terrible. This is terrible.

CLIFF. Nawh, it's not. Now listen to me.

CHUCKIE. Awww . . . Cliff . . . please. Let me get outta here.

CLIFF. Look, Chuckie. I need you. We got to get rid of this body.

CHUCKIE. Nawh, man. I can't.

CLIFF. Yes, you can. We'll take it down the back stairs and load it in the car. Okay?

CHUCKIE. Oh, man, I'm gonna be sick again. All that blood.

CLIFF. We'll drop it in the swamp.

(CHUCKIE *rushes into bathroom again.*
STEVE *stands, looking out front.* CLIFF
opens the last beer.)

Want any of this?

STEVE. Nawh . . . I don't want anything.

CLIFF. Not anything?

STEVE. No . . . just to tell you what I got to say.

CLIFF. That you leavin' . . . now or after the job tomorrow, brother?

STEVE. I need some travelin' money.

CLIFF. Okay, then. That's what we get.

STEVE. Always my big brother.

CLIFF. Always. That's the name of the game.

STEVE. Well, forget it . . . don't waste it on me.

CLIFF. You're all I have . . . might as well spend it here.

STEVE. You love me so much . . . and I hate both of us.

CLIFF (*goes to phone*). Look, man . . . I got my woman to meet . . . (*Gestures to body.*) . . . and the night still ain't over. Talk about it tomorrow . . . after the job, if you want.

STEVE. I'm leavin' as soon as we count the money.

(CLIFF *dials.*)

CLIFF. Leavin', huh?

STEVE. Yeah, leavin'.

CLIFF. Damn . . . this phone is still busy . . . I wonder if she could be talkin' to anybody? (*Hangs up and shouts.*) HEY, CHUCKIE, GET OUT HERE! We got work to do! (*He pulls a sheet from the bed and covers the corpse. From the table drawer he takes a small automatic pistol and puts in his pocket.*) Anything more ya gonna do, Steve?

STEVE. Yeah, man, lots more. A whole lot more . . . Pray for winter 'n head north.

(CHUCKIE *enters, looking empty but resigned. He has a clothes line in his
hands.*)

CHUCKIE (*mutters as he begins to tie up the body*). But I knew him . . . I knew him . . . I knew him . . .

(*Curtain.*)

The King of Soul or The Devil and Otis Redding

A musical tragedy
A one-act play

by Ben Caldwell

CHARACTERS:

OTIS
OTIS' MOTHER
CHURCH WOMAN
BLACK LAWYER
TWO TEEN-AGED GIRLS
BLACK EXTRAS (scene fillers)
TWO BLACK MEN (in bar)
PILOT (white)

THE DEVIL (the sequence of his disguises) as the devil/A&R man/master of ceremonies/aircraft salesman/airport mechanic/policeman

SCENE 1

(We see a church in a Black community. Down South. A sign says, "Macon County Baptist Church." It's Sunday—services are over. We see a group of PEOPLE going, slowly, in different directions. Walking and talking, or just standing, enjoying the sun-bright morning. We focus upon a conversation betwn two middle-aged WOMEN. One of them is the mother of a young MAN who sings in the church choir.)

WOMAN. It sure was a lovely service today. The reverend spoke just beautifully. You know that boy of yours sure can sing! My goodness! The sisters get happy everytime he open his mouth! He sound like he got more God in him than all the rest of us.

MOTHER. Yes, Otis makes me so proud. I feel like I was blessed to birth him. He such a good boy, too—he worries so much 'bout me and his daddy, and his sisters and brothers—he wants so much for us. He's all the time talking about how much money he might make if he went and made some records. He wants to do so much. Well, sister, I'm gon' get on home and fix dinner for that family of mine. Give my love to all of yours.

WOMAN. Alright now.

(Fade out on this screen, and we go to:)

SCENE 2

(A barely lighted room. OTIS lays sleeping. He is startled awake (he is really dreaming) by a flash of red light that flickers like a fire. A figure, a WHITE MAN, is standing at the foot of his bed, like an apparition. His suit looks red, and has a high white collar like a priest's. (Throughout the play, which is Otis' life, we see the same WHITE MAN. We witness him as he changes costumes & disguises. He is the Devil. Keep your eye on the Devil.)

OTIS. What?! Who's there? What you' doin' in here?

DEVIL. Who I am is not important—you are the important one.

OTIS. Well, whoever you are, you got no business in here! *(Not frightened, but suspicious.)*

DEVIL. Don't be afraid, you're only dreaming—but the dream is real. I can't harm you unless you let me. I only want to make a deal with you.

OTIS. What kinda deal?

DEVIL. I'll explain. You want to do a lot of things for your family—for yourself. You want to move them out of this old house and into a new one. You want all kinds of things that you think will make you and your family happier, right?

OTIS.   Yeah, you' right.

DEVIL.   As I said, I wish to make a deal with you. I will see that you have all that you want, but I want something that you have.

OTIS.   If you can give me everything, what could I possibly have that you want?

DEVIL.   You have something I don't have . . . that's the thing I want.

OTIS.   What?

DEVIL.   I want your soul. Truthfully, I don't have one. And that's the only weight that will hold me here.

OTIS.   That sounds stupid to me—how can I give you my soul?

DEVIL.   If you agree to give it to me it's mine!

OTIS (*not serious*).   Okay you can have my soul! Now where's the house and cars?

DEVIL.   It's not that easy. We must draw up a contract. I will give you all the things you want, and when that's done (to your satisfaction) you will willingly give me your soul.

OTIS.   Suppose I take what you offer and then don't give you my soul?

DEVIL.   Then your life would be forfeited as payment. But you're too honorable to do that. Is it a deal?

OTIS (*mumbled in his sleep*).   Yeah, uhhuh!

(*The red light stops flickering, and the rm is dark again.*)

OTIS (*loudly—now awake*).   Is somebody in here? Is somebody in here? Man, I musta been dreamin'.

HIS MOTHER'S VOICE (*calls from another rm*).   Otis, is somethin' the matter?

OTIS.   No, ma, I'm alright. I just had some kinda funny dream. It woke me up.

(*In a dim lighted corner we see the*

DEVIL-APPARITION *change costume and wait for the scene to change.)*

SCENE 3

(Small town "downtown" scene. Signs identify the various stores and buildings. Emerging from a store, laden with packages, is a big, young, BLACK COUNTRY BOY. His strength is his handsomeness. He's accosted by (the Devil comes out of the shadows as) a well-dressed WHITE MAN.)

DEVIL. Say, young man, stop a moment! You're Reverend Redding's son aren't you? (OTIS *nods and says, "Yes.")* I've heard a lot about you, son. I want to do something for you. I want to help you make a lot of money.

OTIS *(anticipating a scheme).* I don't wanna be no prize-fighter, mister!

DEVIL. I don't mean fighting, boy, I mean with your voice.

OTIS *(some interest).* How?

DEVIL. My name is Mr. Jacobs. I represent Antis Records. You have a beautiful sound, Otis. If you were singing somewhere besides church you could make a lot of money.

OTIS. My daddy says my voice is God's gift—I'm supposed to share it! They enjoy my singing like I enjoy some of theirs—it would be like selling smiles! And my daddy says it's wrong to sing anything but church music.

DEVIL. Your daddy's wrong. He just doesn't know. Anything you do with your voice will be holy and spiritual— your father just doesn't know. Furthermore you can reach more people outside the church. You'll be sharing this God-gift to a much greater extent. I'm telling you, you can make a lot of money!

OTIS *(not quite persuaded).* I don't know. Hey, do I know you? I have the strongest feelin' that I've met you before— or somebody look 'xactly like you.

DEVIL. It wasn't me, but we're the same. But that's not important to me, the important thing is you. You can have all the things you want. Everything for your mother, and father, your brothers and sisters—see the world—you can leave this *little* town if you want to—buy a new house—a car! *Give me* your voice and I'll get you everything you want.

OTIS. I don't believe it, but I'd like to try it! It sure sounds good! What do I have to do besides say, "It's a deal"? (*They shake hands.*)

DEVIL. I'm going to have to work hard in order to sell you to the public, but we're both gonna make a lot of money—here's the deal. Our contract will state that after you've made (*He says this slowly to make the figure sound more impressive.*) one million dollars, all rights and royalties to your singing belong to me!

OTIS (*amazed*). A million dollars! (*Pause.*) Wait—how come only a million for me?

DEVIL. *Only* a million! Boy, what other opportunity would guarantee you a million dollars?

OTIS. But it just don't seem sensible to sell *my* voice completely for *just* a million dollars!

DEVIL. Look, you may be screaming your lungs out in that church from now to eternity and won't make anywhere near a million dollars. (*Pause.*) Now is it a deal?

OTIS. Yeah. Okay.

DEVIL. Good. Meet me here tomorrow, six o'clock, and I'll have all the papers. You're on your way, Otis.

(*They part company.* OTIS *right.* DEVIL *left. The* DEVIL *hurriedly changes into his next costume of deception.*)

SCENE 4

(*We hear the final strains of "Satisfaction," the bedlam of a crowd screaming its appreciation. A* WHITE MAN (*the Devil in a tuxedo*) *rushes onto the stage, saying:*)

DEVIL. How about that? How about that? Let's hear it!

The great Otis! Let's bring him back out. Come on back, Otis!

(A tall BLACK MAN, *in a bright/orange suit, comes back on stage. He is glistening with perspiration from his efforts, and breathing heavily. The* WHITE MAN *puts his arm over* OTIS' *shoulder, and puts the microphone to his face. The Devil is congenial.)*

DEVIL. How 'bout that, Otis? They really love you out there. How does it feel to be the hottest thing in the country?

OTIS. Oh, Jack, it feels just great! I still can't believe it! I want to thank all my people—my fans—for all they've done for me. They're the ones truly responsible for my being here today!

DEVIL *(put-on sincerity).* I wanna tell you Otis, it's really a sign of greatness when you attribute your greatness to the people. *(Brief applause).* Tell me, what's the secret of that special sound of yours?

OTIS. Well, Jack, I believe it's sincerity. I just sing and sound the way I feel—and that's the truth. The things I sing I really feel them from my soul on out! No secret or no trick.

DEVIL *(put-on sincerity. Pretending to understand).* That's just beautiful, Otis. Ladies and gentlemen, Otis Redding! OTIS REDDING! One of the truly great ones!

(Applause, screams, as OTIS *leaves the stage. The* DEVIL *goes to a dark corner, changes his disguise and waits.)*

SCENE 5

(A record shop. Two teen-age GIRLS *emerge with their record purchases.)*

1ST. What you buy?

2ND. I bought Otis' new side. It's baddddd!

1ST. Oh yeah, Otis is *my* man! You see that house he bought for his mother?

2ND. Yeah. You seen him in person yet?

1ST. Yeah, girl, that is one big, good-looking nigger! You know what I wish I could do?

(She is telling her giggling GIRL FRIEND *her wish, as they continue on their way out of sight. The* DEVIL *is in the shadows, watching and waiting.)*

SCENE 6

(An angry BLACK MAN *is pacing the floor. He has a piece of paper in his hand.* OTIS *is seated, looking dejected. The* MAN *is saying:)*

LAWYER. As your lawyer I should have known about this from the very beginning. A contract like this is not only illegal, it's immoral! How did you go for a thing like this? (OTIS *shrugs.*) Oh I know—this isn't the first time a white man has shown a poor Black boy a picture of success and made him pay a ridiculously high price for it.

OTIS. But isn't there something we can do about it? It's my voice. Mine! I can say I don't wanna sing for that m.f. no more! I can say I changed my mind. *It's my voice!* I'll keep on singing! For someone to *own* my voice is damn near as ridiculous as someone owning my sou . . . see what you can do about it, huh?

LAWYER. We'll see what the courts have to say about it.

SCENE 7

(Court corridor. OTIS, *his lawyer,* MR. JACOBS, *stand as a group.)*

DEVIL. A bargain is a bargain—you weren't man enough to live up to it.

LAWYER. What the hell you mean! That was an unfair, unethical, contract. You were taking unfair advantage of this man!

DEVIL. If it wasn't for me he wouldn't be where he is today! I didn't twist his arm and make him sign. I explained everything to him. I performed a service in return for his agreement to the terms of the contract.

LAWYER. What the hell is your gripe, Mr.? You've made a few million from singing, and you can't carry a god-damned tune! You . . . the judge allowed you the rights and royalties to *all* of Otis' past recordings! Stopped all future recordings—what more do you want? Why should you make it all?

OTIS (*interrupting*). Well, you got the records, but the things I'm gon' do gon' make the things I've done seem like nothing. I still got my voice! You won the records, but I still got my voice!

DEVIL. The only "voice" you have is what I have on rec-ords! To me, the real value of the things you've done comes after you're gone. Remember Sam? What I have will be all that's left of you! (*The* DEVIL *rushes to a dark corner and changes his disguise.*)

LAWYER (*in disgust*). Ain't that a bitch! Well, that m.f. has a temporary victory. You can still make plenty of money. He has no claim to your live appearances. And maybe we'll get that injunction on future recordings settled soon. A few appearances around the country and you can make enough to finance your own record company.

(*They are about to leave—*DEVIL *approaches carrying attaché case.*)

DEVIL. Mr. Redding! Mr. Redding! I'd like to speak to you a moment. (OTIS *and the* LAWYER *stop to listen.*) I repre-sent the Fall-T Aircraft Company. I have a proposition, which you'll probably find very interesting. (*Shows picture.*) Your own personal aircraft. A twin-engined jet. You no longer have to be bothered with airline schedules. You make your own schedule. A private jet is a convenience and an asset to the modern businessman. All the top names have one today.

OTIS. Sounds good. Look, contact my lawyer tomorrow and he'll take care of the deal.

DEVIL. Thank you, Mr. Redding. I think you'll be pleased. *(Smiling.)*

(They leave. The DEVIL *returns to the dark corner to change again.)*

SCENE 8

(We see a WHITE MAN *in a phone booth, talking to someone. We hear the airport/ airplane sounds.)*

PILOT. Yes. I'm at the airport now. I have to have the battery changed. No, it's just a minor thing. The mechanic, here, says he'll take care of it. It'll be ready to take off as soon as you get to the airport. Alright. Okay. Yeah, the weather's bad, but I think we'll have a good trip. *(To* MECHANIC—*who is the Devil in another disguise.)* You'll take care of Mr. Redding's plane?

DEVIL *(slightly sinister)*. Yes, I'll take care of Mr. Redding's plane.

SCENE 9

(The same two TEEN-AGERS *are dancing to the music from a radio—a soul station—the music is interrupted by a bulletin.)*

ANNOUNCER. Rhythm & Blues singer Otis Redding was believed killed, today, when his private, twin-engine jet crashed into icy-cold Lake Monona, in Wisconsin. It's an unconfirmed report, let's hope it's not true. We'll give you details as we receive them.

(Starts playing records again. Second record finishes and the ANNOUNCER *says, sadly:)* Ladies and gentlemen, a great voice has been silenced. The king of soul is dead. The

report has been confirmed. Otis Redding was killed when his jet aircraft crashed, early today, in Wisconsin. He was truly, appropriately called "the king of soul." Otis was soul. The existence of this intangible was proven by Otis' sound. You know, like you don't believe there's a voice like Otis' til you hear it. And it sounds like what began as perfection—needed no cultivation. You got to believe in soul once you've heard Otis. He's gone, but the inspiration of his soulful voice, singing his songs, still belongs to us. It's really a great, great, and tragic loss.

(The DISC JOCKEY *plays "Try a Little Tenderness." The two* TEEN-AGERS *are seated on the floor, beside the radio, showing their sorrow in silence. The lights and the sound fade, as the* DEVIL *is huddled in his corner, changing his costume for another appearance.)*

SCENE 10

(Sad, sorry PEOPLE *dressed in black. Some of them are crying. The* DEVIL *is on the scene in a policeman's uniform. We hear the people's comments.)*

PEOPLE. "I ain't never seen so many flowers." "Yeah, they sure put him away nice." "I didn't know he was so big!" "He looked like that statue of that Egyptian king, Khafre."

OTIS' MOTHER *(escorted by other members of the family).* Remember how the house used to seem just to vibrate when he use to sing. It sounds like I can still feel Otis' presence.

(The DEVIL *disappears into darkness, and we don't see him again.)*

SCENE 11

(Dimly lighted bar. Two MEN *seated on high stools, drinking. They are loudly discussing the singer's death.)*

1ST MAN: That's right, man, whitey is a cold motherfucka!

2ND MAN.   Aw man you' crazy! You always get some crack-
pot ideas! What the white man gon' kill Otis Redding for?

1ST MAN.   Anytime a Black man start doing something for
his people whitey kill 'im—one way or another!

2ND MAN.   What was Otis Redding doing for his people? All
he was doing was singing and making a lotta money!

1ST MAN.   WE WAS PROUD OF HIM, IF NOTHING
ELSE! Look at what they did to Muhammad Ali!

2ND MAN.   They just took his title, they didn't kill him! If
whitey so cold why didn't he kill him?

1ST MAN.   They tryin' like hell to kill him! Financially!
They cut-off his livelihood! And tryin' to put him in jail!
They tryin' to kill his proud, strong Black image! They
tried to make it look like the white man giveth, and the
white man taketh away. But the champ had enough sense
to say the only way you take this title is in the ring
where he won it. He made Black children say, "I'm the
greatest!" He made the world realize that Black is beautiful
and strong!

2ND MAN.   I can't see anything they'd have to gain by killing Otis—he was making a lot of money for them.

1ST MAN.   He makin' more money for them now that he's
dead, cause now they don't have to pay him! That's part
of their game! The white man sells *you,* and you only get
a part of the money! He even got the nerve to take the
lion's share! Otis was moving in the direction to get more
of it—or all of it! Didn't you read where he was startin' his
own record company? And he was gon' manage other
talent! Now to the white man it's hard enough to take a
nigger makin' *some* money, but when that nigger want *all*
the money—when he start goin' for himself—competing—
the white man say, "He's got to go!"

(2ND MAN *is beginning to give these
ideas serious consideration.*)

1ST MAN.   Another thing, like I say, the white man was
sellin' Otis—Otis was a product to the white man—like
cornflakes! That's all! He want to make as much money off

his "product" as he can. What increases the value of the
product more than a great demand for it? What creates
more of a demand for a great singer's records than his
death? And whitey has no scruples, 'specially when it
comes to the dollar!

2ND MAN. You soundin' foolish again—why the man gon'
get rid of somebody makin' as much money for them as
Otis was? Otis was young, and still had a lotta songs in
him.

1ST MAN. Man, that whitey know he can find another
young, hungry, Black soulbrother, to take Otis' place! Like
he change car styles every year—same quality, different
body!

(2ND MAN *is considering these points of
view seriously again.*)

1ST MAN (*reminiscing*). Yeah, man, Otis was sayin' somethin'. I could just look at my woman, sometimes, and feel
and understand what Otis meant when he sang, "I Can't
Turn You Loose." I've often thought about the good and bad
about my woman when he sang "Respect" and "Security."

It made me think about this jive-ass, frustrating country
when he sang, "I Can't Get No Satisfaction." All Otis'
music had a message. Tellin' us 'bout ourselves, in a way.
Make you happy, or sad, or sorry. Made you "feel" and
"think." Made you examine yourself, and try to get yourself together. Yeah, man, don't tell me whitey didn't want
him out of the picture. For more reasons than one.

2ND MAN. You know, I think you right! It'd be good if we
didn't have to have *no* dealings with the devil!

1ST MAN. Yeah.

(*They drink their drinks in silence. Jazz
comes from the jukebox. The lights dim
to black, ending the play.*)

Family Portrait

(or My Son the Black Nationalist)

A One-Act Play

by Ben Caldwell

CHARACTERS:	(THEIR NAMES)
FATHER:	FARTHEST FROM TRUTH
MOTHER:	NOWHERE NEAR TRUTH
SON:	SUNSHINE ON TRUTH

(Lights up. *Scene: Family trio is seated at breakfast table. Fluorescent bright lighting.* FATHER, MOTHER, SON. FATHER *is fortyish and graying. Casually dressed in sportshirt and slacks. A frown is frozen on his face, from years of unexpressed complaint.* MOTHER *is seated directly opposite him. She wears a colorful housecoat. Her face is almost hidden by the big red wig.* SON *is early-twenty-something. He wears his hair long, natural. He looks dissatisfied. He looks anxious— impatient—as though to say something that is on his mind. There's something he must do. Restless, as he is certain he doesn't belong here. They're eating bacon & eggs. Son is eating cereal. Radio is on, low—early morning rb dj.* FATHER & SON *will soon engage in an argument that seems a ritual practiced for hundreds of years and millions of lives.* FATHER *is saying, over and over:*)

FATHER.   We got to stay out of trouble. That's the way to get ahead. We've got to show the white-man that we are ready and good enough to live with him. We have to prove we are just as good as he is.

(The SON *finally hears this and becomes annoyed.)*

SON *(arguing).* Prove we're as good as the white-men?! How good is the white-man? I can't even think of anything good about the white-man! Daddy, we don't have to show them anything! We don't have to prove anything to them! The white-man who murders us—you have to prove you're good enough to live next door to him? DO YOU WANT TO LIVE NEXT DOOR TO HIM TOO? All we've got to show the white-man is that we resent the treatment we've received from him—the conditions he's imposed upon us—and prove to him that we won't let him get away with it any longer!

FATHER *(repeating the same speech, in very sincere-meaningful tones. Stops abruptly. Thinks, quickly, on an old oft-repeated thought. Pounds on the table. Talks fast. Angrily).* Goddamit, boy, why don't you get a job? I worked hard to see that you went thru school and got the proper training. And look at you! Walkin' 'round here lookin' like a bushy-head savage! A bum! Preaching hate. Making me and your mother ashamed to show our faces on the street!

SON *(sarcastically refers to* MOTHER's *wig).* Mama doesn't have to worry about anybody seeing her face anywhere!

MOTHER *(pulling her wig from over one eye to glare and fuss at him.)* You hear the way he talks to me! Insults me! He has no kind of respect. He's my own son, but I don't want him in the house if he can't respect me!

FATHER. That's right, I can't have you upsetting your mother! Why' you so disrespectful and hateful, boy? *(He goes back to repeating his speech, while looking into his paper. Then loudly, proudly, says:)* No here's a colored boy made something of himself. "Socrates P. Chamberpot." They made him the vice-president of "High-Time Liquors." And he's only seventy-five years old! First negro to have such a high position with this company! *(He goes back to his speech.)*

SON *(angrily).* Damn, daddy, you sound like a broken record! What are you trying to do to me?

FATHER. I'm trying to *convince* you of the right thing to

do! I'm trying to keep you out of trouble! I don't want no
trouble!

MOTHER. And that's all he's going to bring us—running
around with all those ol' ugly girls that don't fix their hair.
And those wild-looking bushy-head, bushy-face niggers.
They don't look like nothing but trouble!

FATHER. That's right! *AND I DON'T WANT NO
TROUBLE! (Emphatically.)*

SON. You never wanted "no trouble," that's why *all* you got
is this house, to hide in; that big-ass Cadillac, out front to
ride in; and a retirement plan, to take pride in. You' got
everything but your freedom, your self-respect, your
manho . . .

FATHER. Boy! What you talkin' 'bout? I got as much as any
white-man got!

SON. Oh yeah, how many niggers *like you* you got working
for you?

MOTHER *(excited. Angry. Frantic).* Listen to the way he's
talking to you! We don't have to take this from him! Put
him out! Put him out!

SON *(yelling. Quickly, without thinking).* You don't have to
put me out! I'll get out—cause one day you might make
me so mad I'll kill you!

FATHER. You threatening me? You threatening me? In my
house! *(He lunges at his son, almost upsetting the table.
Grabs* SON *by the throat.* MOTHER *is screaming,* "Don't kill
him, Father, he didn't mean it!" SON *breaks his hold and
backs away from him.)*

SON. I did mean it. If I don't kill you the white-man will—
he's got no more use for niggers like you! Look at you!
They wouldn't even let you work as long as you wanted.
Retired two years early 'cause the white-man replaced you
with a machine!

*(*FATHER *is standing, gripping the back
of the chair, as if restraining himself from
violent action.)*

Look at you! Ready to hurt me from what I'm saying—
and you've never done anything to any white-man for any-

thing he's done to you—not so much as give him a dirty-look! What are you, anyhow? You really feel you were born to be the head of a goddam shipping dept. for twenty years? Do you feel your primary purpose is to serve the white-man?

Whether you like it or not I won't live my life just to serve the white-man. Who does the white-man serve but himself? The white-man has no use for me now because I won't be what you are—because I won't let the white-man rule my world!

You know the white-man is wrong-as-hell! That's the only thing you and I agree upon. You're just too scared to do anything about it! So scared that, to keep from look-ing at the world and the truth, you hide behind a job, and let these few little creature-comforts compensate for your suffering and your loss of manhood. You close your eyes, and shut off your mind, and you can only hear *my* com-plaints. You can't feel or understand what makes me com-plain. And you open your mouth *only* to tell me to "shut up," or that I'm "wrong" or "hateful." You ain't never said nothin' to the white-man 'bout how wrong and hateful he is!

The white-man unreasonably controls our lives—he has no right to this! He has no right to keep us this way! Niggers like you allow it! Kissing him instead of killing him! You think I want to grow old like you and all I have to look back on, as accomplishment, is "twenty-five years of faithful service," and a goddam retirement plan? And mama waiting for you to die so she can collect a "lump sum," and live even more like a "high-class white-lady"!

(MOTHER *draws up, gasps in shock.*)

FATHER.   Get out! You're not my son! I disown you! *(With a wave of his hand.)*

SON.   You don't have anything to disown! When the white-man took your body and soul I wish he'd taken your right and ability to have sons, then I wouldn't be here for you to disown!

FATHER.   Hateful! Disrespectful! Now standing there yell-

ing—raising your voice at me in my house! Get out! No
man raises his voice in *my* house! (*Bangs chair on the floor
and lunges.*)

SON.   The house still belongs to Schwarts Real Estate. You
don't own anything until you repossess yourself!

FATHER (*softly, subduing anger.*)   Get out! If I have to put
my hands on you I'll kill you!

MOTHER (*comforting*).   Honey, don't let him get you all
excited—that's what he's trying to do.

(*He is visibly upset. She seats him.
Calms him. He starts repeating his
speech.* SON *leaves the room—returns putting on a jacket.*)

SON.   If twenty years of whitey puttin' fire to your ass didn't
excite you I don't see how I can make you so angry.

(*They both give him cold, hard glares.
He says into his* FATHER's *ear:*)

You tried begging your way into this society and failed.
That's why I'm not what you want me to be. Trying to be
white. You die waiting to turn white, and be "accepted"
into this white society. I intend to fight my way out of it!
I AM A BLACK MAN! I'm going to stay black if it kills
me! I'm not going to change my mind, my thoughts, my
personality, till they fit some white standard of accept-
ability. I'm not going to let them fuck-up my life anymore.
You stay here and die!

(*Walks out and slams door. They sigh
a simultaneous sigh of relief, and shake
their heads out of pity.* FATHER *begins
reciting his speech, in very conversational
tones.* MOTHER *is adjusting her wig,
reading the paper, and nodding in agreement to the speech. Lights fade to black.*)

Growin'
into
Blackness

by *Salimu*

CHARACTERS:

MOTHER
LOLITA
SHIRLEY
PEARL
SANDY

(Scene: *Living room. Sister with a natural, pants, shoes off, stretched out on sofa reading (about blackness). Key opens door.* MOTHER *enters, dressed like she's been to business (she's a domestic), with a package.*)

MOTHER. Aw shit! What the hell you done did to yo hair? You might as well go straighten it rat now cause ain't no chile o mine gon walk around with no nappy head.

LOLITA (*looks up at her, rolls her eyes, and goes on reading*).

MOTHER. Dammit, you hear me talking to you. Jes keep sitting there, you gon get the shit knocked outta you. (*Goes to put down the package.*) Lolita, you lik narrow behin heffa, jes git up rat now.

LOLITA (*trying to maintain calm*). You always gotta yell and scream like somebody ain't got no sense? But I guess if you had sense you wouldn't go out here and clean no cracker lady's house every day.

MOTHER. An don't go gitting fucking smart, cause I'll break yo lil' ass. Now you do somethin to yo head.

LOLITA. Do what to my head?

MOTHER. Straighten it, that's what.

LOLITA. Straighten it for what?

MOTHER. Cause you ain't gon live in my house wit no nappy head.

LOLITA. First of all, it ain't nappy, it's natural. An what's so bad about having a natural?

MOTHER. I ain't go to answer to you, you my chile—an dammit don't you forget it.

LOLITA. All I wanna know is what's so bad about a natural? If you tell me what's bad about it then maybe I'll straighten it.

MOTHER. It's disgraceful, that's what it is. Whatcha mean "maybe" you'll straighten it? When you git so grown that you can't do what I say, then dammit you can git the hell out.

LOLITA. Ohhhhhhh! Disgraceful? My brothers can't let theirs grow because you say *(pointing to her)*, you say they don't comb it. An when I git a natural you tell me it's disgraceful. You think it's a disgrace for me to be who and what I am. You think it's a disgrace for me to wanna be Black and beautiful.

MOTHER. You better shut the fuck up before I knock the shit outta you.

LOLITA. Maybe if you listen to somebody sometime you'd learn something.

(A knock on the door just as the
MOTHER *starts toward* LOLITA. SHIRLEY
opens the door and walks in.)

SHIRLEY *(wearing mini dress, makeup, etc. To* MOTHER). Poochie, what the hell you yellin' about now? You're always screamin and cussin.

MOTHER *(half smiling)*. An dammit don't you come in here fuckin with me either.

SHIRLEY *(to Lolita)*. What she fussin with you about now?

LOLITA. Cause I won't straighten my hair.

SHIRLEY. Oh, Poochie, it looks nice. You just ain't hip to what's happenin.

MOTHER. Who ain't hip? Shit, she ain't stayin here lookin like that.

SHIRLEY. C'mon, Poochie, make this run aroun the corner wit me.

MOTHER. Shirley, if yo ass gits drunk umma leave you.

SHIRLEY *(laughing).* I never get drunk.

MOTHER. An when I git back, you better have your head together.

SHIRLEY. An don't pay her no attention. You know how she is.

MOTHER. Bring yo ass on before I change my mind. *(They leave.)*

LOLITA. Man, mothers are too much!

(Knock on door. PEARL *comes in wearing Eastern style dress, natural.)*

PEARL. Peace, sister, how you doin?

LOLITA. Goin through mothafuckin changes.

PEARL. Your hair looks beautiful.

LOLITA. Um glad you like it. My mother says I gotta straighten it or get the hell out.

PEARL. I can dig it. My mother took me through some changes too. But um still there.

LOLITA. Yeah, but you don't know my moms, she'll put me out.

PEARL. I don't think so. Once you explain what it's about she'll dig it.

LOLITA. How you gon explain something to somebody who won't listen?

PEARL. Yeah, well . . . Remember, it was a long time before we listened.

(Another knock. SANDY *comes in wearing natural, pants.)*

SANDY *(very excited).* Ohhhh, you did it! It looks beautiful! Whatcha you moms say about it?

LOLITA. Straighten it or get the hell out.

SANDY. Mine told me I got until this weekend to make it. I don't know what the hell to do.

PEARL. Now listen, sisters, that language got to go. That's no way for Black women to talk. And you ain't supposed to wear pants either.

LOLITA. Uhmmmm. Sounds like you been with Rahim again.

PEARL *(smiling)*. That's right. An I was with Ahmed and Abdullah too. They asked me to give yall the peace.

SANDY. Well seein them ain't helpin much. I mean, they teach us a lot about bein Black, but how umma be a Black woman and live with my messed up mother?

LOLITA. That's right. It got to be one or the other, not both. I can't be goin through no changes all the time.

PEARL. Umma have to talk to um and find out what you should do. I know ain't no brothers gon let no sisters get put out in the street.

SANDY. But you gotta dig that we only 16. They could put us out, call the cops, and have us sent away until we 21. Now you know I can't go for that.

LOLITA. Well all I know is I ain't gon straighten my hair back for nobody—unless it's absolutely necessary. If I git put out, I just have to find somewhere to go. Now don't talk about it no more. *(To* SANDY.*)* So what else did you learn today?

PEARL. Wow! A lot.

SANDY. Well teach, sister.

PEARL. I'll tell you as much as I can remember cause I don't wanna get nothing wrong. We must help to build a strong Black nation. You know, we got to have babies cause without children there can be no future. An like they're trying to kill us off with wars, birth control pills, shootin down brothers and sisters, children, in the streets—and like just any way they feel like doin it. Oh yeah, I almost forgot. I met the most beautiful sister in the world today. You gotta meet her—she's outta sight. She told me a lot too. We're supposed to inspire our men and make um feel like the kings they are. I learned so much I can't even talk about it all now.

LOLITA. We shouldn't have to depend on you to tell us anyway. We should be able to learn whatever we want. But, no, we gotta stay home with our little sisters and brothers.

SANDY. That's what happens when you gotta live with pork

eaters and alcohol drinkers. I be so hungry sometimes my stomach be talkin to me.

LOLITA. Mine talk to me all the time. But um not stayin aroun no ugliness that's gon stay like that when I should be learnin what Black and beautiful is about—and teachin other Black people.

SANDY. Well, um down with whatever you wanna do cause I came too far now. I ain't turnin back to a pork eater and I ain't turnin back to no carbon copy, imitation cracker lady.

PEARL. Then we just have to hustle aroun and find somewhere for yall to go. I just hope your folks don't call the cops.

LOLITA. I don't even care about my moms no more cause like Abdullah said, it ain't about us. If they loved Black people, they would wanna see us doin' what has to be done—and they'd be helpin too. But they too busy drinkin to care about anything.

SANDY. That's right. They'd be out there wearin naturals and would have taught us. And they wouldn't be takin no birth control pills.

LOLITA. So we leavin, right?

SANDY. Right.

PEARL. Remember, sisters, word is bond.

LOLITA. Dig it. They left a big job for us and it's time we got to work on it. From now on my life is dedicated to Black people.

SANDY. Sister, our lives are dedicated to Black people.

PEARL. Alhumdullah!

El Hajj Malik

A Play about Malcolm X

by N. R. Davidson, Jr.

she who stands in tan   committed before a rougher skin
dangles summer panties in long-fingered hands
she who stands in tan   in midnight perspiration dries in her
    vacuum loins
death for the dream children   destroys an art invents a
    death

*(The stage is black at the rise. In the first
seconds of darkness we begin to hear
Archie Shepp's "Malcolm, Malcolm,
Semper Malcolm." After the poem is begun, the lights come up slightly, enough
for us to make out the dark shapes of
the ACTORS arranged on the levels.
Throughout the rest of the poem, projections are flashed on a retractable screen.
The slides are of the anguish suffered by
Afro-Americans since they were first
brought to this country as slaves: slides
of slave trading, of slave dwellings, people working, dancing, crying, finally several slides of lynchings. After the poem
is completed, the music which follows is
faded at an appropriate point. As the
ACTORS begin their opening chant, the
lights are brought up full.)*

ACTOR THREE.   Maaaaaaaaaaaaal-colm!
ALL *(chanting).*   Mal-colm
    Mal-colm   ,
    Mal-colm
ACTOR ONE *(through the chanting which dims).*   *Mal-colm*
    man
    Mr X man
    Reach out and touch this land

ALL *(chant rises)*.   Mal-colm
    Mal-colm
    Mal-colm
ACTOR TEN *(through dimmed chant)*.   Mr X man
    We touch your hand
    And filter out like bitter sand
ACTOR TWO *(through dimmed chant)*.   Preach it man
    And preach it grand
    And scourge it with your burning hand
    Touch us with your finger-fan
    And tell us where to make our stand
ALL *(chant rises very loud)*.   Mal-colm
    Mal-colm
    Mal-colm
ACTOR FIVE *(screaming)*.   MALCOLM!

(Three beat pause.)

ACTOR SIX.   Out of Michigan running
    fire and green-hot trees
ACTOR SEVEN.   And with them the glory blaze of life
ACTOR EIGHT.   Burst from that Northwestern womb
    Be born to the hoofbeats
    riding out of the South
ACTOR NINE.   and across the nation
ACTOR TEN.   And watch with infant eyes
    the light racing deep within the forests
ACTOR ONE.   watch the incendiary venom of the masked
    aurora
ACTOR SIX.   Watch the flaming Jesus turning the leaves
ACTOR FIVE.   and his army cleansing the hooded night of
    you
ACTOR FOUR.   Watch black baby
    from the shadows of your skin
ACTOR NINE.   My earliest memories are of the Klan
    And the violence done to us . . .
    My earliest memories are of the threats and shouts
    and angry curses spat upon my frightened mother
    My infant memories are of the righteous Klan
    sailing like white-hot ghosts in the night
    settling on our house flaming it

and sending it into a thousand sparks and shuddering ash
My prenatal dreams fled naked and vulnerable
from that burning house
In my mother's belly I was the hunted

(In the following sequence, ACTORS FIVE,
SEVEN, EIGHT, NINE *and* TEN *speaking
urgently in hushed tones and half-whis-
pers, like Halloween spooks, create a
night of terror.)*

ACTOR FIVE.   Ooooooo, lady, ooooooo
ACTOR EIGHT.   Hide your husband and your sons
ACTOR FIVE.   Ooooooo, ooooooo, lady
ACTOR TEN.   Hide your husband and your sons
ACTOR EIGHT.   There's a awful wind out tonight
ACTOR FIVE.   Ooooooo, lady, awful mens ridin' out tonight
ACTOR SEVEN.   Ooooooo, ooooooo, lady
ACTOR NINE.   Hide your husband and your sons
ACTOR EIGHT.   Keep 'em outta sight
ACTOR SEVEN.   Put your daughters underneath the bed
ACTOR TEN.   Ooooooo, lady, ooooooo
ACTOR EIGHT.   Quiet! Here they come
ACTOR FIVE.   Ooooooo, look at the whip
ACTOR NINE.   Ooooooo, look at the gun
    Ooooooo, look at the horses breathin' fire
ACTOR EIGHT.   And see the blood, oooooooohh, the blood
ACTOR SEVEN.   Oooooohh, lady, hide your husband and your
    sons
ACTOR TEN.   Put your daughters underneath the bed, ooooooo
ACTOR FIVE.   Ooooooo, lady, ooooooo
ACTOR SEVEN.   Oooooohh, that awful wind, ooooooo, them
    awful mens
ACTOR EIGHT.   They out killin' tonight, lady
    They killin' everything in sight
ACTOR NINE.   They killin' everything black in sight
    It's terrible, lady, it's terrible
ACTOR TEN.   Ooooooo, hide your husband and your sons
ACTOR SEVEN.   Keep 'em outta sight
    Keep'em livin' through the night
ACTOR TEN.   Ooooooo, ooooooo, lady

ACTOR FIVE. If they can't find the one they want

ACTOR NINE. Ooooooo, they kill the first black man they see
  They leave him hanging from a tree

ACTOR EIGHT. 'Cause when that man done met his end
  They let him blow in the midnight wind

ACTOR SEVEN. Ooooooo, ooooooo, lady

ACTOR FIVE. KEEP 'EM OUTTA SIGHT

ACTOR EIGHT. Keep 'em livin' through the night

ACTOR NINE. Say your prayers, bow your head

ACTOR TEN. Keep your daughters underneath the bed

ACTOR FIVE. Keep your men from being dead

ACTOR SEVEN. Cry and pray, cry and pray

ACTOR EIGHT. Cry your tears and pray for day

ACTOR NINE. For the killin' night to go away

ACTOR TEN. Ooooooo, lady, ooooooo

ACTOR THREE (*taking stage*). My father was a Baptist
    minister and disciple
  of Marcus Garvey, Black Nationalist
  and dangerous man of 1925
  My father preached that cause and
  they got him for it
  They fired his house those good Christian white people
  and sent his family wailing and frightened into the night
  But my father was not afraid
  He continued to spread the word of Marcus Garvey
  He dared to persist and they killed him for it
  When I was six they killed my father

ACTOR TWO. Quiet! Here he comes!

ACTOR NINE. Hey, boy! Hey come here!

ACTOR EIGHT. Come here, nigger!

ACTOR NINE. Come here! Come over here!

ACTOR EIGHT. Come here, nigger!

ACTOR TWO. He's backing away!

ACTOR FOUR. Don't be afraid, boy. Don't we know you?

ACTOR EIGHT. You scared him. He's trying to get away!

ACTOR NINE. Get him! Get him!

ACTOR TEN. POW! POW!

(ACTOR FOUR *screams*.)

ACTOR TEN. POW!

(ACTOR FOUR *screams again*.)

ACTOR TWO.   POW! POW!

(ACTORS TEN *and* FOUR *scream*.)

ACTOR EIGHT.   He's down! Get him!
ACTOR TEN.   Still breathing . . .
ACTOR TWO.   He ain't dead yet.
ACTOR NINE.   Look at his eyes! Hit him! Hit him!
ACTOR FOUR.   His head! His head!
ACTOR TEN.   Clang-clang-clang! Clang-clang!
ACTOR NINE.   Drag him over here. Lay him there!
ACTOR TEN.   Clang-clang-clang!
ACTOR EIGHT.   Scatter!
ALL (*except* TEN *who is clanging*).   Braddul-la-dul-la-dul-la-
    dul-la-dul-la-dul-la-dul-la-dul . . . UUUUHHHHhhhhhhhhh!

(ACTOR FOUR *with a scream that becomes
a moan*.)

ALL.   Ooooooooo, shhhhuuuuuuuuish, ooooooooo, shhhuuuu-
    ish
    Clit-clit clitter-clit clit clit-clit (*and on*)
ACTOR TWO.   The wind. The midnight murder wind
    Like a rake dragging dried leaves across the concrete
ALL.   Ooooooooooo, ooooooooooo, shhuuuuuuuish
ACTOR TEN.   Blip-blip-blip-blip Blip Blip Blip-blip Blip
ACTOR TWO.   And too much blood in the wind, too much
    fallen on the leaves
ACTOR TEN.   Blip Blip Blip Blip Blip
ACTOR THREE (*taking stage*).   My father went out one day
    when I was six and didn't come back
    He went out one day and they attacked him
    They smashed in one side of his head
    Then they layed him across some tracks
    And ran a streetcar over him
    Cut his body almost in two
    Cut him with those big scissor wheels
    And in that condition he lived
    for nearly two and a half hours more
    My father was a tough and angry man

ACTOR ONE.   But with him dead
  his family struggled to stay alive
  We struggled to keep together to keep our pride and
    dignity
  That's when the social workers came

ACTOR SEVEN.   Why are your children different from each
    other, Mrs Little?

ACTOR FOUR.   Why are some of your children lighter than
    each other, Mrs Little?

ACTOR ONE.   Came like the plague

ACTOR FIVE.   Were you ever pregnant for any man other
    than your husband, Mrs Little?

ACTOR SEVEN.   Have you had a man since your husband
    died, Mrs Little?

ACTOR ONE.   Sliding out of the filth under the rocks

ACTOR FOUR.   Do you make money *just* by taking in ironing,
    Mrs Little?

ACTOR ONE.   They came at us like the plague those welfare
    people

ACTOR SEVEN.   Why does Malcolm steal, Mrs Little?

ACTOR FOUR.   Why don't you eat pork, Mrs Little?

ACTOR FIVE.   Why are you poor, Mrs Little?

ACTOR SEVEN.   Why is Reginald stupid, Mrs Little?

ACTOR FOUR.   Why don't you feed your children better, Mrs
    Little?

ACTOR FIVE.   Why don't you dress your children better, Mrs
    Little?

ACTOR SEVEN.   Why are you poor, Mrs Little?

ACTOR FOUR.   Why won't you go on relief, Mrs Little? Why
    won't you take our money?

ACTOR ONE.   They came hard and tenacious
  until we were destroyed until my mother caved
  under their incessant pressure

ACTOR FIVE.   Waaaaahhh (*making siren wail*), children,
    there's something
  the matter with your mother

ACTOR ONE.   They hauled her off my mother
  shut her up in a mental ward and
  sent her six kids packing

ACTOR TWO.   My earliest memories are of the Klan

shrouded in righteousness
burning our house
My childhood memories are of that white Black Legion
invisible in this land
murdering my father
and I do not forget them
Nor do I forgive

ACTOR EIGHT. And what do you feel Malcolm now?
And how do you think Malcolm now?
When your mind goes back to that

ACTOR SIX. It could make me a vicious and dangerous person knowing that they looked at us as numbers and as a case in their book, not as human beings. And knowing that my mother in there was a statistic that didn't have to be. That existed only because of a society's failure, hypocrisy, greed and lack of mercy and compassion. Hence I have no mercy or compassion in me for a society that will crush people then penalize them for not standing up under the weight.

ACTOR TEN. And how old were you then?

ACTOR NINE. Then I was thirteen

ACTOR ONE. And what happened to your brothers and sisters?

ACTOR NINE. We were split up

ACTOR TWO. And where did you live?

ACTOR NINE. With some people

ACTOR THREE. And what did you do?

ACTOR NINE. Went to school

ACTOR THREE. And what else did you do?

ACTOR NINE. Stole

ACTOR FIVE. And why did you steal?

ACTOR NINE. 'Cause I was hungry

ACTOR EIGHT. And how was school?

ACTOR NINE. Got kicked out

ACTOR SEVEN. And why'd you get kicked out?

ACTOR NINE. Put a tack in the teacher's seat

ACTOR ONE. And then what happened?

ACTOR NINE. Got sent to reform school

ACTOR THREE. But first . . .

ACTOR NINE. But first they sent me to the detention home
and I got to tell you about that

ACTOR ONE *(taking stage).* The detention home was where
they sent you before they sent you to reform school, and
it was run by these two people, Mr and Mrs Swerlin. I
liked Mr and Mrs Swerlin: they were nice to me. I even
liked the detention home. It was the first time in my life
that I had had a room all my own . . . even if it was in a
big dormitory. And the Swerlins liked me. Right off, not
too long after I got there, they had me doing things around
their house: cleaning up; sweeping and dusting, mopping
and scrubbing. And the next thing I knew, when I looked
up and realized it, I was their mascot. I'd be there cleaning up and they'd talk about any and everything with me
right there. That's what I was: their mascot. You know the
way you see people discussing private things in front of
their dogs? That was the Swerlins. You ever see people go
naked in front of their dogs? That was the Swerlins. Why,
they'd even talk about me and "niggers," with me right
there, as if I had no understanding and didn't know what
it all meant. They loved to talk about "niggers," and they
knew a lot of "nigger" stories.

ACTOR SEVEN. Honey, don't they all.

ACTOR FOUR *(having put on a white mask).* Why, dear, niggers are just happy people. You don't have to tickle niggers
to make them grin.

ACTOR FOUR. But these niggers all live in shacks and hovels
and have big fine shiny new cars parked out front.

ACTOR TEN. Honey, niggers are just that way . . .

ACTOR FOUR. Tell me, passion pie, how big are niggers' feet?

ACTOR TEN. Why, I don't know, goody-stick, how big are
they?

ACTOR FOUR. Big enough to leave holes in the ground
instead of footprints.

ACTOR TEN. But tell me, dingus-heart, is it true that all
nigger men have tails? Long black tails?

ACTOR FOUR. Well, I wouldn't know about that, love-dip,
but I have heard it said that niggers have claws instead
of toe-nails.

ACTOR TEN. Niggers are so close to the earth . . .

ACTOR FOUR. Here's a riddle for you, sweet fuzz: why do niggers have such big thick lips?

ACTOR TEN. Why, honey-staff, I would hardly know . . .

ACTOR FOUR. From doing this all the time. (*Makes sound of humming and rapidly brushing his fingers over his lips.*)

ACTOR SIX. And I was there all the time . . . mopping and dusting. But I may as well have been the doorstep. When local politicians would visit the Swerlins, I would be ushered in, and the visitor would look me up and down, and express his approval, like I was a fine pony or a pedigree pup. It never dawned upon them that I could understand, that I wasn't a pet, but a human being. They never understood. They never credited me with the same sensitivity, intellect and understanding that they would have been willing to recognize in a white boy in my position. They never did really see me. But I never got to reform school. My name came up three times to be sent there, and each time it was ignored. It was Mrs Swerlin's doing. One day she told me that I was going to Mason Junior High, the only school in Mason, Michigan. No ward of the detention home had ever gone there. I was the first . . . two ways. Everybody called me "nigger," but they meant no more harm by it than did the Swerlins. It was their way. But as class "nigger" I was very popular . . . as long as I stayed away from the white girls. I was a novelty. It was hard for me to get through the day without being asked to join up this or head up that . . . and I never turned them down.

ACTOR NINE. And it wasn't bad there until one day. And the way it was was that I somehow found myself alone in the classoom with Mr Ostrowski, my English teacher. Now I was one of the school's top students, and I had made some of my best grades in Mr Ostrowski's class. Mr Ostrowski was a natural-born adviser. He'd advise you on anything . . . what you ought to read, think, do, anything. I often think of Mr Ostrowski in the light of how things turned out. Anyway I knew Mr Ostrowski had been advising all the white kids in my class to strike out into

new fields; to try to make more of themselves than just
farmers, and housewives. So Mr Ostrowski said to me:

ACTOR EIGHT (*playing* MR OSTROWSKI). Malcolm. You know
it's time you began thinking about a career for yourself.
Tell me, have you given it any thought?

ACTOR ONE. Uh . . . well, sir, yes. I've, uh, been thinking
that . . . I'd . . . well . . .

ACTOR EIGHT. Now, Malcolm, don't hedge. You've got to
get into the habit of saying straight out what's on your
mind. Now out with it, boy.

ACTOR FOUR. Well, sir, I've been thinking sort of deep on
it and I think I'd kinda like to be a lawyer.

ACTOR EIGHT. Now, Malcolm. One of life's first needs is to
be realistic. Now don't misunderstand me. We all like you,
you know that, don't you. Of course you do. I myself am
very fond of you. But you are a nigger. You understand
me don't you, Malcolm. You have to be realistic about
being a nigger. Now a lawyer . . . that's not a realistic goal
for a nigger. You need to think about something you *can*
be. Now your people are very good with their hands.
Always have been. I've seen your work, the work you do
in carpentry shop. Everyone talks about it and admires it.
People like you as a person . . . you'd get all kinds of work.

ACTOR SIX. It was after that that I began to change inside.
I drew away from white people. Where the word "nigger"
had slipped off my back before, now whenever I heard it,
I stopped and looked at whoever had said it. And they
were surprised that I did.

ACTOR THREE. Then, in the nick of time, blazing out of the
East with the sun, appearing out of the dust and steam
of the black animal train . . . the majestic ebony princess,
half-sister, woman full grown, indomitable and prideful . . .
ELLA!

(*At this point, the retractable screen is
lowered, and projections of Negro women
are shown. The women in these slides
must combine the elements of the well-
dressed finger-popping momma, and the
strong-willed household manager.*)

ACTORS THREE & TEN.   Ella!

ACTOR FIVE.   Child by my father's first wife

ACTORS THREE & TEN.   Ella!

ACTOR SEVEN.   Down two husbands and working on the
   third

ACTORS THREE & TEN.   Ella!

ACTOR FIVE.   Knowing who and where she was

ACTORS THREE & TEN.   Ella!

ACTOR SEVEN.   Shrinking from no man; saying what she
   pleased

ACTORS THREE & TEN.   Ella!

ACTOR FIVE.   Going where she pleased

ACTORS THREE & TEN.   Ella!

ACTOR SEVEN.   Out of fantasy Boston

ACTORS THREE & TEN.   Ella!

ACTOR FIVE.   Property owner and manipulator

ACTORS THREE & TEN.   Ella!

ACTOR SEVEN.   A natural fighter

ACTOR FIVE.   Like no one I'd ever seen

ACTORS THREE & TEN.   Ella!

ACTOR SEVEN.   Moving in the strength of her blackness

ALL.   ELLA! ELLA! ELLA!

ACTOR FOUR.   I had never seen any black person like Ella,
   unless it was my father. Ella was not just black, she was
   jet black . . . but she was not ashamed of it. There was no
   shame in Ella for what she was. She moved with majesty
   and grace like a dark empress in her African palaces.
   Nothing and no one stood in her way . . . what she
   wanted, she got. All I knew was that if Boston held
   Negroes like Ella, it was where I wanted to be. I wrote to
   Ella that I wanted to come to Boston, and SHAZAM! I
   don't know how she did it! and you didn't ask how Ella
   did things, but somehow she got custody of me. I went to
   Boston.

ACTOR SEVEN.   It's time to tell about Boston!

ACTOR EIGHT.   Who's gon' tell about Boston?

ACTOR ONE.   We need somebody to tell about Boston!

ACTOR TWO.   I'll tell it

ACTOR TEN.   You sure you gon' tell it right?

ACTOR TWO.   I'll tell it right

ACTOR FOUR. Will you tell it like it is and not pull no
  punches?

ACTOR TWO. I'll tell it like it natural-born is! I'll even tell
  Harlem!

ACTOR THREE. No you don't! We'll all tell Harlem!

ACTOR NINE. All right! All right!

ACTOR SIX. But tell about Boston! I wants to hear

ACTOR TWO. Do you want me to fill your ear?

ACTOR FIVE. Honey, we want you to preach us the truth!

ACTOR TWO. Well, gimme a chance an' I'll raise you the
  roof!

ACTOR FIVE. Get away, cat, you just lyin' an' buzzin'

ACTOR TWO. Gimme some room, I'm gon' preach you the
  dozens!

ACTOR TEN. Great God A'mighty, lan' sakes alive
  Let this cat through with that strong jumpin' jive

ACTOR TWO. But I need some help, I mean wit' the start
  Cause when I get goin', I'm goin' straight to the heart

*(From this point on to the Harlem
sequence, ACTOR TWO is alone in speaking. Behind him, the others hoot, yell,
comment and give prayer meeting type
encouragement.)*

ACTOR TWO. This here story covers a whole lot o' ground
  So I need you with me and not foolin' 'round

  I want whoopin' and howlin' and singin' so sweet
  I want bumpin' and jumpin' and stampin' o' feet

  Momma, I want cryin' and sighin' when I talk about fate
  I want moanin' sweet chocklet, like you do when it' late

  Cause I'm lyin' and flyin' and jazzin' the June
  Like I do with the boys in the back o' the room

  I'm gon' preach you the truth, gon' preach it straight
  But when I get through don' accuse me o' hate

  Now stand back, gimme room, I'm gon' start off this letter
  And don't stop me friends, till the times they get better

  I broke in on Ella wit' country on my feet
  She looked and smiled and said "Aaaawww reeeeet"

She wined me and dined me and treated me fine
Then she showed me a room and said it was mine

She told me to cool it on findin' a yoke
Cause I was wit' her now and not out broke

She told me to get out and wander around
Cause that was my chance to view Boston town

But I kept seein' Boston's uglier side
Didn't mess wit' no Negroes wit' that so called "pride"

I went through Boston where the niggers were bad
And I saw things there that made me mad

But the cats were the hippest in that part the world
Everybody was sharp, includin' the girls

Cats leaned on the lamp-posts like walkin' cane sticks
No greater sight for this Northwestern hick

Ella didn't appreciate me hangin' down there
But I had all o' them "good" spooks a body could bear

See I was just sixteen but looked a lot older
At first I was timid but then I got bolder

That's where I went to find me a slave
Though Ella said it would lead to my grave

She said I would die, and quicker than soon
But I dug that scene, that jazzin' the June

That's where I met Shorty, rackin' the balls
And keepin' things cool in the Ace Pool Hall

Now Shorty was a homeboy, a cat wit' a heart
He hunted up a yoke and got me a start

He taught me to jive and swing wit' the cats
He turned me on reefers, cause that's where it's at

My job was at the Roseland . . . a real jumpin' ball
To my hick eyes it was a heavenly hall

I was shinin' up shoes . . . that means in the john
First cat hit his number and had to get on

I was slappin' on paste and poppin' the rag
I was givin' out towels and jiggin' the jag

I start sellin' out condoms and steerin' for whores
I'd hustle you man if you came through that door

    I let my hair grow. It looked like a rag
    The Roseland was fine but it had one real snag
ACTOR EIGHT.   It had music!
ACTOR ONE.   And music
ACTOR THREE.   and music
ACTOR FOUR.   and music!
ACTOR FIVE.   That pretty jazz sound!
ACTOR SIX.   The Roseland State Ballroom
ACTOR SEVEN.   Had music all around!
ACTOR NINE.   One night for colored
ACTOR TEN.   And two nights for white
ACTOR EIGHT.   The swingingest bands
ACTOR ONE.   It was clean out of sight!
ACTOR SIX.   It had dancing and drinking . . . illegal
   It had honey brown chicks
   Who were made to look regal
   When white folks danced
   They knocked off four or five fifths
   After colored folks night
   Cleaned bottles with shovels and lifts
   At the Roseland Ballroom you couldn't keep still
   Natural Rhythm comes out when music gets shrill
ACTOR SEVEN.   Basie and Duke
   Chick Webb and Hamp
   They all played fine
   From the Roseland ramp
ACTOR EIGHT.   It had music!
ACTOR ONE.   And music
ACTOR THREE.   and music
ACTOR FOUR.   AND
   MUSIC!
ACTOR FIVE.   That pretty jazz sound!
ACTOR SIX.   The Roseland State Ballroom
ACTOR SEVEN.   Had music all around!
ACTOR NINE.   One night for colored
ACTOR TEN.   And two nights for white
ACTOR EIGHT.   But the one night for colored
ACTOR ONE.   Was clean out of sight!
ACTOR TWO.   That was the night when we blew off the lid
   And the boss Lindy Hop was the dance that we did

ACTOR FOUR.   We gon' show it to you!

ACTOR SEVEN.   Yes, yes, oooooooohh, yes!

ACTOR THREE.   Dig my grave and bury me wit' it!

ACTOR ONE.   We gon' sock it to you! We gon' sock it to li'l
ign'ant!

*(The ACTORS and a number of DANCERS
who enter from offstage do the Lindy
Hop. The dance may be authentic or
stylized and in silhouette.)*

ACTOR TWO *(after dance is over).*   Aaaaahhh, sweet babies,
    it set me on fire
  I'd party all night and never get tired

  I lost my job, cause o' tingling feet
  But then I had time to dance and be sweet

  Now, my children I knew where it was at
  And I went all out to be a hep cat

  I got my hair zonked
  I got it extra conked

  Flame red in the wind
  I started suckin' up some gin

  Pulled in one mo' notch
  And I was suckin' up Scotch

  Had my pointy-toed shoes
  Man, I didn't sing no blues

  Had my wild green zoot suit
  Everything was aaawwww root

  Had my gold-plated watch chain
  It didn't even dare to rain

  Folks watched my real slow tamp
  As I cooled it up and down the ramp

  And you could see me off a mile
  With my Cab Calloway smile

  And did I dance?
  I'm here to say I pranced
  I leapt till night turned day
  And I leapt till day turned gray

And I leapt and leapt some mo'
Ain't nobody never leapt befo'

Beep de bop, de beep bop biddy
Man I was diggin' that there city

I had things all my way
And I had planned to let it stay

Until that unlucky day
They went and start the war

Maaaan! They start snatchin' cats off the block
And cuttin' off them well conked locks

Start battin' reefers out them lips
Say, you be'd not make no slips

Start pullin' needles out them arms
Say they was doin' GI issue bodily harm

Tell the man you had flat feet
Man tell you you drive a jeep

Tell the man you fulla fright
Man say fine, you fight at night

Tell the man your wife was big
Man say, that don't spring you from this here gig

Tell the man you wild stone crazy
Man say, Yeh, that means you just plain lazy

Cats was jumpin' blacker and meaner
The Army come through wit' a vacuum cleaner

They was snatchin' cats right and lef'
All of 'em claimin' that they was 4F

All them cats was gettin' hung
'Ceptin' your boy, your boy was too young

They even took Shorty, quick and soon
They bout had to reach on top the moon

But they took my man, my ace-boon-coon
He say:

ACTOR ONE.   This here's a white man's war
What the hell I got to be fightin' for?

I wants to stay in my momma's lap
What I got against them Japs?

ACTOR TWO.   He say:
ACTOR ONE.   White man, they shootin' at you
   I like them Japs, they colored too

   An' my natural-born name is Alex Herman
   Ain't got a thing against them Germans

   But just as like a do's a do' [door]
   The U.S. Army done got me sho'
ACTOR TWO.   And after they took everybody's game
   I got me a job on a pullman train

   I hawked and squawked
   Did the Uncle Tom walk

   I smiled, sold sandwiches and things
   I done it all except catch brass rings

   I stooped and grinned and scratch my head
   I swept the floors and made the beds

   I wash the dishes pots and pans
   They gimme a tip and I kiss their hands

   But all the while it was in my mind
   To get to New York and Harlem just one time
ACTOR NINE.   Lemme work wit' it for a minute, brother
ACTOR TWO.   Just a minute now, I got a tale to tell
ACTOR FOUR.   Your tale's over, Jim, we done rung the bell
ACTOR NINE.   Your part is over, and you did real well
ACTOR TWO.   Cast me aside, send me to hell

   We gon' pause, people and open the do' [door]
   To let this cat tell you what you all must know

   It don't say much about this play
   But it say a lot about Yesterday
ACTOR NINE.   It got to do wit' *everyday*
   Step aside, you had your say
ACTOR TWO.   How this fit in wit' the Harlem tale
ACTOR NINE.   Fit in? Wit' a slow blues wail!
ACTOR FOUR.   The blues! The blues!
ACTOR TEN.   Everybody dig the blues!
ACTOR FIVE.   Go on home wit' it!
ACTOR NINE.   Start them blues, I got somethin' to say

(A raunchy blues begins.)

This cat done took up your time
Tellin' the tale and talkin' in rhyme
And that's okay, that's okay
It ain't no crime
'Cept I'm another bag, a separate way
I'm a different thing
My rhythm is different
And I want to ask you if you know my name
Do you know my name?
Of course you don't,
because I am representative
I am the Negro entertainer
I dance and sing,
prance and strut;
I am painted a gay shade of black
I grin and smile my teeth,
I bug my eyes and
bug my eyes, wiggle my ears
and flare my nose . . .
. . . You know . . .
Your beloved ones like
Jolson and Cantor
are made of me
Did you know?
Yet I am shadow
I am Bert Williams
after the show
without a bed or place to eat
Did you know?
I am Canada Lee
after the show
lost in an alcoholic stupor,
because after "The Emperor Jones"
and "Native Son"
what plays are written
for me?
Did you know?
Though "Hamlet" may
scream 'gainst heaven in my breast,
for you I am minstrel

I am Steppin and Mantan
and Willie Best,
and for you I die laughing
Or I am sound:
I am the frustration of
Fletcher Henderson,
When my foot touches that
train bound for Harlem,
there's real minstrel in my blood,
I get a banjo for a heart,
and cabbage likker on my breath.
Whenever I touch a Harlem train

ACTOR THREE.   The Harlem train! The Harlem train!
ALL *(singing it)*.   Catch that Harlem train

(Repeat it three times more.)

ACTOR FOUR.   Like Malcolm caught it!
ALL.   Catch that Harlem train!

(Repeat three times more.)

ACTOR EIGHT.   Like old conk-head Malcolm caught it!
ALL.   Catch that Harlem train

*(Repeat it three times more, then half
the cast makes the sound of a train, like
"Choo, choo, choo" and so on, while the
other half continues with "Catch that
Harlem train." Finally, the train stops.)*

Wwweeeeeeeee! Shheeeeeeeeee. Shhoooooooooooo

(ACTOR FIVE screams joyously.)

ACTOR ONE *(using a hand microphone)*.   YOU ARE NOW
    ARRIVING IN HARLEM, THE FUN CAPITAL OF
    THE   WORLD!   IT'S   BIGGER,   BETTER   AND
    BLACKER THAN DISNEYLAND!
ACTOR THREE.   Harlem, Harlem, children!
ACTOR TEN.   Harlem Harlem HARLEM!
ACTOR NINE.   Harlem is a mad sun-burst
    The swingingest place in the Universe!

*(Here begins Charlie Mingus' "II BS"
and following Jitterbug dance.)*

ACTOR FOUR *(with the opening bass solo)*.   That's a Harlem
 sound
 Pretty is what
 When the restless African spirit
 Parades in night funerals
 But mostly makes itself manifest
 In a dance
 A Harlem dance
 Of joy and pain and pulsing insanity

(Beat increases and dance starts.)

ACTOR FIVE *(as the brass joins in)*.   Look: we are ugly cheap
 and wicked
 But we fling our bodies into the dance
 With the ritual fury of ancient warriors
 See us as you see us!
 The wild and careless spirits
 Of Harlem
ALL *(with long brass phrases in background. This comes
 twenty-four bars into the number)*.
 Haaaaaaaaaaaaaaarlem
 Haaaaaaaaaaaaaaarlem
 Haaaaaaaaaaaaaaarlem
ALL *(with phrasing behind sax solo)*. Make your game
 All the same
 There you went
 Pay your rent
 Make your game
 All the same
 Don't ask now
 You know just how
 Make your game
 All the same
 Bust out nnnoooooowwww

(DANCERS go really wild.)

ALL GIRLS *(with piano solo)*.   Pretty pretty Harlem chicks

Pretty pretty chocolet Harlem chicks
Pretty pretty chocolet Harlem chicks

(They dance.)

ALL *(with brass phrases behind piano solo).* Make your game
    All the same
    There you went
    Pay your rent
    Make your game
    All the same
    Don't ask now
    You know just how
    Make your game
    All the same
    Bust out NOOOOOOWW

(Dance continues to the end.)

ACTOR ONE *(with dance over).* Hey, Red, what you doin'
    man?

ACTOR EIGHT. Man, I got this room in this house fulla
    whores.

ACTOR ONE. Man, you sure that's where you wants to be
    livin'? I mean it ain't hardly a conducive atmosphere.

ACTOR SEVEN. Stay out of this, little man, Red's steering for
    us . . .

ACTOR THREE. An' pimpin for me!

ACTOR FIVE. An' he's learnin' a whole lot about women . . .
    an' men!

ACTOR EIGHT. Tell him 'bout it baby

ACTOR SEVEN. Red, here, steers all these crazy old white
    mens to me. All of 'em wants to get whipped. I got these
    here whips . . . good leather whips that I keeps oiled an'
    Red steers 'em to me so I can beat 'em. An', baby, they
    pay good for that kind of cookie.

ACTOR THREE. The service that Red performs for me is
    more . . . conventional.

ACTOR ONE. Dig it, Red man, it's a alright hustle, I know,
    but come on in with me pushin' reefers an' things. It pay
    good. It pay more! Come here, Red, try some o' this stuff.
    It's cocain.

ACTOR EIGHT.   Yeh, man, I'm right wit' ya, baby.

*(BLACKOUT. Change the actor play-
ing* MALCOLM.*)*

ACTOR SIX *(taking stage as the others become wavering
    ghosts behind him).*   Your rocket heart
  punches through the clouds
  laughing above the city.
  The night is speckled;
  lights, hot and cold, of
  many colors seed your mind,
  moving in and out of focus, like
  translucent snakes wiggling through
  one another. You go into a soft nod.
  Nod. Nod. Nod. You touch the reaches of
  a brilliant nova. You suck
  through its bristling fires into
  the core of your inner universe.
  Nod upon the velvet fruit of space.

  You hurtle great areas of your heart
  driven by no sound winds. The
  channels of your ears echo winter
  with the titillated rattle of
  your heartbeat leaves. You
  search out your supple, fluid fingers.
  They are sea vines. You suck them to your eyes,
  compute the tides of color.

  Whisper on your panther feet
  to the edges of gray curb cliffs,
  glance deerlike off the sun-bellied
  sidewalks . . . avoid the fissures, the faults . . .
  clutch the earthquake in your belly.
  Nod. Nod. Step cloud free, descend into
  the tangled dream forests. Nod. Nod.
  Pleasant just to nod. Hear the
  rush of slow rivulettes; the slither-
  ing alleys, the gurgling streets,
  the tender moans of liquid females.
  Nod. Nod. Nod.

ACTOR TWO.   Hey, Red, where you been?

ACTOR FOUR.   Man, I had to split for a while. It was gettin'
    hot for me. Crazy detectives followin' me around all the
    time. Crazy junkies followin' me around all the time tryin'
    to steal my shit. Man, I was HOT! I been pullin' so much
    jive on people, I got to carry me *three* guns. But I'm back
    now, you dig?

ACTOR TWO.   Well, what you gon' do now, Red?

ACTOR FOUR.   Well, I figure I lay off peddlin' shit for
    awhile an' get back to steerin' for whores. Last couple o'
    days, I been runnin' the Murphy Game.

ACTOR TWO.   There's money in the Murphy, man, but they's
    cops all over.

ACTOR FOUR.   Well you know, like I got to get into some-
    thin'.

(BLACKOUT. *Change actor playing*
MALCOLM.)

ACTOR NINE.   Hey, Red, I hear that West Indian Archie is
    gunnin' for you.

ACTOR SIX.   Yeh, man, I heard that too. But I ain't scared.
    I kill that mud-dumper quicker than look at him.

ACTOR NINE.   But they say, like, West Indian Archie is the
    baddest cat in Harlem. He done already shot five studs an'
    done been to Sing Sing.

ACTOR SIX.   That don' scare me, man. I'm bad too, in case
    you ain't heard. I'm Detroit Red. I got the Mafia lookin'
    for me . . . besides West Indian Archie. When I run up on
    any of 'em, there's gon' be dyin' three, four ways.

ACTOR NINE.   I'm for you all the way, Red, but wit' all this
    happenin', don't misunderstand if I don't stand too close
    to you, baby. Line o' fire an' all like that, you dig.

(BLACKOUT.)

ACTOR TEN.   Billy Salter was pushing shit. He'd got busted
    once and sent up, and when he got out, he went back to
    pushing. Well, these junkies got uptight for some shit one
    night, and they broke in on Billy's pad, real late this night,
    and they killed him cause they couldn't find no shit, and
    he wouldn't give 'em no money. Billy always said he wasn't

scared of no junkies and so he didn't carry no protection. They took 'bout everything they could carry, and hocked it to get 'em some shit.

ACTOR SEVEN. And 'bout the same time it was old Lonnie Blake had his thing. He was married to this old broad Leslie, but when he got busted trying to knock over a drugstore, and got sent up, Leslie started making out with this white dude. When Lonnie got out he got the wire on it, and he never let on to Leslie that he knew, but he followed her up to this white dude's place one night, and he cut 'em dead with this butcher's knife he had. They said he cried the whole time he did that.

ACTOR FIVE. Bertha Taylor had this wild man for a husband who used to get drunk every Saturday night and put her in the Hospital for Sunday. But she kept going back to him 'cause she said that was just the way he knew how to love.

ACTOR THREE. Willie Morrison ain't had nothing but bad luck: got high one day and fell off a roof and broke his hip so where he had to walk with a limp, then his little girl got run over by a car, and his wife left him after another man, and he couldn't keep no kind of job, and so finally he got himself hooked. And being as he was real uptight this night, he tried to rob a plain-clothes cop with a penknife and got shot through the brain.

ACTOR TEN. And Bob Foster got into this fight with these drag queens, and got his belly slashed open. Them gay ladies will do it to you.

ACTOR FIVE. Anabelle Roach was out on the block hustling for her old man, who was hooked and pimping for her. Then she fell for this young kid, and started keeping him in Scotch whiskey and sharp clothes. She'd just tell her old man that business was bad, and that she didn't have no money to give him. And he used to go around asking people how "business" could be bad with a war going on. So finally he got the wire, and one night Anabelle came home, and her old man, well, he just beat her head in for holding out on him.

ACTOR SIX. That's the way it was: day in, day out, but I never noticed cause I was IN it. It was a way of life, my

way of life. I was pushing shit, ducking cops, cheating on
people, and carrying guns. And I knew that some day some
cat was going to back me up against a wall, and he'd have
to be a dead cat!

ACTOR TWO (*taking stage, the rest of the cast wavering
ghosts behind him*).

In the basement of my anger;
In the bright foliage of my drug garden;
In my hard nights,
      How am I like my father?
In my egg hidden in my mother;
Free yet chained in my wet amorphous bed,
      How am I like my father?
How do I rot in life
Like he dismembered in his grave?
How does the passion of his ego
Continue in me, mildewed in this life?
The answers like evening smoke
Dance through my vacuous lungs,
They shriek in my brain,
Crowd my loins,
Paralyze my limbs.
    I nod
    I nod
    I nod
In the black cistern of Harlem
In the swirling jazz dance
In breathy female hours
    I nod
    I nod
I nod my father's death which is my own
I am wintered
I am held inside
a dome of colored glass
in solitary ignorance
The variegated smells
of another life permeate
my soul; my eyes burst
into drugged and wavering
Blossoms.

In the purple-green odor of this life
How am I like my father?
>   I nod
>   I nod
>   I nod
>   my own nigger nod. I nod.

ACTOR EIGHT. Hey, Red, I understand you got a silk that's somethin' else.

ACTOR ONE. Yeh, man, that's right.

ACTOR EIGHT. Well, look a here, why get you a white woman when there's plenty o' spade chicks that would be for you all the way.

ACTOR ONE. Cause I got me this silk, that's why.

ACTOR EIGHT. You got somethin' against colored women? What's a white broad got that a colored girl ain't?

ACTOR ONE. Well, for one thing, her hair don't go back when she sweat. An' for another, your fingers don't get all greasy when you run 'em through her head. An' her lips don't look like hog maws. Man, I don't care if she the fattest, ugliest, dumpiest woman on earth, she white, an' that mean she precious. An' it make me a bad moten-gator cause she do anything I say.

ACTOR FOUR. Now, how these here white chicks gon' work in on this here racket?

ACTOR ONE. Simple; they go out an' case out everything in the daytime an' at night we go back an' clean the joint out. Simple as that. Ain't no way we can get caught. I got it figured.

(*BLACKOUT. Change actor playing*
MALCOLM.)

ACTOR TWO (*a judge*). Malcolm Little: are you sure your friend understands the meaning of the word "concurrently"?

ACTOR SIX. No, your honor, I'll explain it to him. Now look a, Sammy, they got us on fourteen counts of burglary. Now it work like this: count one, eight to ten years. Count two, eight to ten years. Count three, eight to ten years, and so on like that. Now "concurrently" mean that you

serve 'em one right after the other. So that mean if you
add 'em up all together you got . . .

(SAMMY *faints. BLACKOUT. A sound
cue of either a prison blues or slow, eerie
electronic music. This goes on for a few
seconds before the lights dim up again.*)

ACTOR FOUR. I got ten years. I wasn't even twenty-one. I
hadn't started to shave yet. I was sent to the Charlestown
prison. It had been built in 1805, in Napoleon's time . . .
and it hadn't changed much. The cells had no running
water, I could lie on my cot and touch both walls. The
toilet was a covered pail. I lived with the smell of my own
urine and defecation. I stopped believing in God right
there: I was already in hell.

ACTOR SEVEN. You a regular troublemaker ain't you boy?
Droppin' your tray in the chow line, always screaming out
at night in the cell block. You're gonna be here for a long
time. What's your number, boy?

ACTOR FOUR. I don't know. I forgot.

ACTOR SEVEN. You don't forget your number, boy. That's
who you are. You live in a society where your number is
who you are. Who are you, boy?

ACTOR FOUR. I am the pungent smoke rising into the nos-
trils of your cities.

I am the flesh you clean from your windows with rasping
flat knives

I exist like death

Like smoke and formless shadow in the corridors of your
bowels.

ACTOR SEVEN. SOLITARY CONFINEMENT!

ACTOR SIX. I might have died in prison. I might have spent
the rest of my life, the rest of my days in prison and died
there. I might have rotted in prison if Reginald, my
brother, had not brought me the word of Allah and the
Honorable Elijah Muhammad.

ACTOR TEN (*offstage with microphone*). Malcolm, don't eat
pork. Don't smoke cigarettes.

ACTOR SIX. Why? Why not, Reginald? Why shouldn't I do
these things? Why?

ACTOR TEN. Trust me, Malcolm. I'll explain. I'll explain . . .

ACTOR SIX. Reginald, I've stopped smoking. I don't eat pork any more. Like Momma. Tell me why I did it?

ACTOR NINE (*offstage with mike*). They are the symbols and the filth of the devil.

ACTOR SIX. What are you talking about? What devil?

ACTOR NINE. The white man, Malcolm, the white man is the devil.

ACTOR SIX. Man, you've flipped your wig.

ACTOR NINE. No, Malcolm. Look around you. Look at your life. Who are you?

ACTOR SIX. Don't be crazy, Reginald, I'm me. I'm Malcolm.

ACTOR NINE. No. You are who and what the white man tells you to be. Don't turn away, Malcolm, listen to me. Listen to me.

ACTOR SIX. Okay, I'll listen. But you got to do a whole lot o' talkin'.

ACTOR NINE. You don't know who you are, Malcolm. You don't know who you are because you are your history, and your history has been hidden from you. You don't know that the white devil in his evil has hidden your identity from you. Your history! He has hidden it from you that you are from a race of people of ancient civilizations, and riches and gold and kings. You don't even know your true family name, and you wouldn't recognize your true language if you heard it. The white man has hidden from you knowledge of your own kind. You have been the victim of the devil white man ever since he murdered and raped and stole you from your native land in the seed of your forefathers.

ACTOR SIX. I see. I see. I see.

ACTOR NINE. What do you see, Malcolm?

ACTOR SIX. I see that the white man has stolen my birthright from me. I see that he has kept me in ignorance and killed my father. I see that he has raped the mothers of my people and hidden in the lie that it was love of some kind. I see that the white man is a devil. I see that he has made me a clown on a stage of his own purpose. I see that he is losing his power to oppress and exploit the dark world, and that that world is rising to dominate again, as it has before. I see the fear of the white man as he sees himself on the way out.

ACTOR NINE.   You are saved, Malcolm. You have received the word.

ACTOR FIVE.   He was saved. While in prison, he continued to receive the teachings of Elijah Muhammad from his brothers and sisters who visited him frequently.

ACTOR THREE.   I'll tell you how the white devil came to be on earth. First the moon tore loose from the earth, and settled itself out there where it's at now. It was after this had come about that men were formed, and they were all black, these men that were formed, the first people. They founded the Holy City of Mecca. Now this was a long time ago. Then about six thousand years ago seventy percent of the people were satisfied, and the rest were dissatisfied.

ACTOR ONE.   Did they start a fight?

ACTOR THREE.   No. A man got born among them who had a head that was bigger than normal. His name was "Yacub." He was so brilliant and smart that by the time he was eighteen, he had finished all the colleges and schools his nation had. This was the nation of Shabazz. People called him the "big-headed scientist." And he was just born to make trouble. He carried on so, until the authorities banished him and his 59,999 followers to the island of Patmos.

ACTOR ONE.   Good.

ACTOR THREE.   Don't interrupt. Now this big-headed Yacub was angry with Allah and decided to spite him by making a devil race. A race of weak, bleached out people. He took his 59,999 followers and started messing with nature. He started using the ideas of what they call "recessive gene structure." He started changing people. He even set up a eugenics law on the island. Now all his people were black, but every third child would show traces of some brown. When these children started to grow up only brown and brown could get married.

ACTOR ONE.   That's not right to do that!

ACTOR THREE.   Let me finish! It was a long step by step process, but in about six hundred years, a starch white race had evolved on Patmos. They ran around naked, living in trees, ready to start trouble at the drop of a hat. The still all-black people living on the mainland, seeing what had happened, realized that they had waited too long to step in. But they took all of them mean white folks and shipped them to Europe to live in the cold and in caves. In the next two thousand years they prospered these devil people. It had been written that they would rule the world for six thousand years and turn it into a living hell . . . until the original black people would rise up and take power. That time is almost up.

ACTOR ONE. Wow! Oh, maaan!

ACTOR THREE. Do you believe, Malcolm?

ACTOR ONE. Yeah, I guess I do. I do.

ACTOR THREE. You are saved, Malcolm, you are saved.

ACTOR FIVE. And he was saved. He was sent to the Norfolk Prison Colony where he read every book he could get his hands on, where he memorized the dictionary! He worked at many jobs, while continuing his religious conversion. Then after joining the Islamic faith, he himself began to carry the words of Elijah Muhammad to his black brothers across the country.

ACTOR ONE. The devil white man does not want the Honorable Elijah Muhammad stirring awake the sleeping giant of you and me, and all our ignorant, brainwashed kind here in the white man's heaven, and the black man's hell, here in the neon of North America! I turn my back on all that I have been. I do not deny my past, but it is past! I have sat at our messenger's feet, hearing the truth from his own mouth! *(Down on both knees.)* I pledge on my knees to Allah, without hesitation or fear, to tell the white man about his crimes, and the black man the true teachings of our Honorable Elijah Muhammad. I don't care if it costs my life . . .

ACTOR SEVEN *(quietly)*. My, my, such intensity.

ACTOR EIGHT. Shut up.

ACTOR FIVE. A man exists in his pride, in his faith, in his dreams, in his clawing thoughts. He may be now what he thought would never be achieved. But alone, without the impulse to share the things which make him . . . he is empty. Not knowing this, ignoring it, turning away, not being allowed to do it, in time, dissolves the core of his manhood.

ACTOR SEVEN *(drily)*. In other words, a man needs a woman.

ACTOR EIGHT. But not just any woman. Listen.

ACTOR FOUR. I took no personal interest in any of the Muslim sisters. I took great care to avoid any closeness between myself and any of the sisters. My commitment to Islam was total, and complete, and I felt that it left no room for other interest . . . especially women. Besides, my experiences in the streets of Harlem had taught me to be wary of women, all women. Many times in lectures I spoke very hard about them. Yet, at almost every temple I visited, there was always one sister who would drop the ponderous hint that "perhaps" I should get married. I was too busy to love anyone. *(Smile.)* Marriage was out of the question. Pretty soon, not only the sisters were at me, but also many of the brothers.

ACTOR NINE. Brother Malcolm . . .

ACTOR FOUR. Yes?

ACTOR NINE. You got a few seconds, Brother Malcolm?

ACTOR FOUR. Yes. Sure. What is it?

ACTOR NINE. Well, I don't know how this gonna sound, but you know I been listening to you talk a few times, and you come down pretty hard on women, you know. Pretty hard. You ought not do that like that. They ain't all THAT bad.

ACTOR FOUR *(smiling)*. Maybe not, maybe not.

ACTOR NINE. Yeah. You know, you ought to give a woman a chance before you come down on her like that. You ought to give 'em a chance.

ACTOR FOUR. Maybe. But lemme ask you a question, brother. How old are you?

ACTOR NINE. Twenty.

ACTOR FOUR. Twenty. Yeah. Well, I got the edge on you, and let me tell you, brother, there's nothing worse for a man than to be tied body and soul to a woman that's not right for you. And you don't find too many that are right. You don't find too many women who care to understand a man, and most of them will kill you in their sniping, sucking ways before they let you be a man.

ACTOR NINE. But now, brother Malcolm, I'm not married, but don't you think . . .

ACTOR FOUR. No. No. I don't think. I've seen them in action too many times. I KNOW. There are no creatures on the face of this planet more wanton in their desire, more tricky, deceitful and untrustworthy in their flesh, and WITH their flesh than women. Any woman. You get yourself bound to their flesh and you're on a sled headed in just one direction . . . downhill! At a moment's notice, as soon as not, she'll shed you for the next smiling sincere face or the promise of a more exciting bed partner, and never look back.

ACTOR NINE. But . . .

ACTOR FOUR. No buts, brother. They are hungry sucking animals who crave only full bellies. No matter how you try. And no matter what you say, you can't give enough to fill those bellies. There is nothing more devastating to a man, and his work . . . except the constant cackling about wife problems . . . than the sound of that flesh saying, all iceberg and frost, "Get lost, sucker John, I don't need you no more."

ACTOR SEVEN. Now just a minute.

ACTOR TWO. Keep quiet. *Woman.*

ACTOR EIGHT. Then there was this sister that came to us . . . I noticed her . . . took no interest in her; just noticed her. But then she was one of the few of our people that we had reached who had been to college. For about a year I'd see her . . . coming and going . . . I'd just see her you know. I already knew things about her. She came from Detroit . . . she had been to college at Tuskegee Institute and was studying to be a nurse. She taught health and hygiene to our women's and girls' classes. For about a year I just noticed her, watched her working in her classes, and then I got the idea that taking her to the Museum of Natural History might help her better understand Mr Muhammad's theory of the evolution of the races. She thought it was a good idea and went. She was very likable. We became friends. It's funny how these things grow to the point where you fantasize about how it would be to be married to her, how it would be to do this or that with her.

There was something about her . . . this Sister Betty. I did not take back what I said about women . . . but this one, this one was different. She was different. We saw a good deal of each other, and I decided to marry her.

ACTOR SIX. Hello . . .

ACTOR SEVEN. How are you, Minister Malcolm.

ACTOR SIX. Sister Betty, where is the class?

ACTOR SEVEN. I sent them home today. I couldn't meet with them today.

ACTOR SIX. Is something the matter, Sister Betty?

ACTOR SEVEN. They came here, and I tried to have class, I tried, Minister Malcolm. They were so excited that you were coming here again.

ACTOR SIX. Is there something the matter, Sister Betty? Are you sick?

ACTOR SEVEN. Sick? No.

ACTOR SIX. What is it?

ACTOR SEVEN. Oh, it's really nothing. I suppose I exaggerate it all in my mind. I'm really very sorry about the class, Minister Malcolm.

ACTOR SIX. Do you want to talk about it? I mean it helps sometimes to talk to people. When you have problems.

ACTOR SEVEN. Oh, well, I guess so. It's really nothing though. It's nothing for you to concern over.

ACTOR SIX. What is it . . . ?

ACTOR SEVEN. Uuuuhhh . . . Well, my foster parents, you know I told you I lived with them. (MALCOLM *nods.*) Well, uh, they're very nice people, I mean I'm very grateful for what they've done for me . . . taking me in and financing my education and everything. Like I told you. (MALCOLM *is silent, listening.*) But, uh, well, they're very conscientious Baptist people, and they don't really like me being a Muslim . . . and, well, last night they called me when I came in, and they gave me a . . . uh . . . what do you call it?

ACTOR SIX. What?

ACTOR SEVEN. Uh, a thing . . . a thing where you tell people to do this or that or else. What do you call that?

ACTOR SIX. An ultimatum.

ACTOR SEVEN. That's it. The precise word. An ultimatum. Thank you.

ACTOR SIX. Go on.

ACTOR SEVEN. Well, like I said, they're very Christian Baptist people and they got no fondness for Muslims, and they particularly don't like me being a Muslim. Well, they gave me this ultimatum last night. They told me either stop being a Muslim or I would have to quit nursing school and move out of their house. I understand their feelings, but, well, I can't give up my faith. I mean I just can't give up my faith. I'll have to move because I told them that . . . that I wouldn't give up my faith for them. I have no place to go, Minister Malcolm, nowhere to go. I don't know anything about how it is out in the streets. And I'm afraid.

ACTOR SIX. Sister Betty. People are constantly put upon, you know that. But if you have looked at something with your own eyes and your own mind and heart, and it is what you want, then you are right in defending and upholding that something. And Allah will help you, you know that. *(He laughs.)* He may have already seen your plight and sent an agent to help you.

ACTOR SEVEN *(a bit confused, laughing, not quite sure why).* Yes.

ACTOR SIX. Yes. *(Silence for five beats.)* This has nothing to do with your personal trouble, Sister Betty; I mean I came here today not specifically to talk to your class. *(She looks more confused.)* I'm glad you dismissed the class, because I was hoping for the chance to talk to you for a little bit. *(She looks at him.)* I want to ask you something, Sister Betty.

ACTOR SEVEN. Yes. What is it?

ACTOR SIX. How would you like to get married, Sister Betty?

ACTOR SEVEN *(shocked, then smiling to herself the way women do).* To you?

ACTOR SIX. Yes . . .

ACTOR SEVEN *(pause).* Yes.

ACTOR SIX. It won't be anything elaborate.

ACTOR SEVEN. No.

ACTOR SIX. No.

ACTOR SEVEN. I don't care.

ACTOR SIX. I have very little money.

ACTOR SEVEN. Yes, I know.

ACTOR SIX. You know my work. It will be hard.

ACTOR SEVEN. Yes.

ACTOR SIX. I will have to leave you at times. I will be away a lot.

ACTOR SEVEN. Yes.

ACTOR SIX. Don't expect me to be a Hollywood type of husband.

ACTOR SEVEN (*laughing loudly*). No. You are definitely not the Hollywood type of husband. A woman doesn't really look for that you know. I don't anyway.

ACTOR SIX. Some women do. That's why I said that. (*Laughs to himself.*) I, uh, won't carry you over the threshold or any of that, you know. I don't believe in it.

ACTOR SEVEN. Neither do I.

ACTOR SIX. When I come home, I'll be tired, and overworked, and you'll see me not at all the way you see me now.

ACTOR SEVEN. I know. (*Pause.*)

ACTOR SIX. I expected you to say "yes." Do you know that?

ACTOR SEVEN. Yes.

ACTOR SIX. I made up my mind I would ask you. It was a surprise, wasn't it.

ACTOR SEVEN. Yes.

ACTOR SIX. You do understand what it is I have to do, and what being married to me will mean?

ACTOR SEVEN. Yes. Yes.

ACTOR SIX. Why are you looking that way?

ACTOR SEVEN. I don't know.

ACTOR SIX. Are you happy?

(*She runs to him and throws her arms around him. BLACKOUT.*)

ACTOR FIVE. He was saved. Yes, he was saved. He was saved to become the Malcolm you all know. He was saved to become the Malcolm some of you feared. And what of this, all of this? Why this was prologue. This was the bitter road he trod. This was the wilderness in which, like Moses,

he wandered and was purged. This is what a man sometimes must be before he knows he is a man. But we are
incomplete. Hear Malcolm X in his black magnificence!

*(A ladder is set up on stage and the
ACTORS gather around it while one of
their number ascends with a microphone
and begins speaking. At several points
the speakers are changed.)*

ACTOR ONE. One day a young white girl came to me and
said:

ACTOR THREE. Minister Malcolm, what can I do?

ACTOR ONE. Nothing. (ALL *chant* "Nothing, nothing, nothing . . .") After three centuries you wonder what it is you
can do. After three centuries in which our backs were
beaten raw you now ask what it is you can do. After three
centuries in which we were lynched and forced to strangle
on our manhood, and our women forced, forced to submit
to white men, *you* ask what it is you can do. And what
have you to offer? The glory of Western civilization and
your white breasts. They are worthless. The field nigger
lifts his massive black head and you scream. You scream
because what's in his head could erupt in his hands and
devastate this precious glass palace you've built for yourselves out of the blood and bone of his generation. Your
breasts are full, but your heart is empty!

ACTOR TEN. More! More! We want to hear more!

ACTOR TWO. And what did he say, sisters?

ACTOR FIVE. In one generation the black slave women in
America had been raped by the slavemaster white man
until there had begun to emerge a homemade, brainwashed race that was no longer even its own true color,
that no longer even knew its true family names. The slavemaster forced his family name upon this rape-mixed race
which the slavemaster began to call "The Negro." This
"Negro" was taught of his native Africa that it was peopled
by heathen, black savages, swinging like monkeys from
trees. This "Negro" was taught to worship an alien God
having the same blond hair, pale skin and blue eyes as the

slavemaster. He was taught that black was a curse. He was taught to hate everything black, including himself. He was taught that white was good and to be respected, admired and loved. He was brainwashed to believe he was superior if his complexion showed more of the pollution of the white slavemaster.

ACTOR EIGHT. And what did he say, brothers?

ACTOR FOUR. The social philosophy of black revolution only means that we have to get together and remove the evils, the vices, alcoholism, drug addiction and other vices that are destroying the moral fiber of our community. We ourselves have to lift the level of our community, the standard of our community to a higher level, make our own society beautiful so that we will be satisfied in our own social circles and won't be running around trying to knock our way into a social circle where we're not wanted. So I say, in spreading a gospel such as black nationalism, it is not designed to make the black man re-evaluate the white man . . . you know him already . . . but to make the black man re-evaluate himself. Don't change the white man's mind . . . you can't change his mind, and that whole thing about appealing to the conscience of America . . . America's conscience is bankrupt. She lost all conscience a long time ago. Uncle Sam has no conscience. They don't know what morals are. They don't try to eliminate an evil because it's evil, or because it's illegal, or because it's immoral, they eliminate it only when it threatens their existence.

ALL. And what else did he say?

ACTOR TEN. As long as the white man sent you to Korea, you bled. He sent you to Germany, you bled. He sent you to the South Pacific to fight the Japanese, you bled. You bleed for white people, but when it comes to seeing your own churches being bombed and little black girls murdered, you haven't got any blood. You bleed when the white man says bleed, you bite when the white man says bite, and you bark when the white man says bark. I hate to say this about us, but it's true. How are you going to be nonviolent in Mississippi as violent as you were in Korea? How can you justify being nonviolent in Mississippi and Alabama, when your churches are being bombed and

your little girls murdered, and at the same time you're
going to get violent with Hitler and Tojo and somebody
else you don't even know?

ALL. And what else did he say, brother?

ACTOR NINE. I believe that it would be almost impossible
to find anywhere in America a black man who has lived
further down in the mud of human society than I have; or
a black man who has been more ignorant than I have; or
a black man who has suffered more anguish in his life than
I have. But it is only after the deepest dark that the
greatest joy can come; it is only after slavery and prison
that the sweetest appreciation of freedom can come. For
the freedom of my 22 million black brothers and sisters
here in America, I do believe that I have fought the best
I knew how with the shortcomings that I have had. I know
that my shortcomings are many. My greatest lack has been
that I don't have the kind of academic education I wish I
had been able to get . . .

ACTOR SIX. And what else did he say?

ACTOR TWO. Now in speaking like this, it doesn't mean
that I am anti-American. I am not. I'm not anti-American
or *un*-American. And I'm not saying that to defend myself.
Because if I was that, I'd have a right to be that . . . after
what America has done to us. This government should feel
lucky that our people aren't anti-American. They should
get down on their hands and knees every morning and
thank God that 22 million black people have not become
anti-American. You've given us every right to.

ALL. And what else did he say?

ACTOR THREE. I have never heard any woman, white or
black, express any admiration for a conk or a process. Of
course, any white woman with a black man isn't thinking
about his hair. But I don't see how any black woman with
any pride could walk down the street with any black man
wearing a conk . . . the emblem of his shame that he is
black.

ACTOR ONE. And what else did he say?

ACTOR FOUR. When I say love each other, I mean love our
own kind. This is what all black people need to be taught
in this country because the only ones whom we don't love

are our own kind. Most Negroes you see running around here talking about love everybody . . . they don't have any love whatsoever for their own kind. When they say "Love everybody," what they are doing is setting up a situation for us to love the white people. Or when they say "Suffer peacefully," they mean suffer peacefully at the hands of the white man.

ALL. And what else?

ACTOR EIGHT. In the past I have permitted myself to be used to make sweeping indictments of all white people, and these generalizations have caused injuries to some white people who did not deserve them. Because of the spiritual rebirth which I was blessed to undergo as a result of my pilgrimage to the Holy City of Mecca, I no longer subscribe to the sweeping indictments of one race. My pilgrimage to Mecca . . . served to convince me that perhaps American whites can be cured of the rampant racism which is consuming them and is about to destroy this country. In the future I intend to be careful not to sentence anyone who has not been proven guilty. I am not a racist and do not subscribe to any of the tenets of racism. In all honesty and sincerity, it can be stated that I wish nothing but freedom, justice and equality: life, liberty and the pursuit of happiness . . . for all people. My first concern is with the group of people to which I belong, the Afro-Americans, for we, more than any other people, are deprived of these "inalienable" rights.

ACTOR TWO. Travel broadens one's scope. Any time you do any travel, your scope will be broadened. It doesn't mean you change . . . you broaden. No religion will ever make me forget the continued fighting with dogs against our people in this country. No religion will make me forget the police clubs that come up 'side our heads. No God, no religion, no *nothing* will make me forget it until it stops, until it's finished, until it's eliminated. I want to make that point clear...

ALL. More! More! Tell it all!

ACTOR SIX. When I left the Black Muslim movement, I stated clearly that it wasn't my intention to even continue to be aware that they existed . . . But they were fearful . . . So they had to try and silence me because of what they know I know. I think that they should know me well enough to know that they certainly can't frighten me. But there are some things involving the Black Muslim movement which when they come to light, will shock you. The thing that you have to understand about those of us in the Black Muslim movement was that all of us believed one hundred percent in the divinity of Elijah Muhammad. We believed in him. We actually believed that God had taught him and all that. I always believed that he believed it himself. And I was shocked when I found out he didn't believe it himself. And when the shock reached me, then I began to look everywhere else and try and get a better understanding of the things that confront us so that we can get together in some kind of way to offset them.

ACTOR NINE. But at the same time I want to point out that no white man or white group or agency can use me against Elijah Muhammad or against the Black Muslim movement. When you hear me open up my mouth against another black man, no white man can put words in my mouth, nor can any white man sic me on another black group.

ALL. More, more . . . Let it out! Bust it out!

ACTOR FOUR. Any Negro who teaches other Negroes to turn the other cheek is disarming that Negro. Any Negro who teaches Negroes to turn the other cheek in the face of attack is disarming that Negro of his God-given right to defend himself. Everything in nature can defend itself, and is right in defending itself except the American Negro. But when the black man begins to explode and erupt after he has had too much they say that the black man is violent, and as long as these people are putting out a doctrine that paves the way to justify their mistreatment of blacks, this is never called hate.

ACTOR TEN. And what else did he say?

ALL. Yeah! Yeah! More! More!

ACTOR TWO. This year will be America's hottest year: her hottest year yet; a year of much racial violence and much racial bloodshed. But it won't be blood that's going to flow only on one side. The new generation of black people that have grown up in this country during recent years are already forming the opinion, and it's a just opinion, that if there is to be bleeding, it should be reciprocal . . . bleeding on both sides. An example of this was in Cleveland, where the police were putting water hoses on our people there, and also throwing tear gas at them . . . and they met a hail of stones, a hail of rocks, a hail of bricks. A couple of weeks ago in Jacksonville, Florida, a young teen-age Negro was throwing Molotov cocktails. Well, Negroes didn't do this ten years ago. But what you should learn from this is that they are waking up. It was stones yesterday, Molotov cocktails today; it will be hand grenades tomorrow, and whatever else is available the next day. The seriousness of this situation must be faced up to . . . You can take it or leave it. You should not feel that I am inciting someone to violence. I'm only warning of a powder-keg situation. You can take it or leave it. If you take the warning, perhaps you can still save yourself. But if you ignore it or ridicule it, well death is already at your doorstep. There are 22 million African-Americans who are ready to fight for independence right here. When I say fight for independence right here, I don't mean any non-violent fight, or turn-the-other-cheek fight. Those days are gone. Those days are over.

ALL. Yeah, yeah, yeah, yeah! Tell it to us, brother! (*Then they cheer unintelligibly.*)

ACTOR ONE (*who drives it to a hysterical pitch*). White society hates to hear anybody, especially a black man, talk about the crime the white man has perpetrated on the black man. I have always understood that's why I have been so frequently called a "revolutionist." It sounds as if I had done some crime! Well, it may be that the American black man does need to become involved in a *real* revolution. Revolution is bloody, revolution is hostile, revolution knows no compromise, revolution overturns and destroys everything that gets in its way. And you sitting around here like a knot on the wall, saying, "I'm going to love these folks no matter how much they hate me." No, you need a revolution. Whoever heard of a revolution where they lock arms, singing "We Shall Overcome"? You don't do that in a revolution. You don't do any singing, you're too busy *swinging*. This is a real revolution! Revolution is never based on begging somebody for an integrated cup of coffee. Revolutions are never fought by turning the other cheek. Revolutions are never based upon love-your-enemy, and pray-for-those-who-spitefully-use-you. Revolutions are based upon bloodshed. Revolutions are never compromising. Revolutions are never based upon negotiations. Revolutions are never based upon any kind of tokenism whatsoever. Revolutions are never based upon that which is begging a corrupt society or corrupt system to accept us into it. Revolutions overturn systems!

(At this point, two PLANTS *sitting in the first rows of the audience rise, pull hidden pistols and fire at* ACTOR ONE *who is on the ladder. He falls from the ladder into the arms of the other* ACTORS *gathered around it. They all duck and the* PLANTS *race out through the aisles. After a short delay, the* DANCERS *do a dance to show the chaos and confusion of the black community.)*

ACTOR FOUR *(dance over)*. They shot him. They shot Malcolm X. They galloped in straight out of a wild west shoot-em-up. They gunned him down before your lacquered eyes . . . with shotguns, with .45's and .38's. They shot him to death, and you did not see, and you hardly heard. They fired at him even after he had fallen to the floor, and you hardly saw that they were killing you.

ACTOR SEVEN. Malcolm X died broke leaving behind his pregnant wife and three children.

ACTOR EIGHT. One dead nigger adds up to one dead nigger. Nothing else.

ACTOR FOUR. You did it! Whoever killed Malcolm was formed in the crucible of Western Civilization.

ACTOR THREE. Malcolm X committed black suicide.

ACTOR ONE. All this about a Negro, an ex-convict, ex-dope peddler who became a racial fanatic . . .

(The cast arrange themselves on the lev-

*els, facing front, their faces unemotional
masks. They address the audience.)*

ACTOR TWO.　And now
ACTOR THREE.　now the prowling dogs of summer
　nose out your brain
　dig up its treasure carefully hidden in winter
ACTOR FOUR.　And now
ACTOR FIVE.　Now you know you're dangerous and must not
　say it
ACTOR SIX.　But still you see
ACTOR SEVEN.　And how
ACTOR EIGHT.　how do you smile
　when you see
　the bodies
　of your seed
　sliding naked
　through the heat
ACTOR SEVEN.　And how
ACTOR NINE.　how do you dare
　to touch
　to gauze the wound
　mouthed
　in your chest
ACTOR TEN.　How do you answer questions simply put
　or end this whiskey dance in its spin
　Yet you see
　the century old mask wears thin
　They are stealing from you
　they are sucking at the nectar of your life
　trampling your empty hat
ACTOR TWO.　Don't let them shut you up
　Suspend the drunken jazz
　Dress your pain in red satin
　Stalk concrete summer with madness
　Burst rockets from your yellow eyes
　Rampage twirling
　Scream midnight lightning
　Don't let them shut you up
ACTOR FOUR.　For now

ACTOR FIVE. Now there's white paint on your coat

ACTOR SIX. There's blood on your alligator shoes

ACTOR SEVEN. the vampires are at you and

ACTOR EIGHT. and there are no golden metaphors

ACTOR NINE. except in exploded bricks

ACTOR ONE. Tsk. All this about a Negro, an ex-convict, ex-dope peddler who became a racial fanatic . . . (*Sigh.*)

(*BLACKOUT.*)

PRODUCTION NOTES

This play can be done as reader's theatre, or it can be done as a full production with all the indicated action. As it was done originally at Dillard University, it can be a synthesis of the two. It is not a Theatre Game, though it grew out of a group improvisation by M.F.A. actors at Stanford University in the spring of 1967.

The set should consist of a number of levels, not unlike the indications of landscaping in architectural models. The actors should be able to play on these levels, group themselves, or sit on them. (It is the director's option whether or not to have chairs on stage.) And though they are not indicated in the script, there should be many light changes specifically for mood. The lighting for the Lindy Hop and Jitterbug dance sequences should come close to being light shows. There should also be chances to do this at several other points in the show. Where no such lighting facilities are available, the lighting should be straight, with only the indicated blackouts.

It is essential that Charlie Mingus' "II BS" be used for the Jitterbug number, as I wrote the words to match that music. It can be found in the album "Mingus Mingus Mingus," Impulse label, Mono A–54, Stereo AS–54. The dance after the murder should be a modern dance, and the music that seems to work best for it is from Mingus' album "The Black Saint and the Sinner Lady," band three, side one, entitled "TRACK C: Freewoman and Oh, This Freedom's Slave Cries." Only the last two minutes and thirty-two seconds should be used. This is also on Impulse label, Mono A–35,

Stereo AS—35. In the original production we were unable to find authentic music for the Lindy Hop, and we resorted to Les McCann's number "Fake Out," which can be found in his album "Bucket o' Grease." It's on Limelight label, LM 82043, LS 86043.

Though the play was written for young Negro actors to be performed before an audience of young Negroes, this should not be considered a restriction. The play can be informative and enjoyable to adults, and any whites who are interested in seeing it. If the play is done before an all-Black house, the "Negro entertainer" speech and its lead should be cut (from page 218, just after Actor Two's line: "To get to New York and Harlem just one time," to page 220, just before Actor Three says: "The Harlem train! The Harlem train!").

The cast consists of six men and four women (Actors One, Two, Four, Six, Eight and Nine are male; Three, Five, Seven and Ten are female). In addition it might be a help to have about four dancers who are offstage except for the dance when they would come on. All the actors should be able to dance.

The play should be played without a break or intermission, but if the actors find it too exhausting to do it that way, an act break can come after the Jitterbug dance.

There are a number of quotes interposed and interpolated into the script, particularly at the end, from Alex Haley's *The Autobiography of Malcolm X*, which is the primary source for material dealing with Malcolm's life, and from *Malcolm Speaks*, a collection of his speeches edited by George Breitman. There is also one quote from an interview with Kenneth B. Clark. This information should be included in any program notes.

The Rise

A Play in Four Acts

by
Charles H. Fuller, Jr.

CHARACTERS:

BROTHER MARCUS, leader of the Universal Negro Advancement Association

HENRY JEFFERS, one-armed veteran of World War I

RETHA JEFFERS, his wife

AIJA, confident and associate of Marcus

MAN, Marcus's bodyguard

REUBEN HALL, local Harlem politician

MARVIN, an aide to Hall

STEELE, an aide to Hall

BLACK LEADER, voice of Negro leadership

DEAN, white district attorney

CURTIS, stenographer

WHALAN, white owner of ships

RUTLEDGE, sea-captain

Three COPS

CROWD

MAN'S VOICE

WOMAN'S VOICE

PROLOGUE

(To precede opening.)
(Darkened stage. In the center is a large black box, on which stands a dark-skinned BLACK MAN, *dressed in a light-colored suit, and wide brim hat. When he speaks his accent with his actions will be dis-*

*tinctly West Indian. In the background
is the sound of "Swan Lake," and the
repeated bellows of a ship's foghorn. On
the backdrop is projected the year date
1916. The* MAN *is waving and smiling,
there is cheering in the background.)*

BROTHER MARCUS (*loudly, with an exaggerated air*). It is
time for the Universal Negro Advancement Association to
grow fat, with Black men! (*Cheers.*) In America, there are
over fifteen million of our brothers under the whip of the
white man! We cannot wait any longer! Good Jamaicans
have been in the United States for months, and they report
to me that the entire country awaits the arrival of Brother
Marcus! Mr. Booker T. Washington himself has sent a
letter to me! Come, he says, come Brother Marcus, America
has great need of you! (*Pause.*) We will take America, as
we have done in every country where white men grow rich
on the fruits of our labors! We will unite all Black men to
one aim, one God, one destiny! The bell of history is ringing for the day when Black men throughout the world will
join as one, in their own kingdom, with their own leaders,
loving blackness as they would their God! (*Builds momen-
tum.*) And it is also tolling for an end to colonialism and
Black slavery! In America, we will build a rich, powerful
organization! The Black man there is ready—and we bring
him strength and power! (*Ship's horn blows again, and as
curtain closes slowly, there is the sound of explosions, and
a loud ominous voice in the background.*)

MAN'S VOICE (*loud, harsh*). WE DON'T NEED NO DAMN
BROTHER MARCUS IN THIS COUNTRY! WE GOT
OUR OWN LEADERS! GO BACK WHERE YOU CAME
FROM, JAMAICAN!

WOMAN'S VOICE (*shrieking, sarcastic, troubled*). I, FOR
ONE, DON'T LIKE THE WAY HE'S ALWAYS SAYIN'
NEGRO AND BLACK! WE COLORED PEOPLE—
EVERYBODY KNOWS THAT!

MAN'S VOICE. MARCUS AIN'T NOTHIN' BUT A TROU-
BLEMAKER! COLORED PEOPLE IS DOIN' FINE, WE
DON'T NEED NO TROUBLEMAKER! (*Curtain begins*

to open slowly.) TROUBLEMAKER! TROUBLEMAKER! TROUBLEMAKER! TROUBLE——

ACT 1

(*A relatively bare stage darkened at the rear. To the left is a table chair and stool. Seated at the table is a young* BLACK WOMAN. *On the stool, a young* BLACK MAN *with one arm, dressed in the French uniform of World War I. In the center is the large black box, it can be sat on or used as a platform. To the right is a lonely American flag. From the right comes the loud playing of the song "Over There" in ragtime. The time is 1916. On the backdrop is the projected image of President Wilson, hitting the campaign trail.*)

HENRY (*looking to his right*). Listen to it, Retha. (*Turns to stage right.*)

RETHA (*looking up*). What?

HENRY (*annoyed*). The music! That damn "Over There"! They been playin' it on that gramophone all day long downstairs!

RETHA (*unconcerned*). Oh? (*Pause.*) I's got so I don't even hear it, Henry.

HENRY. How can anybody not hear that? (*Angrily leans forward toward floor.*) Turn off that goddamn music, Kissinger! *You go over there,* you coward sons-of-bitches!

RETHA (*scolding*). Henry! You don't have to do that! If he puts us out—where we gonna' go? Mr. Kissinger and Miss Connie jest let us stay here, 'cause I've been with them so many years. (*Pause.*) Miss Connie ain't used to no strong language.

HENRY (*laughs*). She ain't used to no strong language? She should have heard the language they used in France! (*Grows calm, reflective.*) Do you know what it's like over there? (*Turns to her.*) Do you? (RETHA *looks up silently.*)

They're pretty over there! *(Smiles.)* Lie in the sun, and strut around like birds! Oh, yeah. You ought to see them, walking down the street in their shiny uniforms, too brave, too big, too—sick, to return a nigger's salute. So you stop salutin' them. *(Laughs.)* But ole Henry Jeffers had the last laugh! *(Reflective.)* Ole pretty white boy drivin' that ole ambulance big as hell, and them damn German shells screamin' over us—wheeeeeee, wheeeeeee, and he takes one—kabooooom—right in the ass, and blew him right outta that damn truck into my hole. He cried like a baby! And blind as a bat he was, layin' there stretchin' out his arms jest begging for some help. *(To* RETHA.*)* You know what I did? I patted that ole white boy on the head, and told him to calm down, 'cause his Mammy and Pappy was on the way. Yes I did! *(Pause.)* Till he found out I was a Black boy. *(Reflectively.)* I guess it was in my voice—I never knew before that we sounded colored—but he found out, and you know what he did? He got up enough spit in his mouth, to spit in my face, and call me nigger. *(Smiles.)* And I shot that old white boy. I laid that pistol upside his head, and blew out his white brains! Yes I did!

RETHA. Why you got to tell it? *(Backdrop is dark.)*

HENRY *(quickly).* 'Cause I know them whites for what they are! *(Lower.)* Playin' that damn "Over There," and talkin' about joinin' in the fight to end tyranny, and that bastard calls you a nigger when you save his stinkin' life— *(Loudly.)* I know 'em Retha, that's why I talk about it! *(Slight pause.)* And I wish to God, he could have been all of 'em! *(*RETHA *seems startled. To the center of the stage comes a* BLACK LEADER. *He is well dressed, in dark clothes. In his hand are several sheets of paper. He mounts the box, followed by a small group of people.)*

RETHA *(softly).* I think it's wrong to eat yourself up like that.

HENRY *(shouts, overlapping* LEADER'*s speech).* Give me back my goddamn arm then!

LEADER *(addressing his audience loudly).* Now just wait one minute! *(*HENRY *and* RETHA *seem to take notice of him.)* Let's face something squarely! After all, this is nineteen-sixteen—and today is not the time to hold grudges! Now

is not the time to start licking old wounds! (*Behind him, a
projection of a Preparedness Day parade is flashed on the
backdrop.*) The entire world is preparing for the war in
Europe! And we've got to face this. (*Pause.*) The enemies
of Europe are the enemies of us all! That's right—black or
white, it don't matter none to the Kaiser! (*Pause, he looks
around at some of the faces.*) All right—so we haven't gotten the best deal—we all know that! Is that any reason to
be unfair in a time of world crisis? We're all needed in this
fight! This is our country too! (*The group of* PEOPLE *is unre-
ceptive. Behind him from the right comes a silent funeral
procession, in which there are three small coffins. The*
GROUP's *attention is slowly turned to the procession.* WIL-
SON's *face, smiling, is projected on the backdrop.*) We've
got a helluva better chance to make it if we join in the
fight. Europe needs us all! We've got to put down our
grievances and follow the path of truth! (*He begins to be
distracted by the procession. His group of* PEOPLE *walk
away, joining the funeral.*) No man— (*Louder.*) No man can
ask for what he's not entitled to (HENRY's *speech should
overlap.*) and unless we Blacks join the efforts of free
people everywhere against the tyranny of the Kaiser— (*He
is very suddenly silent.*)

HENRY (*to* RETHA). What's that Retha? That funeral, who
is it? (RETHA *looks quickly in direction of the group walking off.*)

RETHA. The Johnson girls. (*To* HENRY.) Died in that fire
that white man set. You know the one—thought his wife
was down here wif' some colored man? I told you about
it—the one where the woman was really in New Rochelle?

HENRY. You told me.

RETHA. They's two more children left—least that colored
woman got something left.

HENRY (*annoyed*). She had five, Retha! (*The* LEADER *takes
notice of him.*)

RETHA (*defensively*). Well, it ain't my fault! (*Quickly.*) You
know you can't never tell what them white people gonna
do! Sometime, they just plain crazy!

HENRY. We ought to string that bastard up, and burn him,
like he burned them damn kids!

LEADER (*addresses audience, as though he heard* HENRY). We can't do that, Harlem! There would be blood flowing in the streets—our blood—BLACK BLOOD! There's been enough killing!

HENRY (*to* LEADER). Tell that to the white man who killed those children!

LEADER (*to* AUDIENCE). I know you! Your kind are all over our streets these days! You would have every Black man, woman, and child slaughtered because of a few lives!

HENRY. A few lives? There were seven last week, and—

LEADER. Quote your statistics! You corner preachers always have statistics! You get all your facts from Black papers down South, or RUMORS, or *he said, I said,* and you go around talkin' about the white menace, and some kingdom you're gonna build in Africa—I say, if you really want respect, you got to go out and earn it! Your country needs you behind her now!

HENRY (*waving disdainfully*). Damn the country! (*Turns to* RETHA.)

LEADER (*turning toward* HENRY). Harlem, this is nineteen-sixteen! We're civilized! Why do you think we're going to war? (*Faces audience again.*)

HENRY. They're fools, Retha! Do you hear them? They've got colored men recruiting colored soldiers for white officers to kill.

RETHA. What you say, Henry?

LEADER (*overlapping*). You think the white man's gonna forgit we helped him in this? We've been honored too, you know! We've gotten our share of medals—and statues too! (*Slight pause.*) For valor, and bravery—we've had great men—and right here in Harlem!

HENRY (*overlapping*). You don't half-listen. None of you women do—I was talkin' 'bout the war.

RETHA. That's all you talk about! I git tired!

LEADER. Look at Larry Thomas—first colored man ever got the Congressional Medal of Honor! We must join this war! It's our only hope! We'll be decorated, appreciated—

HENRY (*overlapping*). What?

RETHA. Nothin'!

HENRY. Well say somethin' loud enough to hear! Don't just move your lips!

LEADER *(loud).* You're not listening, Harlem! This is the only chance we've got! *(Pleading.)* Fight his wars, then make demands! We'll have a base!

HENRY *(irritated).* Retha! You hear what I said?

LEADER (RETHA *looks up at* HENRY *disdainfully, as light begins to fade over left and center of stage).* Listen! This is 1916—not 1851! We're being accepted more and more!— every day in more places than before! Things ain't bad as they used to be! *(Loud.)* Well, they ain't! This is America! *(Light fades out. On the right a* BLACK MAN *in uniform is saluting the flag, as several* WHITE ONLOOKERS *stand and laugh. The* MAN *notices their laughter, is embarrassed by it, and finally stands rather awkwardly staring down at his uniform. Light fades, comes up on center.* MARCUS *enters from left, walking slowly to the box, where he stops. He seems disturbed, and is quickly followed by* AIJA *and a tall* BLACK MAN. *On the backdrop, a projection will show the headlines of the sinking of the French ship* Sussex.)

MAN *(to* BROTHER MARCUS*).* Marcus! Where did you get to man? We looked everywhere for you! The people were yelling for you!

AIJA *(overlapping).* Why did you leave? You had some of them!

BROTHER MARCUS *(annoyed).* Some of them? And the others, they treat me like a dog? *(Shakes head.)* These Blacks in America welcome you like they welcome the clown—and I just been here three weeks! They don't even know yet what I stand for! How can they boo me, and shout me down, when they won't even listen long enough to hear what I got to say? I am Brother Marcus, not some jack leg preacher they can treat like dirt!

MAN *(smiling, a little relieved).* I am glad you said it, man. I feel the same thing. These Negroes here don't understand anything! Anything! They're like cattle! The white man's emissaries lead them by the nose, and they wait for the whip before they move—I think we should leave, it's been a bad trip.

AIJA *(overlapping).* I agree.

MAN (*overlapping*). What is there here worth saving—?

BROTHER MARCUS (*cutting them off suddenly*). No! (*Looks at them.*) I am angry—but I didn't come to this huge, troublesome country for nothing.

MAN (*quickly, surprised*). You were just for leaving, man!

MARCUS. No!

AIJA (*annoyed*). Why Marcus? We're foreigners here—do you know what they call us?

MARCUS (*quickly*). So what? (*Softens.*) You think I don't know they call us voodoo men? I know it! (*Loudly.*) I know what they say, and I know what they are! (*Intensely.*) They are like children, these Black men here!—infants! whose strength is untested! Untried! They know nothing because they have been fed the wrong food! They must find out who they are first—didn't we prove that in Jamaica? You forget, it was not easy there either. Here it is new to them—perhaps, we judge too quickly. (*Looks down at himself.*) I don't even look like they do—my clothes I mean. The others on the platform had on dark suits—

MAN (*waves annoyingly*). Marcus, what difference does that make? I'm telling you, these people—

MARCUS (*quickly*). Did you see some of their faces, when I said, Back to Africa?

MAN. Well—

MARCUS (*sharply*). Well, did you?

MAN (*shrugs*). I saw them.

MARCUS (*annoyed*). You saw them! What did you see man? Did you see their faces light up that crowd?

AIJA. In that crowd there were a lot of pigs!

MARCUS (*angry*). Pigs? Yes pigs! Always and everywhere there are pigs! Pigs booed Marcus (*Mood change.*), but there was something else there! (*Reflectively.*) And it was not just in what I said about Africa. Their faces lit up because I dared to say, we are one people—because I had dared to say what they felt—I shared blackness with them! (*Softly astonished.*) Didn't you see that?

AIJA. Jamaica is warmer in April.

MARCUS (*disgusted*). Jamaica is warmer in April! Damn Jamaica! We are here Aija, not Jamaica!

MAN (*confused*). You want to stay then?

MARCUS. I will stay.

AIJA. Even if they laugh?

MARCUS. They won't laugh long—and besides, it took lots of money to bring us here to see Mr. Washington. I do not intend to spend Jamaican money foolishly.

AIJA. But Washington is dead.

MARCUS *(irritated)*. Marcus is not, and he will not be stopped by boos or laughter! *(Turns from them.)* Today was a mistake—it will never happen again. I know how to reach them.

MAN. What do these pigs know? Do you think they want to hear about themselves or how Black men can improve? *(Laughs sarcastically.)* I tell you, only from the white man's emissaries do these people want to hear anything! And he gets up on the platform, waves a few pieces of paper at them, and says, "We colored folks ain't got it as bad as some people in Europe!" and these people love it!

AIJA *(to MARCUS)*. What if he's right, Marcus?

MARCUS *(smiling reflectively)*. We have a culture all our own—and in Africa all our ancestors were kings. *(Turns to them.)* Some of them were ready to leave then—can't you see it? Once they begin to think as one mind about Africa, and share that thought, we've got them!

MAN *(cynically)*. In this country we will grab nothing!

MARCUS *(smiling)*. You are too pessimistic.

MAN. Marcus, I see what my eyes tell me is there! You asked me did I see them when you spoke—I saw them! I saw them boo you! I saw them stand up and call you witch doctor, and voodoo man! I saw them take your speech, and strip it naked, and word by word justify their continued slavery! I saw weak, frightened, stupid Black men! I saw nothing, and no reason for us to remain in their company! *(Sarcastically.)* See? I see the truth!

MARCUS *(loud, angry)*. Then see that the truth is, Black people have nothing in a world of plenty! *(Softer.)* See that unless we give them strength they will go on being slaves! *(Coldly.)* And do not ever address Mr. Marcus, if you value your— *(Hesitates.)* position, in that tone again! *(MAN lowers his eyes.)*

MAN. I'm sorry. *(Silence.)*

AIJA. We would be better off at home!

MARCUS (*smiling to her*). Home? This is home! Harlem, New York!

MAN (*sullenly*). It is not as peaceful as Saint Ann's.

AIJA. And there were Jamaicans in that crowd today! Jamaicans booing!

MARCUS (*annoyed*). Saint Ann's? Jamaicans booing? What is Saint Ann's but another place where Black men suffer? When was it a paradise, man? In Kingston, Jamaicans tip their hats to the big white man—are we better off there, because we manage to walk lightly out of his way? (*Intensely.*) I am here! (*Silence, stares at them.*) Come on now! What did I bring with me? In Kingston we were anxious about Harlem and America—think of how many Black men there are here! Do you think in Jamaica we could have begun our journey to Africa, and a Black kingdom? Here is where it must happen—here, where all Black men suffer! Stay with me!

MAN (*seriously*). What if they never hear you?

MARCUS (*calmly*). I have thought of it. (*Pause.*)

MAN. Are you afraid?

MARCUS. No. (*Pause.*)

MAN. Be prepared for failure if it comes, Brother Marcus.

MARCUS (*smiling*). You are too solemn, man! Too solemn—

(*From the right a* BLACK BOY *walks on stage with a bundle of papers under his arms. He is shouting.*)

BOY. Colored man gunned down in Induction office! Read all about it! Man killed for enlisting at wrong office! Clean up man at Roxy Theatre shot in the face!

MARCUS (*to* BOY). Hey, you boy! (BOY *turns toward him.*)

BOY. Negro leaders protest shooting!

MARCUS (*handing him a coin*). Let me see that! (*He looks at the paper, and suddenly crumples the paper.*) This devilish white man—what kind of man is this? (*He leaps onto the box, shouting.*) Harlem! Marcus is here! and Black men, we will rise together like a million nights!

(*Light fades. Comes up on the left, where* HENRY *is seated*

*on a stool. On the backdrop is a projection of the June
Preparedness Day parade.)*

HENRY *(looking up as* RETHA *comes in from left).* Hey
Retha.

RETHA. Hello Henry. *(She seems tired. Sits down.)*

HENRY. Seen the paper?

RETHA. No.

HENRY *(turning to face her).* They say they don't intend to
prosecute that soldier who shot that man at the Induction
office last month.

RETHA. I heard them talkin' 'bout it. *(Pause.)* I don't think
he shoulda been in there, Henry. *("Over There" begins to
play again.)*

HENRY *(turning to his right).* Listen to it! Hear it? It's that
son-of-a-bitch downstairs! *(Loud.)* Hey, Kissinger! Turn it
off! *(To* RETHA.*)* All day, all night!

RETHA *(annoyed).* I wish you wouldn' do that Henry.

HENRY. Were you ever over there, Retha?

RETHA. You know I wasn't—you always ask me that, Henry.
You know I wasn't! Don't talk about it tonight, please!

HENRY. Why? *(Silence.)* Then what we gonna talk about
then? *(Pause.)* You wanna talk about this murder down the
Induction office?

RETHA. Why we always got to talk about the white people,
Henry?

HENRY *(exasperated).* Retha, everytime you turn around,
they done killed one of us, or lynched somebody—what we
supposed to do—they gunned down that colored boy for
nothin'!

RETHA *(irritated).* He ain't had no business down there,
Henry! You know that! There's an Induct place right on a
Hunert-Twenty-fif and Lenox Avenue! He ain't had no
business down—

HENRY *(loud).* They ain't have to kill him for it!

RETHA *(sighs).* They do though, Henry, and gittin' mad
ain't gonna change a thing—we ain't people who hit back.
(Silence.)

HENRY. That's why they kill us anytime they get good and
ready. *(Pause.)*

RETHA. Did you find anything?

HENRY (*sarcastically*). What am I gonna find, Retha—with one arm? It takes two hands to sweep a floor, or pick up trash. (*Pause.*) I didn' know that, before.

RETHA. Tomorrow'll be better.

HENRY. Why's it gonna be better tomorrow—'cause they'll turn me down at some high class place? (*Intensely.*) If I worked with a gun, I'd git me some work then! (*He gets off the stool and mimics.*) Put your white hands up— that's right, higher, higher! (*Smiles.*) BLAAAAM! I'd shoot them right in the face! (*Laughs.*)

RETHA (*as though she hasn't heard*). Little Miss Connie? She said, she hope you feelin' better—I swear, sometime that chile acts like she's a grown woman!

HENRY (*turning to her, disturbed*). Miss Connie! Miss Kissinger! Miss Eileen! Miss Catherine! Miss this, Miss that! Stop it woman! Sweet Jesus, stop it! (*Pause, long.*)

RETHA. I brought some ham hocks for tonight. (*Smiles faintly.*) And some greens—I bought a lot of greens, Henry. (*He turns away, as light fades.*)

(*To the right of center is a desk and chair arrangement. Behind the desk is seated a rather obese man in his forties, REUBEN HALL, the committeeman of Harlem. To his right is a tall slender aide, called STEELE, and to his left in front of the desk is another aide, called MARVIN. Toward center MARCUS is standing with AIJA and his MAN; they seem impatient. MARCUS paces back and forth to the box. On the backdrop the Black Tom explosion is projected onto the screen.*)

HALL (*looking at MARCUS*). Is that the one? He don't look like much to me—he certainly don't look like no great leader of people—what are we getting into, Marvin? (*He looks up at the man.*) I don't like the feel of this—and if anyone downtown gets out of hand about it, you'll be out of a job! (*Softer.*) It's taken us too long to build what we've got in Harlem! (MARCUS *whispers something inaudibly to his friends.*)

MARVIN (*leaning forward*). Listen, Reuben, he's a born organizer—a born one! He's already got half of Harlem listening to him—and he hasn't been here six months yet! I say we can't afford to have a man like him with the opposition!

STEELE. He's right Reuben. You know that?

HALL (*harshly*). He'd better be! (*Nervously fingering his tie.*) I don't like these Jamaicans! They're crowding us out of Harlem—and I can't even half understand them! (*To* STEELE.) Who is he anyway? He calls himself Marcus—what does that mean? (*To* MARVIN.) I've heard what he's been preaching in the halls and on the street-corners—and I don't like it! (*Pleased, reflectively.*) I'm not completely deaf, you know. We've got enough problems without every nigger walkin' around thinkin' he's some damn king or queen of some lost African culture!

MARVIN. The people think—

HALL (*cutting him off*). Damn the people! The people don't know what they want!—or who they are! This—this Jamaican is a pompous, psalm-quoting madman who wants to be a Black Napoleon—besides, I don't like talking to every young radical that stands on a box on a Hundred-and-Twenty-fifth Street! (*Sarcastically.*) Twenty-nine years old, and he is going to solve America's Black problems! (*Laughs.*)

MARVIN (*exasperated*). He's no madman, Reuben—believe me! The man's extremely shrewd!

HALL (*looking around at* STEELE, *mock laughter*). Shrewd? (*Coldly.*) Shrewd men don't go around running off at the mouth, Marvin—and they don't go around calling themselves professors—or has he graduated to Doctor now? What do we call him today—his royal highness?

STEELE (*softly, whispered loudly*). Can we really lose anything though, Reuben?

HALL (*annoyed*). Come on, Steele—you should know better! We can lose Harlem, that's what we can lose by getting involved with this Marcus! (*Looks at them.*) What is there about this man? Did you really think I was going to get

involved with some street-corner hustler from Jamaica?
What do you take me for?

MARVIN (*surprised*). But you said, you wanted—

HALL (*cutting him off harshly*). I've changed my mind! Just
now! (*Pause.*) I changed it! (*Silence.*) Do either of you
know when I came to Harlem? Do you?

MARVIN (*hesitatingly*). Reuben, I—

HALL. Thirty-two years ago! Before that boy out there was
born! Thirty-two years Marvin! Thirty years of just lickin'
white boots and runnin' errands down at Tammany before
the lowest white man there would even speak to me!
Thirty years of doin' favors—of listenin' to dumb niggers
with less education than I got, screamin' on every corner
about what they was gonna' do! (*Loudly.*) I'm the boss
here! (*The loudness startles* MARCUS, *and he turns in the
direction of the office.*)

MARVIN (*quietly*). What do you want me to do?

HALL (*reflectively*). It's a bad move all around! (*Waves a
hand.*) Tell him I can't see him—I'm busy! (MARVIN *looks
at him.*) Tell him! (MARVIN *moves in the direction of*
MARCUS. *When he reaches them, they will talk inaudibly
for a few moments.*)

STEELE (*smiling, leaning over* HALL). They do say, he's a
pretty good fund raiser, Reuben.

HALL. I don't— (*Hesitates, looks at* STEELE, *after* MARVIN.
Irritated.) It's too late!

MARCUS (*angry*). What do you mean he won't see Marcus,
man? He has kept me standing here in this hall for twenty
minutes, and he cannot see me? No one does this to
Brother Marcus, man! Where is this—this person?

MARVIN. He won't see you!

MARCUS (*loudly*). Where is he, man? Don't keep telling me
this! I am Marcus—that man must be out of his mind!
(HALL *starts to rise, and move forward slowly, listening.*)
I have no time for games! Where is he?

HALL (*on the edge of the group,* AIJA *studies him*). Brother
Marcus?

MARCUS (*to* MARVIN, *as he faces* HALL). Who is this, man?

MARVIN. Brother Marcus; Mr. Hall.

MARCUS. I don't have all day, you know. (STEELE *moves*

toward them.) Do you think I am a statue, I can stand here all day waiting on somebody? When somebody says he will be somewhere, at a certain time, I don't have to wait like a statue! You called for me, man.

HALL *(smiling).* Mr. Marvin didn' understand me—I said I wasn't going to see anyone but Mr. Marcus. (MARCUS *looks knowingly to* AIJA. HALL *looks at* MARVIN.) You oughta know better!

MARCUS *(irritated).* You want to talk, man?

HALL. Yes. Sure, come on in. *(They follow* HALL. MARCUS *sits down in front of the desk,* AIJA *beside him, his man standing up silently.* MARVIN *and* STEELE *take places beside the desk, as* HALL *sits down.)* Well! *(Pause.)* I'm the committeeman— *(Smiles, looks up at* MARCUS' MAN.) Care for a seat? (MAN *shakes head "No," folds his arms.)* Suit yourself. Well, as I was saying—they call me the Mayor of Harlem! *(Smiles. There is a pause.)* Last year we took the city—and don't think we don't have power downtown! *(Seems embarrassed.)* A—a, they tell me you're an organizer—and a good one! I think we could clean up in Harlem if we worked together—don't you? *(Silence.)* How much do you people—a—well, how much a month can you collect from—

MARCUS *(cutting him off).* You don't know what I stand for.

HALL *(looking at the others, smiling).* Well?

MARCUS *(surprised).* Black people of course—it should have been on your tongue!

HALL. Does a thing like that have to be said, Brother Marcus?

MARCUS *(smiling).* I don't think you understand completely, Mr. Hall. I am not for white interests—or the white man's country. *(Slight pause.)* Or his wars, his peace, his homes or his women! And *(Slowly.)*, I may not be acceptable to the *Mayor of Harlem!* *(Pause.)* Do you know, Mayor of Harlem, why the Negro suffers so much in this country? (HALL *is cut off before he can answer.)* Precisely because he is in it, and not owner of it! We have nothing, man! This white man's whim is our command—his progress, our death sentence! We are still captives here—do you love Negroes, Mr. Hall? Quickly! Don't hesitate!

HALL (*stuttering*). Of—of—of course! What kind of a man do you—

MARCUS (*breaking in*). Good! Then you love Aija here because she is Black, and her nose wide, her lips thick, and her hair short? (*Pause.*) Do you know, Mayor of Harlem, once in Jamaica, I watched a light-skinned colored man, like you, beat that beautiful woman? I watched white men trick her; in her ignorance, rape her—and I watched her bear ugly, half white babies who grew to hate her! Did you know that? (*Pause.*) She has died in every country where white men ruled, where white men sentenced us to death in the name of progress! And do you know what I asked myself? I said, Why is this? Where is the Black man's country? His Parliament, his ministers? Where is his Foreign Office? His diplomats, his tycoons, his generals, his admirals? Nowhere! Nowhere on the face of the earth! And it occurred to me, that Mr. Marcus might make them! (*Silence.*) I stand for that!

HALL (*laughs*). We all do—don't we? (*Pause.*) Like I said though, we're big—real big downtown, and we could use a man like yourself—I don't have to tell you how difficult it might be for a Jamaican downtown—and there's a lot of Negroes don't like Jamaicans too, you know.

MARCUS. We are first Black man!

HALL. I know that Marcus—but see—hell, here we don't have no Parliament! If you want an army, you vote on it—(*Smiles to* MARVIN.) Course with the right kind of money, you could buy an army. (*Laughs.*)

MARCUS. We have the money—but, why does money change you?

HALL. Change? Me? (*Smiles.*) We politicians don't change—do we Marvin? (*Laughs.*)

MAN. Don't think Marcus is a fool!

MARCUS. I think he knows that—right Mr. Hall?

HALL. I wouldn't want to be partners with a fool, Marcus—(*Looks at* MAN.) Assuming we can be partners.

MARCUS. I want no partners who are emissaries of the whites!

HALL (*annoyed*). Do you think that's what we are? Don't

you think I know what they do to us—I ought to be Mayor
of New York, not some Mayor of Harlem—

MARCUS (*smiling*).   I like sincerity in a man. (TO AIJA.) Don't
you Aija?

AIJA.   Real sincerity. (*The* MEN *look at her.*)

HALL (*irritated*).   It's obvious to me!

MARCUS (*standing, seemingly tired*).   So, we are partners?
(HALL *reaches over desk and shakes his hand. He extends
his hand to the others.*) There will be papers to draw up,
Mayor of Harlem.

HALL (*surprised*).   Papers?

MARCUS.   We are an organization of contracts and commit-
ments—this is a business, and we leave nothing to chance
man!

HALL.   I agree! (*Smiling.*) We have papers for you to sign
too! I'll have them made up by tomorrow. We'll do well
together Marcus. (MARCUS *starts to leave.*) Very well! By
the way—what do we call ourselves?

MARCUS (*turning to face him*).   The Universal Negro Advancement Association! (*Light fades.*)

(*Light comes up on* HENRY *on the left. He
is standing beside his stool, fondling a
pistol, and smiling. In the center the light
builds again, and* HENRY *take no notice
of it.* MARCUS *is standing beside the box
with* AIJA *and his* MAN. *On the backdrop is a photo of Vice President Mar-
shall inspecting farms to insure Europe's
food supply. "Over There" begins to
sound ominously in the background.*)

MARCUS.   Did you see his face, when he mentioned money?

AIJA (*angrily*).   He doesn't care about the movement! Why
did you bother with that dog?

MARCUS (*annoyed*).   Are you telling Marcus what to do?—
or what I should have done? You are my associate, not my
master! It is a first step! A first step!

AIJA.   What kind of step is it, when a man walks into the
mouth of a snake?

MARCUS (*quickly*).   I will not have this, Aija!

AIJA.   Why did you bring me with you, Brother Marcus? I am not a statue, either!

MARCUS (*loud*).   You are not my voice!

AIJA (*frightened*).   What am I then? (*He stares at her strangely.*) What? (*Silence.*)

MARCUS (*hesitantly, softer*).   Do you think I like that lackey? That boot licker of the white man? (*Intensely, though low-keyed.*) We must build! We must form alliances, and not be stupid enough to be trapped in them! We must reach the people—we must pretend to carry some banners, to carry our own—how else can we bring them down?

AIJA (*averting her eyes*).   What of Hall?

MARCUS (*smiling*).   He will be the first one to fall! (AIJA *turns away slowly, and he follows her with his eyes. He is troubled.*) Will you draw up the contracts?

AIJA (*sadly*).   Yes, Marcus. (MARCUS *turns to his* MAN, *who has been silent. They exchange knowing glances.*)

MARCUS (*to* MAN).   How does one say to them that all this is larger than we are?

MAN.   You don't say it, Marcus. You don't say it. (*Silence, both* MEN *walk off to the left, as the light builds on the right.* HALL *is still seated behind his desk, and in the chairs are* MARVIN *and* STEELE. *Light is still on* HENRY, *who is playing with the gun childishly.*)

HALL (*laughing*).   Did you see that pompous Jamaican? He really thinks he's a leader! (*Mimics.*) Where is the Black man's country?

MARVIN.   You were right—I think he is crazy!

HALL.   These foreigners! (*Laughs.*) He's crazy all right—crazy like a fox! Here he sits, a little fat, Black Jamaican who's going to take over Harlem—and the whole world, with his great big United—Universal—hell, I can't even say it, much less care about it! Marcus is a pretty good con-man—I wonder what his total contributions are a week? I bet you there's a lot of crazy niggers buyin' that crap!

STEELE.   I've heard he's got a pretty good sized group—and is talkin' about collecting a dollar from every Black man in the world! (*Laughs.*)

HALL.   Did you hear him—There will be papers to sign Mr.

Hall! (*Shakes head.*) What next? (*Laughs.*) It's good politics to be on speaking terms with these religious cult leaders—the people think you're closer to them—listen, I want you two to find out as much as you can about Marcus! . . . write letters, talk to people who know him, find out about where he came from—I want everything, understand? (*They laugh.*) Mr. Black Country may take over Harlem, but Reuben Hall intends to take over the Black country! (*Laughter, light fades.*)

(HENRY *is now to the left of the stage alone. He seems to be waiting. From the left, a* WHITE MAN *walks onto the stage.* HENRY *steps into the shadows. The* MAN *slows down, looks about cautiously, stops.* HENRY *steps forward.* MAN *backs away, tries to run, and* HENRY *shoots him. He waits for a moment, then hastens to the* MAN'S *side and removes his wallet.*)

HENRY (*holding up the wallet, on the backdrop is the picture of German dead*). You wanted me to do something, Retha? (*Mimics.*) Find you a job, Henry! (*Removes money.*) Well, I found me a job! (*Smiles.*) And a damn good one! (*Laughs, stuffs money in his shirt. A police whistle sounds, and* HENRY *stands up and runs offstage to his right. The body is left lying in the light.*)

(*Curtain.*)

ACT 2

(*Early in 1917. In the center of the stage, the* BLACK LEADER *is standing. In his hand is a small newspaper clipping. He seems amused by it, and will address the audience. On the backdrop is projected the march of the suffragettes who are marching on Washington, and being carried away. There is no music.*)

LEADER *(smiling)*. Harlem, let me read you this! It's the funniest damn thing I've read in months! *(Pause.)* January thirteenth, nineteen-seventeen. Marcus claims UNAA Black world's only hope! *(Smiles.)* Marcus, local Negro leader—and I question that—anyway, Marcus said yesterday at a rally given for the benefit of his Black Cross Nurses, and his Black Legion, in their foreign office on One-Hundred-and-Thirty-eighth Street, that joining him was the only hope for the world's four hundred million Negroes. Only through unity, self-reliance, and Black pride can the Negro free himself from white oppression! *(Pause.)* Such big words— *(Shakes head.)* un huh! *(Extravagantly, still reading.)* The wave is growing!, he said—a wave so huge, so powerful, it will drown the whites in a sea of Black faces! *(Smiles, puts article in pocket.)* Now come on! *(Points.)* In the first place—who the hell is Marcus? Has he fought against the white man for you? *(Points.)* Or you? What about you? When did he try to get us the right to vote? Or decent houses? *(Pause. Behind him, Dewey's funeral goes on.)* If you ask me, he sounds more like a census taker than a leader! Four hundred million? Why not eight hundred million—who told Marcus? *(Smiles.)* I wonder if he counted Zulus and Pygmies in that? *(Angrily.)* That crazy Jamaican don't know what the hell he's talkin' about—he ain't worth nothin' as a leader—and pride? We'll have a lot more of it, when we get rid of Marcus! *(Slight pause.)* All our efforts since Emancipation have been to gain rights as free individuals, in a free society, and along comes this arrogant Jamaican in a nightgown, and a row of two-cent medals, and *he's saying* we no longer need them! All we have to do is unite, open up our own stores, and walk around proud of our shoe-shine parlors, and our newsstands! We want to be in America, not out of it! Where are our Negro college graduates? Doctors? *(Pause.)* How many of you want to live in a grass hut, and hunt zebra? How many? *(Looks around.)* We must repudiate this madman! Put him down before he is responsible for getting some of our young people killed! We are a sensible people, who have gotten as far as we have, not with talk of Black people with power, but with a fervent belief in

the American way! *(Pause.)* And lest we forget—our Marcus
has become the young genius of Wall Street now! *He's*
gonna take *our* money and invest it in his companies—
how many of us have heard of the story of the colored
man who ran out with the treasury? *(Shakes head.)* Yeah,
we done all heard it—and we ain't goin' for it anymore!
Everything this great man plans takes our money! And
while he's ridin' around in his fancy cars with them big
time politicians downtown—we still walkin'! I'm wonder-
ing if the D.A. is checking—and if he ain't checkin', colored
people want to know why! We are not about to have
another man run out with our money! *(Light fades. Behind him, President Wilson gives his "Peace Without Victory" Speech, "Over There" begins to play as the light
builds on the left. There is a new table, chair, and stool in
the arrangement. To the right of it is a window frame.
HENRY and RETHA enter from the left. RETHA seems apprehensive at first, then she is suddenly excited.)*

RETHA *(looking around)*. Henry! It's beautiful! *(Pause.)* But
it's too expensive, I think.

HENRY *(smiling)*. Retha! There ain't nothin' too expensive
for us anymore!

RETHA *(sitting down, pensive)*. Henry? Where you gittin' all
this money?

HENRY *(momentarily puzzled)*. I'm workin' chile! *(Smiles.)*

RETHA. In them clothes?

HENRY *(annoyed)*. Retha, all colored men don't hafta wear
work clothes! I got a desk job!

RETHA *(pouting)*. Well, why can't I come and see you at
lunch time? You won't even tell me where you workin'—
Miss Kissinger let me have the time if I ask her!

HENRY *(going to his stool)*. I tol' you, I tol' the man I
wasn't married! *(Turns to RETHA.)* You quittin' Miss Kissinger anyway!

RETHA. I could act like your girl-friend!

HENRY *(waving disdainfully)*. You think I want them dirty
white boys in that office makin' smart remarks about you?
I tol' you how them boys talk to all them other colored
men on the job—"Your girl sure got a big ass, Jeffers!"—
I can just hear them! Leave it alone, Retha!

RETHA *(anxious).* You just don't tell me nothin', Henry! We go for a whole week, and you don't tell me nothin'! You don't even come home tired and disgusted—a man should come home tired and disgusted once in a while! *(Looks at him tearfully.)* Henry Jeffers have you got another woman? *(He faces her quickly.)* A street woman? *(Pause,* RETHA *draws in her breath.)* Are you pimpin'?

HENRY *(louder).* Retha, that's crazy!

RETHA *(drying her eyes).* A man as fine as you look, can find them—you know that! All dressed up! *(Sniffs.)* And I ain't no fine woman—I know I ain't! It ain't sensible for no fine man to stay here, when he got all that money!

HENRY *(softly, stands).* Retha, what you think I am?

RETHA *(runs to him).* I'm sorry— *(Puts his arm around her.)* but it ain't—this just ain't the way it happens, Henry!

HENRY *(tenderly).* Retha, it can happen, baby! I just can't tell you 'bout it, that's all! I ain't pimpin'—I'm just doin' somethin'—gittin' back some of what I gave up in the war! I'm entitled to somethin' for this arm! *(Softly.)* Everything's gonna be all right—I don't want nobody else! *(Smiles.)* Pretty soon, we gonna be movin' out of Harlem—maybe we'll go to Philly, or Detroit.

RETHA *(stepping back, half-smiling).* I can't do that Henry!

HENRY *(bewildered).* Why not?

RETHA. What would I do? *(Walks back to her chair, and sits.)* I been with Miss Connie all her life! She wouldn' know what to do without me! *(Smiles.)* I'm the only one can fix her hair—she won't let Miss Kissinger near it—I'm tellin' you the truth, sometimes I think that chile's full grown! *(Looks innocently at him.)* What would that chile do, Henry?

HENRY. You don't have to do that Retha!

RETHA. But I been doin' it so long, Henry—I wouldn' know what to do if I didn't have Miss Connie to look after— you don't never see my way no more!

HENRY *(disturbed).* Damnit, Retha—your way is old! You can have your own to look after! This is nineteen-seventeen—we ain't slaves no more!

RETHA. I can't! I jest can't!

HENRY *(whispered).* All right! *(Silence. He turns away.)*

RETHA (*staring at table top*).   Henry? (*He faces her silently.*) I'm holdin' you back ain't I?

HENRY (*sighs*).   No, Retha.

RETHA.   How come we always end up arguin'?

HENRY.   I guess 'cause we want to be together, but we just ain't made friends yet.

RETHA.   You plannin' to leave me?

HENRY.   No. (RETHA *sighs, smiles.*)

RETHA.   This place is pretty, Henry.

HENRY (*sighs*).   Yeah. (*Silence.*)

RETHA.   Henry? When we was movin'? I founds a gun—is that your gun, Henry?

(*From the right comes a parade, in the background is "Over There" played in march time. A* CROWD *follows, carrying green, black, and red banners.* MARCUS *is at the rear of the parade, waving and smiling. The* CROWD *will congregate around the black box. On the backdrop is a projection of Russians rioting in Moscow.*)

RETHA (*hearing noise gets up and looks out frame of window, before* HENRY *can answer*).   Look! There's a parade on a Hundred-and-Twenty-fif' Street!

HENRY (*nervous*).   Retha?

RETHA.   Look! They all dressed up, Henry! (MARCUS *mounts box.*)

HENRY (*nonchalantly*).   Probably war veterans.—Retha? That gun? It's—it's a souvenir from the war! I thought I lost it! (*Laughs.*)

RETHA.   I don't think so— (*Looks at him.*) They all colored people! Look!

MARCUS (*overlapping*).   I have gone to our so-called Negro leaders—and what did they tell Marcus? They told me, that the Black man needed no unity! Needed no self-reliance! That Black men in America were contented! (*Loud.*) Are you contented? (CROWD *responds with* "No!")

HENRY (*approaching window*). What did you do with it, Retha?

RETHA (*shrugs*). I don't know—I think it's in the drawer. (*Excited.*) Look Henry!

HENRY (*beside her*). Who is it?

MARCUS (*overlapping*). They tell me that Black freedom must come before Black unity—and I ask, how can you be free, until you unite? (CROWD *cheers.*) I am the equal to white men now!

RETHA. Looks like that man Marcus. I heard Miss Kissinger and them talkin' 'bout him. Seems like he got white people pretty scared around here!

HENRY. A colored man? Let me see him! (*Pause.*) You feel like goin' down?

RETHA. No indeed! I wanna fix dinner. (*She moves toward table.*)

HENRY (*moving away from window*). I'll be right back hear? I wanna see him—all right? (*Starts out.*)

RETHA. Go 'head.

HENRY (*stops*). Retha? (*She looks at him.*) It's a souvenir. I—I took it off a dead German. (*She nods slowly.*) I'd thought I lost it, you know? That's all— (*Smiles, anxious.*) A man deserves something, don't he? After all, I lost my whole arm!

RETHA (*softly*). I know. (*Light fades.* HENRY *goes off to the left.* RETHA *puts her hands to her face.*) I know!

(*Center stage is bright.* HALL *has just come on from the right to join* MARCUS. *The* CROWD *is still clapping. On the backdrop, the headlines will read, "United States Declares War on Germany!" As this headline appears, all the clapping will stop, quite suddenly, and everyone in the* CROWD *will turn, this includes* MARCUS, *and face the headline. Their movement should be stiff, sudden. They will continue this for a few moments, then equally as suddenly return to their*

*original positions, and continue the clap-
ping.* MARCUS *will then wait for the*
CROWD *to subside.)*

MARCUS *(loudly).*   Let no man shrink from this knowledge!
Before white men called England a nation, Black men
were kings! In Timbuktu, Black men built fine universities
when white men were barbarians! *(Points.)* Who gave the
world iron? The genius of Black men! We are a proud
people with a proud history—of what are we to be
ashamed? Our Black faces? *(Raising his arms.)* Let the
world know, they are beautiful! *(Cheering.)* We can only
move forward through unity! Unity of mind and body!
We must begin to see each other clearly—and not through
the glasses of the white man! We must know that we are
one people, and share a common destiny! *(Clapping.)* Let
no one tell you that your collar of white oppression cannot
be removed! We have only to stand as proud as I know we
are!—moving together—Black in thought, and Black in
deed! *(Clapping.)* The white man thinks we are still slaves!
Let him continue to think that, as we rush toward him,
shoulder to shoulder! *(Clapping,* MARCUS *tries to quiet
them.)* But as God is the witness of Marcus, I say to you,
we will never unify, never come together as one body, as
long as we believe, as our great Negro-leaders tell us, that
we must first free ourselves and then unite to act—we are
free when we are together! *(Clapping.)* We must leave this
swamp of American lies, and build a world founded on the
knowledge that we are a great people! (HALL *tries to interrupt,* MARCUS *ignores him.)* A world free of white domi-
nation! A world where Blacks can determine their own
destiny—a kingdom! A kingdom of unity in Africa! (PEOPLE
cheer—he pauses.) The white men are cowards! They fear
our unity— (HENRY *breaks in.* MARCUS *continues for an
instant.)* of action!

HENRY *(shouting, as he enters from the left).*   He's right!
(To CROWD.) Listen to him! (MARCUS *stares at him smiling.)* They *are* cowards! I know them; I fought in the war
with them—they cry like babies! They're weak—and we go
out an' lose our arms and legs for these people! We (HALL

begins to speak inaudibly to MARCUS *who appears to argue with him.*) make them safe, and get nothin' but hell for it!

MARCUS. He's right! When are Black men heroes? (*Slight pause.*) When they are dead! (*Cheering.*)

HENRY (*overlapping*). We should kill them all! (MARCUS *glances at him strangely.*) And anyone who opposes us should be killed with them!

MARCUS (*pointing to* HENRY). Here is a man with grievances! Hear him! We must, if the door is locked, tear it down! But we will build our own doors, which will remain shut to the white world! (*Cheering.*) We will go to our kingdom on our own roads! We will ask white men for nothing! We will build our own businesses—our own shops! And every dime! Every dollar we make will bring us one step closer to each other—to unity! It is our strength that will bring down the old white ways! (POLICE *enter, three of them from the right, blowing whistles.*) What is the meaning of this? (CROWD *begins to panic.*)

HENRY (*overlapping, to* CROWD). Hey! Listen to him! Don't y'all hear what the man's sayin'? Hey! (*Turns to them, just as* AIJA *comes out from the right. She runs to* MARCUS' *side.*) You black cowards! Run then! Go 'head! Run!

1ST POLICEMAN (*shouting, warrant in hand*). You're under arrest Marcus!

HENRY (*turning suddenly in the direction of* MARCUS). You can't arrest him! He's Brother Marcus! (*He reaches one of the* POLICEMEN's *shoulders.*)

2ND POLICEMAN. Get off me, cripple!

3RD POLICEMAN. You heard him, move! (*Starts to strike* HENRY.)

MARCUS (*overlapping*). Wait! There's no need for that! (*To* HENRY.) I have no fear of the police. (HENRY *stands quietly.*) Thank you.

HENRY. Don't let them take you!

MARCUS. While it is necessary, we play their game! (*He smiles, steps down from the box, and takes* AIJA's *hand, and is led off to the right by the* POLICE. HENRY *remains standing, looking after him, and is finally chased a few steps by the* 3RD POLICEMAN.)

3RD POLICEMAN. Move along, boy! Move along! (HENRY

takes a few steps to the left but continues to look after MARCUS. *Light fades, just as a huge headline reads,* "Doughboys Arrive in Europe!" "Over There" *is at its most powerful.)*

(MARCUS *is brought into an office arrangement to the right, and sat in a chair before a desk. The light begins to build after he is seated; as it builds, a* WHITE MAN *enters area, stares at him, and sits quietly behind the desk. He is tall, graying around the temples and is somewhat fat.)*

DEAN *(picks up a piece of paper).* Who are you? *(Silence.)* I asked you a question—who are you?

MARCUS. You know who I am man! You don't have to holler like a cow!

DEAN. Answer the question then, boy. *(Sets paper down.)*

MARCUS *(angry, almost rising).* Wait a minute mister! I talk to no white man as less than an equal—have you become a boy? *(Pause.)*

DEAN *(peering at him).* You hate us don't you? And don't deny it, because I've heard what you're telling those colored people in Harlem! filling their heads with a lot of nonsense about Black beauty and Africa—nobody believes that stuff! I know you Marcus— *(Smiles.)* I've seen hundreds like you. You come into Harlem and stop on the first corner where a crowd will listen to you, and you start screamin' your Black head off about what white people are doing to you! You pass out your filthy pamphlets with one hand, and collect your con money with the other! You won't leave well enough alone! You bleed your own people dry, then run out on them, when you figure you got enough!

MARCUS. I don't need to be preached to by someone like you, white man!

DEAN. Your kind make me sick!

MARCUS. No more than you make me!

DEAN *(shocked).* Curtis! Curtis! Come in here! *(Small WHITE MAN with a note pad enters room.)* Take his statement!

MARCUS. I have no statement!

DEAN *(points as CURTIS sits down).* Take down what he says—every word!

MARCUS. What charge is against me?

DEAN *(arrogantly).* Soliciting illegally—is that good enough for you? And you know who brought the charge against you? Your own people! The good Harlem leaders who are sick and tired of your big mouth speeches— *(Sarcastically.)* Equal to white men? You people will never be equal to white men—you can't even take care of your own problems! Call us! Let us settle it!

MARCUS *(smiles).* We will be rid of you soon, so don't get too upset.

DEAN. Rid of us? You Blacks would starve without us— where do you hatemongers come from? What hole—the colored people were contented—why? You—you stir things up, you steal—

MARCUS. I am no thief!

DEAN. Are you selling stock?

MARCUS. Check my books—and where is my lawyer? And Aija— *(Here DEAN overlaps.)* what have you done with her?

DEAN *(yelling.)* Shut your mouth!

MARCUS. Damn you!

DEAN *(starts to strike him, but pulls back, he stands up, and begins to pace the floor).* Marcus! Marcus, you stop preachin' in this city, you hear me?

MARCUS *(smiles).* If I came to you on my knees, would that please you, white man? *(Suddenly disgusted.)* I want to be rid of you—is that too strong? *(DEAN faces him.)* Rid of you—your white face, your white voice— *(Loud.)* I don't want you! You are nothing to me—and—and I want to be nothing to you!

DEAN *(shocked, defensive).* We freed you!

MARCUS. We were never slaves!

DEAN. You ungrateful—you stop—

MARCUS *(shouting).* Then leave Marcus alone! You arrest me—you question me—you arrest my people—and on what?

For what reason? Because I am Black—because I tell you we no longer want you!

DEAN. Now you wait a minute—I've been fair to colored people! You just wait a minute—what are you trying to say?

MARCUS. White fairness is nothing to me! It is always dressed in slaves' clothing—always robed in silence, in white superiority! (*Waves his hand.*) I want none of your fairness! I want to be rid of you—your God, your churches—

DEAN. You traitor!

MARCUS. This country is yours, and we want nothing more than to give it back to you! We don't hate you, man! We cannot any longer stand the sight of you!

DEAN (*moving toward him, pointing*). Listen—you listen, you! There've been some killings up there in Harlem! You hear me? Three white people—up there, three—you stop it, you hear? You stop it!

MARCUS. What have killings to do with me?

DEAN. You just stop it! Stop your filthy talking—you're responsible! You're the one, if those people get dangerous— you stop it!

MARCUS. Marcus is no murderer!

DEAN. Just stop! Get outta New York! Stop tellin' the niggers that stuff! Now I mean it! You stop it! (*Pause.*) You get out of my office! You just get out of my office! (MARCUS *stands.*) Get out! (MARCUS *looks at him for a moment, and leaves.*) Get out! (*Pause, long.*) And I can't stand (*Turns to left.*) the sight of your Black face either! Hear that? I can't stand the sight of you either—*We* don't want *you!* It's the other way around! (*Light begins to fade. On the backdrop, the East Saint Louis riots break out.*)

(*Light builds in the center.* MARCUS *walks on from the left with* AIJA. *They walk slowly and stop beside the black box. In the shadows on the right,* HENRY *is waiting, watching.*)

MARCUS (*taking a deep breath, softly*). Don't let that man worry you Aija.

Aija. It's not that simple—Dean has informers—Hall, and our leader friends back him! They help him! Why do you think they arrested you in the first place? They want you out of New York—you've started something Marcus! The people are beginning to see—that's dangerous to them!

Marcus *(smiles)*. What have I to fear then, if the people are with me? *(Aija does not answer, Marcus' mood changes.)* They are hunting Marcus, aren't they? *(Aija nods. Marcus intensely.)* Even the Black men hunt Marcus! If I came to Harlem to steal, then lynch me! But I am an honest man, who comes to unite Black men—to call on their strength— *(Bewildered.)* What do I say that threatens us? *(Pause, anger.)* These Black leaders in their dark suits and university educations who submit our race to inhumanity after inhumanity—they threaten us! Not Marcus! I have come to save the Black man! *(Pause.)* And that wolf waits to devour what Black pawns leave—that is what chokes me, Aija! *(Sits down.)* Don't puzzle over what I say—I am not weakening. *(Pause.)* Sit beside me.

Aija. We could go back home, Marcus.

Marcus *(laughs)*. Aija, you are a persistent woman!

Aija *(defensively)*. I am concerned about your welfare, even if you don't think of it, man!

Marcus *(softens)*. I know Aija. Marcus thanks you.

Aija. Do *you* thank me?

Marcus. There is hardly any time left for me. There is only time for Marcus. *(Intensely.)* There is much to do, Aija! *(Pause, tries to touch her, but does not. Reflectively, softly.)* I would be sad, Aija, if you left.

Aija. Where am I to go man? This city is too big! I get lost all the time!

Marcus *(smiles faintly)*. I had doubts. *(Looks at her.)* I have doubts once in awhile—not too often! *(Pause.)* It is when a man has a vision that he doubts. In his vision, he is strength and greatness—he is power. He sees himself at the head of a wave of Black faces—he is king—yes, in visions we are kings, and we see ourselves in the company of great men, of great minds, but we are really confronted always by the weak—the little ones, fighting to hold on to their slavery! *(Pause.)* I am tired! *(Stands, looks back at *her. Reflects.)* Sometimes, I see Saint Ann's, quiet and peaceful, and I wonder why Marcus came here. But I always see the white man in his carriage, and the hats going up in the air as he rides by, and I know. *(Pause.)*

AIJA. The pace has been too fast—and you haven't been careful! You are valuable to us, you know!

MARCUS *(laughs)*. Valuable? (HENRY *moves forward, it surprises* MARCUS.)

HENRY. Mr. Marcus?

MARCUS *(stepping back)*. Who are you man? *(Two of Marcus' MEN approach, and stand beside him.)*

HENRY *(looking around nervously)*. Henry Jeffers—I heard your speech—you were magnificent, Mr. Marcus. That white man has—

AIJA *(cutting him off)*. Mr. Marcus is tired man! (MARCUS *silences her with a gesture.)*

HENRY. I know—but you're right about them! They are cowards! They cry! They get down on their knees like babies and fold their hands and beg you!

MARCUS *(disturbed)*. Do you want to join us?

HENRY *(shocked into reality)*. Yes sir— *(Hesitatingly.)* yes—a—a don't you remember me, Mr. Marcus? I'm the man who grabbed the cop—don't you remember?

MARCUS. Yes. *(Softer.)* I remember. *(Pause.)* Where is your arm?

HENRY. The war. I fought with the French.

MARCUS. We have need of soldiers in the Black Legion—that is our army—a Black army! But without—

HENRY. I'm Black!

MARCUS. I am sorry, man!

HENRY. Give me a test! Any test!

MARCUS *(To* AIJA, *smiling)*. He is proud! We need proud men. *(Pause. He stares at* HENRY.) Tomorrow? Yes, tomorrow come to our Foreign Office. *(He reaches for* HENRY'S *hand, and shakes it.)* Henry Jeffers. We will find a place for you. *(Pause.)* Would you have died out there for me?

HENRY *(draws revolver)*. I would have killed for you. (MARCUS *stares at him silently.)*

MARCUS. We will find a place beside Brother Marcus for you, Henry Jeffers. (*He turns away with* AIJA.)

AIJA (*whispering,* HENRY *stares after them*). I don't like him! Did you see his eyes?

MARCUS (*walking left*). Are you voodoo, woman? (*Laughs.*) Did I see his eyes!

AIJA (*offstage*). Be careful of him! (MARCUS *is heard laughing in the background.*)

(HENRY *is alone on stage and behind him a large picture of Vladimir Ilich Lenin gradually rises until it is directly above him.*)

HENRY (*shouts*). White man! Look out! (*He brandishes pistol.*) I stand beside Marcus now! Look out, you cowards! (*Light fades. Lenin's picture remains. "Over There" is a quiet strain.*)

(*Curtain.*)

ACT 3

(*Late 1917, early 1918. To the left of the stage is an office arrangement, a desk and several chairs behind which is a black, red, and green flag.* MARCUS *is seated at the desk, to his right is* AIJA, *to his left* HENRY *is standing menacingly. The center is still occupied by the box, and to the right the American flag is limp on its pedestal.* MARCUS *is writing. On the backdrop, a picture of Lenin addressing a group of shouting Russians is projected. "Over There" is unbearably loud for an instant, then it slowly dies away.*)

MARCUS (*lowering his pen, and rubbing his eyes, groans a*

little). Aija, I can't think! The words are stuck in my head! *(Smiles.)*

AIJA. You should rest—you won't start again?

MARCUS *(thoughtfully).* No. What I wrote first, I wanted to say—these are simply difficult men to answer with poetry. *(Pause.)* They have the ear of the people—and it is never sensible to answer Du Bois and Randolph too quickly! The people see them as mirrors of their own potential, and if Marcus answers them too quickly, he gives them too much importance— *(Mimics.)* "How could they affect Marcus like that?" *(Sighs.)* You know what they say. *(Intensely.)* If they did not have this insane belief in the possibilities of white justice! It is like an appealing disease— *(Loudly.)* in the future we will all be brothers—equals! And it will never happen, until Black men stand together! The leaders are the fools—they cannot see beyond their light-skinned noses! *They* confound the Black man—do you see it Henry?

HENRY *(smiles knowingly).* The Legion *could* handle it. *(*AIJA *looks as though disbelieving.)*

MARCUS *(glances at* AIJA, *to* HENRY*).* Some situations call for words, Henry—Du Bois would only have fuel for his fires, if he were threatened. The doctors have to be given prescriptions for silence— *(Waves a hand.)* Marcus has his own logic. Their arguments are full of holes!

HENRY. They're tools of white men, Marcus, and he uses them in any way he see fit—he uses them to get at you!

MARCUS *(smiling).* They're his worst tools man—they are sincere. *(Louder.)* But there should be no dead-end streets for the Black man! With Marcus at least there is a way—someplace to go! *(Sighs.)* Well— *(Slides papers aside.)* What is there today, Aija? Should I see someone?

AIJA. Hall is waiting; then there is the review of the Legion.

MARCUS. Let Hall wait! *(To* HENRY*.)* Have you inspected them?

HENRY *(straightens to attention.)* Not this morning, Mr. President!

MARCUS *(annoyed).* Then do it, man! Must Marcus be the mind and voice of everyone?

HENRY. No, Mr. President! (HENRY *turns stiffly, and mili-
tarily marches from the room.* MARCUS *shakes his head.
Silence.*)

AIJA (*softly*). Why do you keep him?

MARCUS. Who? Hall? (*Looks at her.*) Henry? (*She nods.*)
I trust him.

AIJA. He always wants to hurt someone—he is like death!
I don't like him!

MARCUS (*smiling*). Have you become the voodoo woman?
How do you know—

AIJA (*cutting him off*). I see it in him! And you are never
careful enough, I say he is bad luck!

MARCUS. I would feel undressed without the man—for eight
months he has been beside me—remember, he tried to help
Marcus when everyone was running! I will not turn my
back on him that easily!

AIJA. All he did was grab a policeman's hand—and for that,
you give him the highest post in the Legion? What if he
grabs at your hand—or kills you? Besides, you had a bodyguard—Jamaican. What was wrong with him?

MARCUS (*sullenly*). The man betrayed me.

AIJA (*sarcastically*). How, Marcus?

MARCUS (*indignant*). Must Marcus answer every supersti-
tious question asked? Are you the white prosecutor or my
associate? He betrayed me—that's enough! He was to guard
me, not question my every decision! Don't annoy me with
this again, Aija!

AIJA (*softer*). I am just afraid for you— (*She is interrupted
by a voice offstage to the left.*)

HENRY (*offstage*). Mr. Marcus will see you later! (*On the
projection in the background, President Wilson asks for
war on Austria-Hungary—"Over There" grows in intensity.*)

HALL (*angrily*). I want to see him now! I don't answer to
you Legion people!

HENRY (*anger*). No one is above the Legion! (HALL
screams.)

HALL (*loudly*). Marcus! Marcus—get this—Marcus! (MARCUS
stands excitedly moving around the desk.)

MARCUS. What the hell is going on—

HALL (*quickly, as though gagging*). Get this crazy— (AIJA *muffles a scream, standing, facing the left, as* HENRY *backs* HALL *into the room, a gun at his throat.*)

MARCUS (*loudly*). Henry! Put it down! (HENRY *turns momentarily toward him.*) I said, Put It Down! (*He lowers it.*)

HENRY (*almost inaudible, drawing breath*). Yes, Mr. President.

MARCUS. Come in Hall! Sit down!

HALL (*backing away*). Get this crazy man out of here!

MARCUS (*angrily*). Henry, do as I told you!

HENRY (*appealing*). Mr. President, he had no right—

MARCUS (*louder, angrily*). Do as I say! (HENRY *turns and leaves. There is a moment of silence.* MARCUS *takes a long look at* AIJA, *then sits down.*) What is it, Hall?

HALL. I want to see you! Why haven't you answered any of my messages?

MARCUS (*leans back, reflectively*). We found out your man Baker is a thief!

HALL (*suddenly defensive*). So what? (*Looks at* AIJA.) Don't look at me! Can I guarantee everyone that comes to me?

MARCUS (*points*). He's your man! (*Sits back.*) We fired him!

HALL. You didn't speak to me about it! You call that being fair to all Black people?

MARCUS (*irony*). Should I have waited until he stole the entire building? Besides the man admitted it—what proof do I need?

HALL (*to* AIJA). We're supposed to be partners!

MARCUS. Garvey is partners with honest Black men; yes.

HALL. What is that supposed to mean? If you are so honest, why don't you tell me nothin'? No one can see you, until they get through that Black Legion of yours—and—and you act like you don't need the party anymore! (*Stands.*) I'm still Mayor of Harlem, Marcus, remember that! And I didn't get there by lettin' anybody put me off—Baker was my man, and you should've talked to me about it first! It's been a whole year, and you ain't co-operated yet! (*Stammering.*) You—you won't help the party—what the hell are you tryin' to do?

MARCUS *(amused)*. Get some men I can trust, Mayor of Harlem!

HALL *(annoyed)*. That money's a temptation, and you know it! And what are you gonna do with it? You haven't contributed one dime to the party! Nothin'! *(Points.)* You know what I think? I think you want to be in politics yourself, and all that money's goin' to—

MARCUS *(waving a disdainful hand)*. Oh, Hall, shut up! Be sensible, man! (TO AIJA.) Have we found someone to fit Baker's place? (AIJA *shakes head "No."*) See if there is someone now. (AIJA *gets up silently and leaves.* HALL *has continued to talk.*)

HALL *(overlapping)*. Sensible? You be sensible—if we're together, people expect us to do things together! It don't look right if you don't campaign with me—it don't! Where would you be now, if it hadn't been for us? (MARCUS *smiles.*) They come out there to see you, 'cause I'm with you! *(Louder.)* I need you on my platform, not going around tellin' people you gonna use that money to buy some ships, and stirrin' up trouble! *(Pause.)* And what the hell is all this crazy stuff about ships anyway?

MARCUS *(irritated)*. Listen man, I'm gettin' tired of you bellowing like a wounded cow!

HALL. At least I don't bellow like no white man!

MARCUS *(shocked, angry)*. What? *(Stands.)*

HALL *(continuing)*. That's what I said! You think they gonna let you buy ships and sail them—who's gonna sell them to you—who's gonna sail them? (*A light flashes on the right, and in the spotlight is a* BLACK SEA-CAPTAIN. *He is visible for only a second.*)

MARCUS *(overlapping)*. Take that black man!

HALL *(continuing, ignoring* MARCUS*)*. Where you gonna find a Black sea-captain? (*Light flashes again to the right, where the* SEA-CAPTAIN *stands.* MARCUS *moves toward him, raising his hand and slapping* HALL *across the face.*) Why'd you do that? What did I say?

MARCUS. Get out! *(Raises his hand again.)*

HALL. All right! All right! *(He turns away from* MARCUS, *who stands staring at him.)* All right! *(He reaches far left.)*

You won't destroy me, Marcus. I swear to God you won't destroy me! (*Exit.*)

MARCUS (*sits down, sighs, seems exhausted. Moves papers in front of him, just as* AIJA *enters room. She says nothing, they share a long look in silence*). Our worst enemies are Black, Aija. (*Light fades.*)

(*To the right is the table and chairs arrangement.* RETHA, *well-dressed, is seated at the table snapping beans.* HENRY *is seated on his stool, this time it is to the left, and a little forward of the arrangement, facing the audience. On the backdrop headlines are projected about national witch hunting for disloyal statements.*)

HENRY (*turning slightly toward her*). You jest don't understand him, Retha! Mr. Marcus ain't like these politicians and leaders, sell us out to the white man!

RETHA (*looking up*). How you know? I think they jest ain't offered him enough yet—it just ain't right, that no man be that good, like you say he is! Everybody got somethin' wrong wif' 'em! You watch!

HENRY. Watch? You be watchin' for a hundred years, and everythin' run right pass you!

RETHA. Lotta people say he ain't good for us—that he'll run off with all that money he been collectin'.

HENRY (*annoyed*). What lotta people? Miss Kissinger? Them white folks you work for—why you always listen to white folks, Retha?

RETHA (*louder*). They got a right too, Henry Jeffers!

HENRY (*puzzled*). A right to what? To tell us how to think? If you want to know somethin' listen to Marcus—or listen to Black people in Harlem! He's a great man, Retha—he made me the head of the Legion—me, a one arm man, Retha! Head of the whole Black Legion!

RETHA. Humph! Betta watch your money!

HENRY (*angry*). If you don't like the man, don't talk some-

thin' you don't know! He's a good man! *(Reflective.)*
People flock around him everywhere he goes—and you
know why? 'Cause for once in our lives, there's a Black
man who ain't scared of the white man, and ain't afraid
to say he ain't! *(Softer.)* Sometimes, I think of somethin' I
want to tell 'em myself, and before I can say it, Mr. Marcus
done got it out, and is shouting it from the stage! *(Smiles,
pause.)* It's like he says what we all been waitin' so long
to say, and jest couldn't git out! He's like all of us put
together—and when you follow a man like that, you follow
yourself.

RETHA. So what? You know what happens when colored
people gets they hands on money!

HENRY *(shouting)*. He ain't like your stupid colored people!

RETHA. You don't hafta holler!

HENRY *(calms down, softer)*. Retha? Why ain't you satisfied?

RETHA *(unsure)*. It ain't that—I just ain't used to all this
commotion Henry! I just ain't!

HENRY *(intensely)*. Do you know what I've done to make
you comfortable? To make you independent? To tear out
that yassuh boss brain in your head?— *(Louder.)* And you
still do it! You still sit there like some *mammy* in her
rockin' chair!

RETHA. I can't help it Henry! White folks been good to me!

HENRY *(harshly)*. They made you a nothin'!

RETHA *(almost in tears)*. If it hadn'ta been for Miss Kissinger, I don't know what I'da done when you was away!
She was a comfort to me Henry! She used to come up
sometime and set with me—and we'd talk about the war—
and you. And every Sunday, 'cause they knew I couldn'
go out, they'd bring me breakfast—imagine that, Henry—
white folks bringin' me my—

HENRY *(cuttin' her off)*. Why couldn' you go out?

RETHA *(nervous)*. I—I wasn' feelin' well.

HENRY. How come?

RETHA *(shrugs)*. I was jest laid up for a long time—I—I was
nursin' Miss Connie. *(She turns away.)*

HENRY *(surprised)*. Miss Connie? You ain't had no milk!

RETHA *(softly, crying)*. I loss our baby, and—

HENRY *(shocked, standing)*. What? Our baby, Retha?

RETHA (*quickly*). I wanted to surprise you Henry! I did! Right after you left, I felt the signs—but I lost it, and Miss Kissinger, she was just havin' Miss Connie, so—

HENRY. You gave them white folks your milk? Milk from my baby?

RETHA. I was all swollen with it Henry! And I wanted to feel a baby's mouth on it—I did, Henry! I really did! (*Sobbing.*) Miss Connie, she's just like my own!

HENRY. She's white, Retha! (*Turns away dazed.*) Oh, my God—what? (*Angry.*) I swear—Retha, so help me God—I swear, she won't be nobody's no more! (*He starts off.*)

RETHA (*looking up shouting*). What you gonna do Henry? Henry?

HENRY (*stops, turns around*). Retha? Did I ever tell you how I loss this here arm? (RETHA *lowers head, shaking it* "No.") A white man did it! A white man on my side in the war, Retha! (*Turns away angrily.*) Called hisself a doctor! (*Turns back to her.*) I had a bullet in my hand, Retha! An' he laid me down on that bed and said my whole arm had to go, if I wanted to go on livin'! It was poison eatin' me up—so he cut it off! (*Tearful.*) And two months later they found out he wasn't no doctor, and there wasn' no poison— (*Looks at her.*) He cut off my arm for nothin'! (*Whispered intensely.*) Nothin'! (*He starts out, stopping again.*) I'm gonna kill them Retha! Your Miss Kissinger, and her little Miss Connie. (*Walks off.*)

RETHA. Henry! (*Stands, looking around for an instant, suddenly.*) Miss Kissinger! Miss Kissinger! (*Light fades.*)

(*From the left* HALL *enters an office arrangement hurriedly, going behind a desk, opening drawers and slamming them shut, he smashes a fist against the top.*)

HALL (*shouting*). Steele! (*Turns around, as he sits.*) Steele!

STEELE (*entering from left*). I'm right here! What's the matter?

HALL (*ignoring him*). Where's Marvin?

MARVIN *(offstage, approaching).* Comin', Reuben! *(Entering.)* Right here! What's all the commotion about? I could hear—

HALL. My name is Mister Hall to you, you understand?

MARVIN *(stopping on the right of the desk).* Yeah—what's— well, I mean, what is goin' on?

HALL. Where have you been?

MARVIN. I've been here all day!

HALL *(to himself).* You got me into this— *(Louder.)* What have you got on Marcus? *(Reflectively.)* That bastard! What have you got?

MARVIN. Well, we got a letter, the other day— *(Looks at* STEELE.) I don't know how valuable it is—I mean—

HALL. What does it say?

MARVIN. Well, it's from some man named Bey—he claims Marcus used to work for him in London. *(He removes letter from his pocket.)* I have it with me— *(Pause.)* Now there is no guarantee any of this is true—I mean we can't substantiate any of it!

HALL *(annoyed).* I'll decide that! Read it! Read it! You waste more goddamn time—

MARVIN *(irritated).* All right! *(Stares coldly at* HALL.) Listen to it. *(Pause.)* Dear Mr. Marvin, I received your inquiry on the nineteenth. At the time, because of a publication deadline, I was—

HALL. Go on! Don't waste my time with that crap! Read the damn thing!

MARVIN *(sighing).* O.K. Mr. Hall! *(Pause.)* The man in question, Marcus, did work for me during the spring and summer of 1914, and was a most unsatisfactory employee. When he first came into my employ, he was an apprentice, but proved unsuitable for such skilled labors— *(*MARVIN *looks up.)* He says something about himself—about how good a printer he is—

HALL. WILL YOU READ?

MARVIN *(louder).* I then tried him as a bookkeeper, thinking that the simple task of putting down numbers would best suit his abilities; however after several months I found very serious shortages in our income, and a very foolish attempt to cover them with bookkeeping entries. When I confronted this Marcus person with the problem, he grew extremely aggravated—so much so, that I was forced to demand his resignation, and—

HALL *(elated)*. A thief! Our Marcus is a thief!

MARVIN *(quickly)*. He doesn't say that, Mr. Hall—and there's no proof!

HALL *(coldly)*. Proof? Let him find it the same way Baker did—in accusation—who else took the money? A ghost? Marcus took it—I know he did, just like he's gonna steal from the good people of Harlem! *(Points.)* You let one word of this get out, and so help me God, I'll have both your asses, hear? *(Smiles.)* We just gonna sit on it for awhile—at the right moment, we'll send that Jamaican home!

MARVIN. What if it doesn't work?

HALL. It'll work, Marvin, as long as you don't panic! People's tired of Marcus—even the Jamaicans are tired of him! Him and his Black Legion! And the way he's goin' around shootin' off his mouth— *(Rubs face.)* and slappin' people—it'll work all right! *(Light fades.)* Then we'll send that bastard back where he came from! *(Laughter.)*

(On the backdrop news of war continues. In the center, slightly left, the BLACK LEADER *emerges. He walks forward to the edge of the stage, and addresses the audience directly.)*

LEADER *(cynically)*. Harlem? Have you heard the latest? Our obese Jamaican friend? Mad Marcus? He's looking for a sea-captain? *(Smiles. To the right, a* BLACK MAN *dressed in the clothes of a sea-captain walks forward, smoking a cigar. He stops at the edge of the stage, and walks back to the box, where he begins to wait, nervously.)* And he's gonna buy some ships—I suppose, so we can all go back to Africa! Is he serious? Does he expect Harlem to dig into its pockets and finance this scheme? We have already paid for his stores, his laundries—and that monstrosity on a Hundred-and-Thirty-eighth Street! How much more can we afford to give him—and what's happening to all that

money? Has he built any new houses in Harlem? Are any
of us eatin' any better? Hell no—we starve while he goes
out and buys thousands of uniforms for his insane Black
Legion! We've already gone to Dean about this—do we
have to go back? *(Louder.)* If we do Dean, we're gonna
ask for your job, because he must be paying somebody off!
It's time sensible people put a stop to this nonsense! This
is 1918—we weren't born yesterday! *(Light fades on
LEADER. He walks off, just as MARCUS and AIJA walk on
in the direction of the SEA-CAPTAIN. As they approach him,
several shots ring out. MARCUS, AIJA, and the SEA-CAPTAIN
seem not to hear them, and will go on with their conversation. From the right, RETHA will walk on, as though in a
daze. She will look around for a moment, shake her head,
and speak as MARCUS is addressing the SEA-CAPTAIN.)*

RETHA. Miss Connie? *(Smiles.)* Why you runnin' all ova
the house that way? You know what your Mama tol' you,
now! *(Looks up.)* Miss Connie? *(Frightened.)* Henry? What
you gonna do—don't do that Henry! Jesus don't let him
do— *(Screams.)* Henry! *(She looks around, takes several
steps to the left, and sits down on the stage to the left of
MARCUS.)*

MARCUS *(overlapping).* You are Captain Rutledge, man?
(He reaches for RUTLEDGE's hand.)

RUTLEDGE *(moving forward, coughing).* Yes—yes sir! And
you're Mr. Garvey?

MARCUS. Yes. This is my associate— *(Turns to AIJA).* Aija?
Is there anything wrong?

AIJA. No, Mr. Marcus. *(He glances at her for a moment.)*

MARCUS *(to RUTLEDGE).* You come highly recommended.

RUTLEDGE *(coughing).* Thank you—I've been out in open
waters a long time. I've sailed the Atlantic, the Pacific,
the Indian, the Arctic—and there's places, Mr. Marcus,
where I have sailed that no man alive can tell you about—
and they ain't on no maps! *(Coughs.)*

MARCUS *(glancing at AIJA).* You *are* a captain, aren't you
man?

RUTLEDGE. The only tan boy on the seven seas! *(Puffs out
chest, and coughs.)* These is really bad cigars! I usually
git mine out of Havana, see?

MARCUS (*looking rather strangely*). Could you get a ship to Africa?

RUTLEDGE. Africa? Why I been to Africa so many times, I could plot a course blindfold! What's your cargo?

MARCUS. Goods.

RUTLEDGE. Goods? You are *the* Mr. Marcus ain't you? I mean, I heard that you was plannin' to take people—I mean, that's what I heard—you are the one who's sayin' that ain't you?

MARCUS. Do you often listen to rumors, Mr. Rutledge?

RUTLEDGE. No! I mean—

MARCUS. Let me suggest, you tend your own affairs, man! If you are to be a captain, be just that, and nothing more!

RUTLEDGE. Yes sir! (*Smiling.*) I never interfere with my employ——

MARCUS (*snapping*). Do you have papers?

RUTLEDGE. Yes sir! (*Reaches into his jacket, and removes a wallet.*) Right here! (*Hands it to* MARCUS *who studies its contents.*)

MARCUS (*looks at* RUTLEDGE *coldly*). These papers say you are just a first officer—what are you trying to do man?

AIJA. He doesn't even sound like a captain!

RUTLEDGE (*to* AIJA). That's the highest rank of any colored man on the sea! What is the first officer but captain, anyway? (*Coughs.*) I been on ships all my life, and not once got the chance to command one! Not once—and yet there ain't a white captain in the world wouldn' trust his bridge to me! I done it hundreds of time—hundreds! (*Pause.*) All right, I ain't no captain—but neither is nobody else!

MARCUS (*annoyed*). You should not have lied! (*Turns away.*)

RUTLEDGE. Wait a minute! Listen—what else was I gonna do? You think them white men gonna give me a ship? You think they gonna let me sail on the high seas with a crew of white men?

AIJA. He's a liar!

RUTLEDGE. I'm a colored man who wants to command his own ship—and I'll do anything to do it! (MARCUS *stops.*) Mr. Marcus—I'm Black too! Do you have your ship?

MARCUS. No.

RUTLEDGE. I could help you! I know a man! (MARCUS *turns to* AIJA.)

MARCUS. What is it, Aija?

AIJA. I don't trust this man, Marcus! My first look at him— he is no captain!

MARCUS. Is that what has bothered you?

AIJA. Yes.

MARCUS (*to* RUTLEDGE.) How soon can we get in touch with this man of yours?

RUTLEDGE. Tomorrow, Mr. Marcus.

MARCUS. You get him to us! (*To* AIJA.) I am satisfied, Aija! I think we have a captain— (*To* RUTLEDGE.) but a captain who will be cautious. Isn't that right man?

RUTLEDGE. Yes sir, Mr. Marcus. (*Smiles.*)

MARCUS. Do not make mistakes, *Captain* Rutledge.

RUTLEDGE. Yes sir. (*Reaches out to shake* MARCUS' *hand.*) Thank you sir.

MARCUS (*shakes his hand*). Now we have a captain, and by tomorrow our ship! (*Smiles.*) And that devilish white man will be screaming at us! (*He mounts the box.*) Harlem! (PEOPLE *begin to walk on, and crowd around him,* HALL, STEELE, *and* MARVIN *among them.*) You think he will not be yelling at us, and laughing? The white man has always laughed at the Black man! (RETHA *looks up, and* HENRY *enters as though looking for her. When he reaches her side, he tries to lift her up, but she resists, finally he snatches her up, and she pulls away from him cringing. He grabs her violently, she puts up no struggle, and he marches her to the box, and forces her to listen.*) He laughed when we told him we hated slavery, when we told him we could fight for his country! And when we told him we wanted to be men, he rolled into the streets with laughter—let us see now—when we tell him we are one— that we do not need his country—let us see now if he will laugh! (*Clapping.*) We have the strength and power to do all we say—and ten times more! (*Cheers.*) Let them tell you on your jobs, Marcus is a madman! He is mad! Mad to unite his people under one God, one Aim, and one Destiny! (*Cheering.*) Let them wave their fingers and rattle their

tongues, but let them be at the Harlem pier, when the
Black man launches his first ship—the first of a fleet of
ships—Black ships, with Black captains, flying Black flags!
Ships that will make the Atlantic Ocean a Lenox Avenue!
(*Cheering, suddenly on the backdrop, the headlines read,
THE WAR IS OVER! Everyone will turn toward it for a
moment in silence, and turn back to resume the clapping.*)
But that is not enough—not enough, because we will not
go back tomorrow— (*He looks at* RUTLEDGE.) It will take
time to build a fleet large enough to carry fifteen million
Black Americans to Africa—but we cannot wait to begin
building our empire—an empire right here! We will own
everything in Harlem! We will buy from Black stores,
wash our clothes in Black laundries—and Marcus does not
promise you an eternity of waiting! We are ready today
to buy our first ship! (*Cheering.*) Yes! Yes we are! (HALL
moves forward.)

HALL (*yelling*). I've got something to announce!

MARCUS (*annoyed*). Then announce it man!

HALL. Give me a chance to speak up there, where you are!

MARCUS (*vehemently*). Speak damn you! You are like a
child, Hall! And we will be better off without you! Say
what you have to say, quickly! (*To* CROWD.) Someone else
wants to speak to you! (CROWD *boos.*) No, he is our friend!
Committeeman Hall! (HALL *mounts the box,* MARCUS *steps
down. To* AIJA.) This will be the end of him!

HALL (*waits until the* CROWD *subsides*). The man you call
Marcus is a thief! (*The* CROWD *is stunned, then general
disbelief and boos.*) This man who would unite Black men
is a thief!

MARCUS (*pushing forward*). It's a lie, man! Hall, what is
this?

HALL (*waving letter, quickly*). I've got proof! Right here!
Let him deny this! He is a thief! And all the money you
are paying him will never buy ships—it will go into his
pockets—the same way it did in London! He's known there
as a thief! (MARVIN *grabs* MARCUS.) Deny it Marcus! Deny
that you worked for Bey, and that you were fired because
money was missing from his company, and you were the

bookkeeper? Deny it! He's got us right back where we started! He never intended to do anything for us!

MARCUS. It's a lie—let me speak!

HENRY. Tell them it's a lie!

HALL (*overlapping*). Speak? What for—can you deny this?

MARCUS (HENRY *grabs* MARCUS). Get your hands off me!

HENRY. Tell them! (RETHA *walks off slowly.*)

MARCUS. Don't touch me!

HALL. Does the thief deny this letter? Does he? (CROWD *begins to break up.*)

HENRY. Wait! Wait! It's a lie— (*Notices* RETHA *is gone. Pulls out gun.*) Retha? Retha, you come back, you hear? (*Begins to walk left.*)

HALL. And this is the man who talked so much about Africa! (*Shouts.*) Go back to Jamaica, Marcus! We don't want you here!

MARCUS (*overlapping*). Wait! It's a lie! Listen to me! (*Grabs* HALL *from the box.*) Listen! (*He mounts.*) Hall is a paid tool of the white man! Hear the truth—we must redeem— (CROWD *has exited.* HALL *and his* MEN *walk off smiling.* HENRY *has begun to look for* RETHA.)

HENRY. Retha! (*He exits left.*)

MARCUS (*looks at* AIJA, *who has remained. From the right, two* WHITE POLICEMEN *enter*). Listen.

1ST POLICEMAN (*to* MARCUS). Marcus? (MARCUS *faces them.*) You are under arrest.

AIJA. On what charge?

1ST POLICEMAN. Mr. Marcus?

MARCUS. What is it, man?

2ND POLICEMAN. You're under arrest for soliciting funds for stock— (*Looks down at the warrant.*) soliciting without a license, that's it! (MARCUS *steps down slowly.*)

MARCUS. Has that man Dean nothing else to do?

2ND POLICEMAN. Come along, Mr. Marcus. (MARCUS *walks forward.* AIJA *joins him, they walk off left.*)

(*To the left, light builds after* MARCUS *has exited.* HENRY *crosses stage to right, as though looking for him. He stops.*)

HENRY. Marcus! *(Waits for a moment. Looks down at his gun, removes it, stares at it momentarily—suddenly shaken.)* Retha! *(Looks at gun in horror, then throws it away.)* Retha! *(Goes limp, as light fades.)*

(Curtain.)

ACT 4

(The stage is dark, when the light builds the BLACK LEADER *will be facing the audience. He will seem slightly older than before. It is late 1918, and this act will run thru 1919 and early 1920. Behind him, there is a projection of American soldiers coming home.)*

LEADER *(reflectively).* Well, the myth of Marcus doesn't seem quite as ominous today as it was yesterday. The great Black leader who would march his people to their manifest destiny—this spotless Black knight, this noble lord of a new Black kingdom, was, after all, just another man. And a pretty common one at that. No knight, no lord—just someone we would rather forget. *(Shakes his head.)* He was the maddest madman of them all! Waving flags, and parading people dressed in those crazy uniforms—Harlem was like a carnival! But he's gone now, no more power, no more platforms— *(Pause.)* It almost seems a shame to be without him. At least when he was around, the white man trembled—and he could say what we all wanted to say, but didn' have the courage to! Even when he was wrong, you couldn' help but admire him. He was wrong so big! He's make a mistake seem like a triumph! *(Moves forward.)* Where is he? Somebody said they saw him several weeks ago, still running, still agitated, still a bundle of energy. *(Smiles.)* He was so wrong! Sure we want to unite, but free us first! *This* is our country—you know what I mean? *(Turns to left as though answering someone.)* I'll be the first to admit he was a man—I never denied that! And he's still one of us—all right, I'll accept that too! Let's hope all

those people downtown who are persecuting Marcus hear
us! People like Dean, who thinks the Negro community
isn't behind Marcus! *(To audience.)* We in the Negro community call for the immediate withdrawal of all charges
against Marcus! We demand that he be left alone! *(Loud.)*
Stop harassing the man, Dean! Leave Marcus alone! *(Turns
to left.)* What else can we do? *(Light begins to fade.)* I'm
the leader—you don't tell the leader what to do! *(Shouts.)*
All right! We'll do what we can—wait a minute, we're the
Negro leaders—certainly I am, I'm respected, looked up to—
(Frightened.) What else can we do? What else— *(Child-
like.)* I can't help it, if the white man won't listen! *(Light
fades.)* All those people downtown hear us! People like the
D.A., who thinks the Negro community ain't behind
Marcus! *(Turns to the right.)* We heard that you're picking
him up every month! *(Loud.)* Stop harassing the man,
Dean! Leave Marcus alone! *(Faces the audience.)* What
else can we do? *(Light begins to fade.)* It doesn't matter
what we thought of Marcus! Can we let white men intimi-
date him? Can we?

*(To the right is an office arrangement.
Seated behind a desk is* DEAN. *He is reading a newspaper.* MARCUS *is seated in a
chair before the desk. He seems annoyed.
On the backdrop, headlines read "Wilson Dies!")*

DEAN. Did you see this? *(Looks up.)* You people's threat-
enin' to riot if I don't stop harassin' you! *(Puts paper down
angrily.)* What the hell's wrong with them? Eight months
ago, they were screamin' for your blood—today you're their
hero—I'll never understand you colored people! But you'd
better tell them somethin'—white people ain't gonna be
scared by no threats!

MARCUS *(leaning forward).* Why am I here, Dean?

DEAN *(smiles).* What difference does it make to you? Dis-
turbing the peace—resisting arrest—anything I feel like it
being! I asked you a question anyway—what's wrong with
your people?

MARCUS. Whites.

DEAN (*sudden mood change*). Don't get smart! (*Relaxes.*)
I didn't steal no money in London! I didn't expose you!
Hall did—you'd think they'd see that, wouldn' you?
(*Silence.*) You don't have to answer. I know how you feel,
even if you don't! (*Pause.*) I guess you won't be buyin'
no ships now, huh? Lost everything, didn' you?

MARCUS (*annoyed*). Am I supposed to be frightened by all
this, Dean? My lawyer you keep from the room—you question me without charging me with anything—

DEAN (*quickly*). I'm trying to be nice to you, Marcus!

MARCUS (*calmly*). I don't need your friendship.

DEAN (*smiling*). Who else do you have? No one in the
world will trust you now! Who wants you?

MARCUS (*irritated*). What do you want man? Did you bring
me here just to say stupid things? (*Waves disdainfully.*)
Do not worry about Marcus! Marcus will buy ships—and
unite his people!

DEAN (*excited*). What will you buy them with? You pull
any fancy stock deal—or any of that stuff you pulled in
London, and I'll have you deported! (*Cynically.*) Buy
ships! Who the hell do you think you are anyway—the
Black Admiral Jones? (*Loud.*) Don't talk about no ships to
me! What do you know about these six killings?

MARCUS (*smiles*). Dean, you know I will not answer questions like that without the benefit of my lawyer man! We
have been through this seven times—

DEAN (*cutting him off*). You better answer! A member of
your group did it! Your—what the hell do you call it? You
damn people have more names for things—your Black
Legion! (*Shakes head.*) He had on one of those suits
you've been passing out! And his was pretty fancy!

MARCUS. It was a suit that seemed like ours!

DEAN (*pointing*). I say it wasn't! I say it's somebody close
to you, and you know who it is! Don't you?

MARCUS (*smiles*). Are you accusing me, man?

DEAN (*stands*). Let me tell you something, Marcus! No matter what you do, or where you go, to me you'll always be
just another Black boy! (*Loudly.*) I've got the power here!
And I intend to keep it! You can unite a billion Blacks,

or go back to your jungle Africa, I don't care—but wherever
you go, you start some trouble, and the white man's gonna
be there to slap your Black behinds for you!

MARCUS. Are you finished?

DEAN *(loud)*. No! *(Takes a deep breath.)* Now fair is fair—
so let me give you a little bit of advice. Six white people
have been killed in Harlem, by somebody in your group.
You've got two choices—you can find the person, and make
me happy, or forget about it, and I'll hound you until you
break. *(Walks to the side of the desk, and sits on the edge.)*
It's that simple.

MARCUS *(angrily)*. Go to hell, Dean—you waste my time!
If you have no charge let me go!

DEAN *(overlapping)*. Don't talk to me like that! *(Stands.)*
I asked you a question!

MARCUS. I know nothing about your six murders! White
people are killed every day! You kill each other in your
stupid wars and ridiculous revolutions—

DEAN *(interrupting)*. You wait a—

MARCUS *(stands)*. I am talking! You condone it, if we join
in your madness, but let one of you suspect we killed you,
and you move heaven and hell to catch a single Black man!
Did it ever occur to you, I don't give a damn about six
white lives—or sixty? If you are so powerful, man, prevent
another murder—catch the man—and if you can't, leave
Marcus alone! I have a destiny to fill!

DEAN *(laughs)*. Destiny? What destiny? *(Sits back on the
desk.)* To unite a bunch of shiftless Blacks? To rid this
country of its scum? Is that a destiny?

MARCUS. To be rid of you is our destiny.

DEAN *(angry)*. Don't get smart! I could have locked you up
for ninety days! *(Calming down.)* But I'm fair! I try to
treat you like a man! I'm as polite as I can be to you—
(Pounds on desk.) You'll never convince me you're right!

MARCUS. I don't wish to convince you of anything.

DEAN *(puzzled)*. What is it with you Marcus? You don't
understand when a man is trying, do you? I'm the law
here, don't you know that? I can be as partial or impartial
as I want to be—I could give you twenty years—but I don't!
I believe in the majesty of the law—and that's its fairness!

To niggers as well as whites—but you don't see that do you?

MARCUS. If I had said nothing, you would pat me on the head—I would be a good boy! But to be your equal—

DEAN (*excited*). You're not my equal! I'm a—a—I'm a lawyer! I've studied—

MARCUS (*cutting him off*). To be your equal—that is more than you can stand— (*Stands.*) I waste time with you! There will come a time when you will wish to your God you had left me in peace.

DEAN (*shouting*). Get out! (*Turns his back on MARCUS.*)

MARCUS (*begins to walk out, stops, with his back to DEAN*). Dean? (DEAN *stiffens, his back to MARCUS.*) Why do you bring me here for this?

DEAN (*after pause, reflectively*). To defeat you.

MARCUS (*after pause*). You defeat yourself, Dean.

DEAN. You heard me—get out! (*Pause.*) I'll get you Marcus!

MARCUS (*leaving, right*). It's too late Dean. (*Light fades.*)

(*In the center of the stage, the light builds.* RUTLEDGE *is standing with a short white man called* WHALAN, *their voices are heard, even as* MARCUS *leaves.*)

RUTLEDGE (*explaining*). Mr. Whalan, I tell you, he will definitely buy that ship!

WHALAN (*irritated*). He doesn't even have an organization anymore! No one's heard from the UNAA in almost eight months! If he'da had any money he wouldn' have been put down so easily!

RUTLEDGE. He's re-buildin', I tell you! (*Coughs.*) You've never seen anythin' like it in your life! He got hisself a newspaper—and seven or eight stores already! He's the luckiest man I ever seen!

WHALAN. He needs more than seven stores!

RUTLEDGE (*unsure of himself*). Ah, how much more—ah, well, how much more could I git, if I convince him—once he's got the money?

WHALAN (*indignant*). We agreed on a price, Rutledge! I said sixteen hundred!

RUTLEDGE.   Yeah, but I heard you was gittin' a hundred—

WHALAN (*cutting him off*).   Look Rutledge, we made a deal! And in my book a deal's a deal—you don't change it, because you think you can get more at the last minute! My word is my bond—and I expect all my business acquaintances to be of the same character! I won't pay one penny more than sixteen hundred! (*Points.*) You remember this, I'm the one who backed you, when you wanted first officer papers!

RUTLEDGE.   All right! I jest thought— (*Coughs.*) one hundred and sixty thousand was a lot of money—that's an old scow!

WHALAN (*irritated*).   What do you think it cost me—besides, he's got nothin' and our agreement was based on sale!

RUTLEDGE.   He'll be back in three months—I know it!

WHALAN (*slowly*).   If he is—I could consider a bonus, Rutledge—not much! Say another thousand?

RUTLEDGE.   A thousand? (*Coughs.*) All right. He will be back too—ain't he fixing to collect a dollar from every colored person in the world? It's four hundred million of us—and if any man can do it, Marcus' the man!

WHALAN.   Well—if he raises the money, you'll get the bonus—but not before! I've got a lot tied up in this, Rutledge. Don't let me down!

RUTLEDGE (*smiling, as he shakes* WHALAN'S *hand*).   You just keep that twenty-six hundred ready, boy! (*Light fades.*)

(MARCUS *walks on from the left in a pensive mood. He stops at center stage, just in front of* RUTLEDGE *and* WHALAN, *but does not see them.* AIJA *follows him out, but is overtaken by* HENRY. WHALAN *and* RUTLEDGE *watch the proceedings.*)

HENRY (*a newspaper in his hand*).   Mr. Marcus! Mr. Marcus! (*He stops beside* MARCUS.) Is it true? Do we really have a deal for the ship? I've been looking all over for you! (MARCUS *looks at him strangely.*) Is it true? I saw—

MARCUS (*annoyed*).   Where have you been for eight months? (AIJA *moves forward.*)

HENRY (*lowering his head*).   I thought it was all finished, after Hall gave that speech—and Retha— (*Looks at* MARCUS *pleadingly.*) She's dead, Mr. President. She didn't understand—she left me— (*Pause.*) And somebody killed her, and—

MARCUS (*haughty*). What is that to me? I asked you, Where have you been, man? Not would you cry to me about your wife!

HENRY (*excited*). I'm trying to tell you! Retha was scared, Brother Marcus—everybody was running—and they was sayin' the whole thing had broken up, and the cops was lookin' for us! I wasn' thinkin'—

MARCUS (*intensely*). Where have you been for eight months, man?

HENRY (*scared*). I didn' desert the movement—I didn'—I—I still talked about it! Ask anybody that knows me! Ask them!

MARCUS (*angrily*). Don't tell me that! Don't tell me excuses! You were the leader of the Black Legion—Marcus' strong right arm! I can't depend on you! Black people can't depend on you! You run and hide behind your woman when things get difficult! You want to redeem Black men? You can't even redeem yourself—white men frighten you! They chase you off like a rabbit!

HENRY (*almost reaching*). Don't say that! That's not true!

MARCUS. What is true? (*Loud.*) You ran! That's true! You're a coward, that's true! (*He begins to walk to the right.* HENRY *follows.*)

HENRY. I'm not afraid of anyone! I've killed white men! Plenty of them—right here in New York! (AIJA's *face is horrified.*) Six of them! (MARCUS *steps back.*) They deserved it—every one of them!

MARCUS. Get away from me, madman!

HENRY (*grabbing his arm*). Wait, Mr. President—

AIJA. Don't touch him!

MARCUS (*looking at his arm*). You dare to touch the arm of Marcus?

HENRY (*releasing it quickly*). Don't put me out, Mr. President! Please! I didn't betray you!

MARCUS. Get away from me! (RUTLEDGE *walks into the light, smiling.*)

RUTLEDGE (*reaching out for* MARCUS' *hand*). Brother Marcus! (*To* HENRY.) Hello colonel!

MARCUS (*smiling, and walking away from* HENRY). Rutledge, I wanted to see you! This man with his ship? We are ready to buy it—

HENRY (*walking forward*). Please, Brother Marcus!

MARCUS (*turns on him violently*). Get away from me!

HENRY. I'll take anything! Let me work my way up!

RUTLEDGE (*overlapping, reaching for* HENRY). Here now man, be reasonable—

AIJA (*to* HENRY). Leave the president alone, can't you see he's talking business? You are a crazy man—go someplace!

HENRY (*to* MARCUS). Please!

MARCUS (*vehemently*). No man! No! No! No!—coward! (HENRY *backs away as* MARCUS *turns to* RUTLEDGE.) We need new people, captain! The UNAA is rebuilding again!

RUTLEDGE (*smiling*). You've got a man right here—I swear, I've never heard a man say to white— (AIJA *screams*.)

HENRY (*a pistol in his hand*). Marcus! (MARCUS *moves back*, AIJA *tries to stand in front of him, and he pushes her aside*. RUTLEDGE *is frozen*.) Marcus! (HENRY *levels pistol and fires three shots*. MARCUS *falls backward onto the stage, and* AIJA *falls over him trying to revive him. She begins to cry*. HENRY *is suddenly frightened, he glances from side to side and bolts off to the right*.)

MARCUS (*being lifted upright, gasping*). Get him! Get him! (*Lapses into unconsciousness, just as police whistle sounds. Light fades.*)

(*From right and left people run onto stage crying, "Marcus been shot!" "They shot Marcus!" "Marcus! They shot Marcus!" "They tried to kill Marcus!" A chant begins which grows into a wild, loud crescendo. "Marcus!" will be repeated until it fills the stage, then suddenly, everything will be silent. From the rear left, the* BLACK LEADER *will slowly walk forward.*)

MAN'S VOICE *(when* LEADER *first emerges).* I KNOW WHO
DID IT! IT HAD TO BE THAT BUNCH DOWNTOWN!
EVER SINCE HE CAME HERE, THEY BEEN AFTER
HIM!

WOMAN'S VOICE. HALL PROBABLY PAID THEM TO
HAVE IT DONE! HALL, THAT'S WHO DID IT!

MAN'S VOICE. IT WAS HALL! HALL TRIED TO KILL
MARCUS! HALL DID IT!

WOMAN'S VOICE. HALL DID IT! *(Voices overlapping.)*
HALL DID IT! HALL DID IT!

MAN'S VOICE. HALL DID IT! HALL DID IT! RUN THAT
BASTARD OUT OF TOWN! HE TRIED TO KILL
MARCUS! *(Silence.* LEADER *reaches front of stage, just as
shots ring out. The* LEADER *is dressed in black.)*

LEADER *(quietly).* Henry Jeffers is dead. *(Pause.)* Marcus'
one time most trusted lieutenant, head of the Black Legion,
today, October twenty-third, nineteen-nineteen, committed
suicide. *(Pause.)* Harlem mourns, but not for a sick Henry
Jeffers. Harlem mourns for itself. Marcus is still alive, and
as one man put it, "Where will it all end?" Where will it
end? When will the madness that surrounds this man come
to a halt so that Blacks here and elsewhere can get on
with the work of freedom and equal rights? He can bring
us nothing but disaster and ruin! We must repudiate him
before it is too late for all of us! We must— *(He is cut off
by loud music, a march.* MARCUS *enters from the right
alone, though smiling. His arm is in a sling, and he waves
as though there are crowds. He walks to the box, mounts
it, and waves.)* What is he doing now? Hasn't he had
enough yet? Haven't we told him here in Harlem often
enough that we don't want anymore of his madman
schemes? *(Turns to* MARCUS.) Marcus! Get out of Harlem,
hear me? Marcus?

MARCUS *(to the audience).* What do you want man?

LEADER. Get out of Harlem! Haven't you done enough?

MARCUS *(smiling).* You want to hear about the Black People's Steamship Company? Well, it's a part of all that I
spoke of before! The Black man must unite—pull himself
up from the hole the white man dug for him! *(To the right,*